Power in Numbers

JAMES DeNARDO

Power in Numbers

The Political Strategy of Protest and Rebellion

Princeton University Press, Princeton, New Jersey

Published by Princeton University Press, 41 William Street, Princeton, New Jersey 08540

In the United Kingdom: Princeton University Press, Guildford, Surrey

Library of Congress Cataloging in Publication Data will be found on the last
printed page of this book

ISBN 0-691-07682-0

Publication of this book has been aided by the Whitney Darrow Fund
of Princeton University Press

This book has been composed in Monotype Times Roman

Clothbound editions of Princeton University Press books are printed on acid-free paper,
and binding materials are chosen for strength and durability

Printed in the United States of America by Princeton University Press,
Princeton, New Jersey

For Dad and Carol

CONTENTS

LIST OF ILLUSTRATIONS

UPON RARE occasion, a manuscript one is driven to read by one or another form of professional obligation turns out to be a treasure. This is such a book. Like many original and powerful works, it takes a set of old and familiar raw materials and reassembles them in an unexpected way, illuminating them from a new angle of vision which, one imagines, can revise their apperception forever.

The subject and method seem at first glance to be ill-suited to one another. The main ingredients are the letters, polemics, and other works of revolutionaries in our modern period, ranging from Samuel Adams orchestrating the Boston Tea Party to Ho Chi Minh challenging the French and then the Americans in the jungles of Indochina. These original writings, suffused with passion, become the substance for an austere and bloodless model of dissident decision-making, a true rational calculus of revolutionary strategy.

The formal model locates at the extremes of the same simple framework the gentle peace vigil and the underground cell of terrorists. What these actors have in common is a profound dispute with the governing regime. To exert pressure they must in one sense or another create disruption. Disruption, in the bare abstractions of the DeNardo model, is summarized in two dimensions: the "power of numbers" and the escalation of violence. At one extreme, numbers are recruited and violence is eschewed. At the other extreme, numbers, usually small, are hidden and violence is unleashed.

Between these extremes lie most of the phenomena to be discussed—the considerations of strategies that represent various mixes of the three basic options available: compromising demands, recruiting greater numbers, or turning to violence. The dissident group must search for its optimal strategy contingent upon government moves such as varying levels of state repression. Consensus within the group as to ultimate goals, at least to the vague approximation which is all that mere opposition requires, is not hard to come by. But ways and means are another thing again. Leaders of dissident groups vary in their levels of political impatience, as well as their estimates of the environment in which they operate, and hence the group becomes engrossed in factional disputes over the most efficacious procedures or, as Lenin asked more simply if rhetorically in his famous treatise, *What Is To Be Done?* In masterful style, our author uses the sometimes copious records of such persistent debates as a way of validating the major terms of his model: details of time and political context shift enormously, but the basic tensions over strategy recur, and the barebones model puts them in simple order.

I need not do greater justice to the substance of the model, because a better description is about as close at hand as it could be. But the intellectual location of the work, as well as its long-run promise, deserve more comment.

The root inspiration here is, of course, the history of revolution. However, this is history with a difference. Conventional studies of revolution abound, many of them descriptive, but some with nomothetic yearnings. The standard focus of the latter is, as our author discusses, upon the deeper causes and precipitating circumstances of revolutionary episodes, grand and small. If there be a trend in the history of ideas about history, the pendulum has swung far away from local assessments and decisions of "great men," and toward the inevitability of historical outcomes under the weight of ponderous social and economic forces. Whatever happened, we now tend to think, it could not have been otherwise, even give or take a Bonaparte or a Lenin or a Hitler.

The volume in hand cuts across this antique dispute at an oblique angle which is most profitable. The doctrine of inevitability suffers its own curious sterility as an intellectual premise, a matter that our author develops with fair elegance. (It is a delectable irony along the way that the controversies over historical inevitability have figured prominently in schisms among revolutionaries as well as historians.) On the other hand, he shows how we can pay attention to the strategic assessments of key parties at critical junctures in major episodes, and can do so in highly systematic fashion, without capitulating to counterdoctrines of pure caprice and the idiosyncracy of this or that utterly implausible personality.

Our author starts in the first chapter with a modest and diffident claim that however interesting the conventional treatments as to why observed revolutions had to have occurred at the time and place that they did, there still is intellectual room for another way of looking at revolutions, which has to do with their planned trajectories, decision-making about mid-course corrections, and the like. By the final chapter, if I am not overreading, the mood is more assertive. The author's approach is not merely some supplementary alternative or "frill": without it, I think we are being told, it is hard to see how the phenomena of rebellious behavior, including especially their ultimate outcomes, can be understood at all. The argument is compelling, and I am inclined to agree.

There is no point in hiding the fact that even seasoned historians of revolution and other readers unfamiliar with the deployment of formal models will find numerous passages in this book obscure and forbidding. The author does his level best to help, thanks to a most lucid style and charitable tactic of moving from the simplest building blocks to the more complex. Where this is not enough, I would urge the reader to plow on without trying to follow the detailed formal maneuvering, for the text remains intelligible provided only that the reader keep in mind the very few forces that the model encompasses and the common-sense relationships likely to obtain between them, such as that if disruption is increased by a turn to violence, numbers of supporters are likely to shrink. The formal machinery is necessary to keep track of more than two things interacting at a time, but one can take some of the resulting insights on faith, *faute de mieux*.

Even such a rudimentary reading will be richly repaid, for the formal passages are highly interspersed with very readable historical narrative. Indeed, much of the middle of the book is given over to an analysis of the famous episodes at the turn of this century surrounding the schism over tactics between Eduard Bernstein on one hand and Rosa Luxemburg and Lenin on the other. Enriched as it is by the terms of the model, this discussion is in itself worth the trip.

In the final analysis, as it seems to me, James DeNardo has done here for the logic of protest what Anthony Downs did a quarter of a century ago for the logic of candidate strategies in voting systems. In the intervening period, a cottage industry has grown up involved in extending, generalizing, and otherwise plumbing the more detailed implication of the Downs work. I shall be surprised if this book generates any lesser response.

Ann Arbor, Michigan   PHILIP E. CONVERSE
May, 1984

ACKNOWLEDGMENTS

THE IDEAS presented in this book evolved in conversations with an exceptional group of teachers, colleagues, and friends whose generous efforts on my behalf have greatly improved the chapters ahead. The most basic idea of all—that mathematical reasoning can help us understand how politics works—is one that I resisted quite stubbornly when it was introduced to me by Denis Sullivan and David Baldwin in the early 1970s. Their challenging and exciting teaching opened my eyes to a world of possibilities that I would never have discovered otherwise. My desire to learn more about these possibilities then led me to Yale's Department of Political Science where I completed an initial version of the present theory under the watchful guidance of Gerald Kramer and Robert Lane. Their suggestions were always most constructive and I owe a special debt of gratitude to each of these fine teachers.

The final phase of the book's life history unfolded in Princeton where, contrary to the precepts of academic common sense, I spent three additional years elaborating my theory and building a broader empirical foundation for it. During this endeavor I received constant encouragement and intellectual support from my colleagues, particularly Stanley Kelley, Jr., who now holds the world record for reading *Power in Numbers* (three times at least, maybe more). That he would like nothing better than to see his record broken is but one indication of his generosity and kindness. I should also like to thank Stephen Cohen, Amy Gutmann, Harry Eckstein, Walter Murphy, Peter Stillman, Donald Stokes, Lawrence Stone, and Dennis Thompson for their helpful advice on early drafts. Avinash Dixit, Fred Greenstein, and Ronald Rogowski read the final edition in its entirety, providing many useful suggestions for improvement.

For their help in preparing a complex manuscript with skill and precision, I am grateful to June Traube, Mildred Kalmus, Charlotte Carlson, and Avis Kniffin. For their financial support, I am indebted to the Center of International Studies at Princeton University and to the National Science Foundation. Of course, none of these individuals or institutions bears any responsibility for the lapses of judgment, reasoning, or interpretation that remain in the pages below.

Finally, I wish to extend a special word of thanks to Jorge and Luiza de Macedo, Charles Monagan, Michael Doyle, Duane Lockard, Jeffrey Goldstein, David Meerschwam, Dorothy Dey, and Joyce Slack for their friendship and support.

To my wife and father, whose steadfast love and devotion can never be repaid, I dedicate this book.

I hesitated between pure mathematics, to which
I was very strongly attracted, and Revolution,
which little by little was taking possession of me.
—Leon Trotsky, *My Life*

INTRODUCTION

In *What Is To Be Done?* we discover both a careful defense of Lenin's own political strategy for revolution and sharp attacks against opponents he variously identified as "Economists," "terrorists," "Economist-terrorists," "opportunists," "tail-enders," "worshippers of spontaneity," "conciliators," and "Bernsteinians." Lenin's taxonomy of political deviations, polemical though it was, should not be dismissed as the figment of a besieged imagination. Rather, it was an accurate representation of the complex factional divisions within the European Marxist movement around the turn of the century. Nor were these divisions on questions of strategy unlike those to be found in other radical movements that have endeavored to secure political change by disrupting the status quo.

How, then, shall we account for the diverse trends of strategic thought in radical politics? Should they be understood as purposeful adaptations to a variety of political circumstances? Are they reflections of long historical traditions and distinct political cultures? (Is Lenin's thought peculiarly Russian?) Are they manifestations of essentially different temperaments or psychological predispositions? (Do terrorists share a particular "mentality"?) Are they simply window dressing for clashes of personality or struggles for power within incipient organizations? Or, perhaps, are they byproducts of the organizational forms that dissident movements assume?

That the number of plausible explanations approaches the number of trends to be explained suggests correctly that nothing like a unified understanding of strategic behavior in protests, uprisings, and revolutions now exists. In this book, I attempt to lay the foundations for such an understanding by exploring the idea that strategies of the most various kinds, from "drab everyday struggle" (the phrase is Lenin's) to the self-sacrificing extremes of terrorism, can be explained as the outcome of systematic calculations, sharing a common logical structure.

This hypothesis might appear surprising and hard to accept given the bewildering profusion of factions and splinter groups that flourish in radical movements, and the diverse historical settings in which uprisings and rebellions have occurred. Nevertheless, there is good evidence in its favor. Above all, a convincing case for the defense requires a theory that can demonstrate the common patterns of reasoning and calculation that underlie the various strategic perspectives.

In fact, the theory presented here assumes an explicitly mathematical form on a level of generality sufficient to accomplish three basic purposes:

1. To derive from first principles the major strategic alternatives from which radical movements may choose

2. To predict the occasions when each kind of strategy will be preferred, and by whom

3. To generate the patterns of political reasoning developed by articulate representatives of each strategic persuasion, both to defend their choices and to criticize those of others

As an immediate and noteworthy corollary of these objectives, we have as well:

4. To explain the logic of factional splits and combinations among the different trends, and the nature of their strategic debates

None of these tasks can be accomplished without drawing upon the insights to be found in the vast and distinguished literature on political uprisings and revolutions. Nevertheless, our treatment respects several constraints, already alluded to above, that together distinguish it from earlier work on these and related subjects.

A Strategic Perspective

THE FIRST constraint is to remain faithful to the perspective of radical leaders themselves. Since the perspective of radical leaders is articulated most comprehensively in their political writings and manifestoes, the success of the theory shall be measured first by its congruence with those works.

Our preoccupation with the writings of preeminent radical thinkers like Marx, Engels, Lenin, Bernstein, Luxemburg, Mao, and the Russian terrorists is not shared by many historians and theorists who have been concerned with the political, economic, and social causes of revolutions. As a matter of fact, there exists a rather sharp divergence between the concerns and methods of those who ask why men rebel and those who inquire about how they rebel. As Thomas Schelling has written, "Among diverse theories of conflict ... a main dividing line is between those that treat conflict as a pathological state and seek its causes and treatment, and those that take conflict for granted and study the behavior associated with it."[1] In the next chapter, we shall explore more carefully the tensions and discontinuities between the historical, or etiological, perspective on revolution and the strategic perspective. For the moment, let us simply reiterate that our purpose is to understand the logic of struggle between radical movements and incumbent regimes, not to explain why strikes, rebellions, and civil disorders occur when and where they do.

Its focus on the literature of radical thought also distinguishes our approach from the one taken in recent aggregate-level statistical studies of political violence and turmoil.[2] The authors of these studies attempt to infer the political motivations of radical activists by first observing the magnitude, duration, and intensity of political disorders, and then measuring how these quantities covary with a host of political and economic indicators. The statistical approach has yielded mixed results at best, not only because the quality of the aggregate political data is generally very poor, but also because these data are extremely difficult to interpret. The basic trouble is that summary tabulations of strife and turmoil, aggregated over whole countries and long periods of time, invariably reflect the combined efforts of many groups and factions, often pursuing very different goals. The problem is compounded by the fact that most quantitative indices of political violence have ignored (often by necessity) both the identity of the participants and the character of their demands.[3] Even without a

[1] Thomas C. Schelling, *The Strategy of Conflict* (New York: Oxford University Press, 1963), p. 3.

[2] The nature of the statistical approach can be appreciated by reviewing the articles collected in Ivo K. Feierabend, Rosalind L. Feierabend, and Ted R. Gurr, eds., *Anger, Violence, and Politics: Theories and Approaches* (Englewood Cliffs, N.J.: Prentice-Hall, 1972) or Douglas A. Hibbs, Jr., *Mass Political Violence: A Cross-National Causal Analysis* (New York: Wiley Interscience, 1973), which is statistically more sophisticated than its forerunners and presents a good critique of them.

[3] This difficulty is less pronounced in statistical analyses of strikes, which have generally been far more detailed and useful for those interested in problems of strategy than the so-called cross-national studies of political violence. See, for example, Douglas A. Hibbs, Jr., "Industrial Conflict in Advanced Industrial Societies," *American Political Science Review* 70 (1976):1033–58; Orley Ashenfelter and George E. Johnson, "Bargaining Theory, Trade Unions and Industrial Strike Activity," *American Economic Review* 59 (1969):35–49; or Edward Shorter and Charles Tilly, *Strikes in France, 1830–1968* (Cambridge: Cambridge University Press, 1974). The program of research described by Charles Tilly in *From Mobilization to Revolution* (Reading, Mass.: Addison-Wesley, 1978) also promises to provide a far richer body of evidence for statistical analysis than earlier researchers had at their disposal.

technical understanding of statistical problems associated with aggregation, one can easily appreciate the difficulty of trying to infer the political calculations of Bolsheviks, Mensheviks, trade unionists, Socialist Revolutionaries, and other opponents of the tsar simply by observing the scope and magnitude of political upheavals in Russia between, say, 1905 and 1917. One might well gain general insights into the large-scale, structural preconditions that led to the tsar's downfall, but inferences about the strategic plans and reasoning of his radical opponents would necessarily be tenuous and inconclusive.

Comprehensiveness

THE ASPIRATION to explain the entire gamut of radical strategic behavior from a unified theoretical perspective further distinguishes our approach from a large body of research that focuses on particular forms of dissident activity. There now exist separate and specialized literatures on terrorism, protest, nonviolent resistance, strikes, and mass political violence, each rich in factual detail and political insight, but all resting implicitly on the faulty premise that different strategies can be explained and understood independently.

If we want to explain why a radical movement adopts a particular strategy, logical completeness requires that we also explain why other strategies are not pursued. It is not sufficient simply to provide positive reasons in the chosen strategy's favor, without also showing that alternative choices were less attractive, and why. But this enterprise becomes extraordinarily difficult if the historical cases selected for study only provide examples of a single kind of activity (be it terrorism, peaceful protest, or whatever). Such evidence cannot tell us that the positive factors given in favor of strategy X have not also been present in cases where strategy Y was followed. Nor can we know that negative factors given against Y (if Y is considered at all) were in fact absent in those instances where Y was adopted. Explanation and empirical inference in these literatures therefore tend to be partial and incomplete.

Remaining faithful to the reasoning presented by radical leaders in their political writings impels one toward a fairly literal description of ideas, while creating a comprehensive theory of strategy requires sufficient abstraction to subsume apparently dissimilar points of view within a coherent framework. A certain amount of tension therefore exists between the first and second constraints we have imposed. In fact, the two objectives would be inconsistent if our basic hypothesis were false. Only if radical leaders of all strategic persuasions share a common system of reckoning (albeit one that permits different outcomes) can the two constraints be reconciled. Nevertheless, it is important to notice that reconciliation can only be achieved at the expense of literal adherence to primary sources of evidence. In seeking the common logical structure underlying divergent trends of thought, we must to some extent idealize each one, suppressing not only contextual details but also many of the qualifications, refinements, and caveats that embellish each theorist's work. For writings as rich and complex as those of Marx, Lenin, and Bernstein, this is a difficult and delicate undertaking. One tries to capture what is basic and fundamental in each point of view, while retaining enough simplicity to illuminate general connections with other trends of thought.

Formal Rigor

THE FINAL constraint is to strive for a level of rigor and generality consistent with the standards of modern economic theory. This constraint forces disciplined thought in constructing explanations that rest upon explicit axioms of behavior whose consequences can be derived by formal deduction and tested for logical consistency and empirical merit. Recent efforts to build general theories of revolution and civil violence, among which Gurr's and Tilly's stand out as two of the most ambitious and noteworthy,[4] have not achieved these standards. While each theory strives for great generality, it comes at the expense of logical precision; first, because a veritable flood of variables and factors are introduced to explain radical behavior and, second, because basic concepts, which are selected from a variety of disciplines, do not stand in explicit logical harmony with each other. The resulting loss of simplicity makes it difficult to derive clear and definite predictions from these theories, or to establish the logical basis of the empirical assertions put forth by the authors.

In order to achieve both generality and rigor, a formal theory of revolutionary conflict must be abstract and coherent. That is to say, an abstract framework must be devised that allows basic concepts to be defined within a common system of coordinates, in such a way that the logical relationships among them can be made precise. This endeavor is our basic purpose in the chapters to follow.

[4] Ted R. Gurr, *Why Men Rebel* (Princeton: Princeton University Press, 1970), and Tilly, *From Mobilization to Revolution*.

CHAPTER ONE

History and Strategy in Theories
of Revolution

AMONG the many difficult questions that confront theorists of revolution, one of the most enigmatic and elusive goes something like this: Do the grand forces of history or do the calculated strategies of revolutionaries and regimes play a more fundamental role in deciding the timing, the outcomes, and the dynamics of revolutionary struggles?

The Historical Pattern of Explanation

NOW it should be admitted at the outset that many theorists find little occasion for controversy in such a question. Lawrence Stone concludes in his review of the recent theoretical literature about revolutions that

> everyone is agreed in making a sharp distinction between long-run, underlying causes—the preconditions, which create a potentially explosive situation and can be analyzed on a comparative basis—and immediate, incidental factors—the precipitants, which trigger the outbreak and which may be non-recurrent, personal, and fortuitous.[1]

That Stone includes in his list of "immediate, incidental factors" both "an inspired leader or prophet" and "a secret, military revolutionary organization"[2] would seem to dispose of the issue in short order. And it is certainly true that modern theorists of revolution generally ascribe vastly more importance to large-scale processes of historical change like economic development, innovation in the techniques of production and commerce, and revolutions of rising expectations than to the artful designs of radical politicians.

---

[1] Lawrence Stone, "Theories of Revolution," in *The Causes of the English Revolution, 1529–1642* (New York: Harper Torch Books, 1972), p. 8.
[2] Ibid., p. 10.

While the particulars differ in sometimes bewildering ways, the explanatory structure in most theories of revolution can be likened to a simple spark-and-tinder model. The heart of the problem, according to this view, is to explain how the body politic becomes volatile and combustible. Why one spark rather than another ignites the conflagration is an issue of lesser concern. The presumption is not that the sparks don't matter, but only that they happen randomly and with fairly high frequency. It follows that efforts to predict the particular spark and the particular moment are at once hopeless and unnecessary, for if one spark doesn't come along another surely will. The implicit assumption is that a revolutionary explosion will occur with high probability, if not with certainty, when the underlying conditions are ripe, and the paramount issue is to know what conditions constitute ripeness. The burden of the theorist, therefore, is to explain how disharmony arises in the basic components of the social structure—economic, political, or normative—and how the animosities excited by such "disequilibriums" or "cramps" or "contradictions" become focused on the political system. Marx's idea that

at a certain stage of their development the material forces of production in society come into conflict with the existing relations of production, or—what is but a legal expression for the same thing—with the property relations within which they had been at work before[3]

is one classic solution to the problem. In this tradition of explanation, then, the political strategies of revolutionary activists take on potential significance only as excitants or sparks that may ignite the revolutionary tinderbox after the necessary preconditions develop. Nor are the revolutionaries accorded exclusive title to this decidedly secondary role. Economic reversals, military disasters, agricultural calamities, and inopportune repression also intervene as triggers or catalysts in many accounts of revolution. The fundamental idea, in either event, is that revolutionary situations arise from large-scale historical dislocations, operating far beyond the reach of any political movement or organization. The ironic result is that some of the most influential studies of revolution devote hardly a word to revolutionary groups or to their

---

[3] Karl Marx, Preface to *A Contribution to the Critique of Political Economy*, reprinted in *Marx and Engels: Basic Writings on Politics & Philosophy*, ed. Lewis S. Feuer (Garden City, N.Y.: Anchor Books, 1959), pp. 43–44.

strategies, while few accord to them more than a secondary role in the larger historical drama.[4]

According to Hannah Arendt, the classical "historical" pattern of explanation is a legacy of the French Revolution.[5] Her argument traces the metaphorical use of the term *revolution* since it was borrowed from the astronomers' lexicon in the seventeenth century. In those days, the political connotations of the word had nothing to do with newness or violence, but rather were closely associated with the original astronomical idea of a regular cyclical motion or "a movement revolving back to some pre-established point."[6] It was in this sense, Arendt asserts, that the "Glorious Revolution" and the American Revolution were undertaken "by men who were firmly convinced that they would do no more than restore an old order of things that had been disturbed and violated by the despotism of absolute monarchy."[7] The revolutions before the French Revolution were perceived as restorations or renewals, rather than as new beginnings or historical watersheds. Just as the stars revolved in the sky, so "the few known forms of government revolved among the mortals in eternal recurrence."[8]

The awesomeness of the French Revolution transformed the way people thought about revolutions and deprived the astronomical metaphor of its original connotations. The emphasis shifted away from the idea of lawful, cyclical behavior to another characteristic of the stars—the irresistibility of their motion. The metaphorical imagery of revolution was suddenly filled with volcanic eruptions, raging torrents, violent tempests, and other natural calamities that were at once awesomely destructive and utterly beyond human control. Revolution

---

[4] This is a fair description of the following works, classical and modern, despite their widely differing substantive conclusions: Alexis de Tocqueville, *The Old Regime and the French Revolution*, trans. Stuart Gilbert (New York: Doubleday Anchor Books, 1955); Karl Marx, "Wage Labour and Capital," and Karl Marx and Friedrich Engels, "Manifesto of the Communist Party," in *The Marx-Engels Reader*, ed. Robert C. Tucker (New York: W. W. Norton, 1972); Harry Eckstein, "On the Etiology of Internal Wars," *History and Theory* 4 (1965): 133–63; James C. Davies, "Toward a Theory of Revolution," *American Sociological Review* 27 (1962): 5–18; Stone, *The Causes of the English Revolution*; Chalmers Johnson, *Revolutionary Change* (Boston: Little, Brown, 1966); Ted R. Gurr, *Why Men Rebel* (Princeton: Princeton University Press, 1970); Neil Smelser, *Theory of Collective Action* (New York: Free Press, 1963); Theda Skocpol, *States and Social Revolutions* (Cambridge: Cambridge University Press, 1979).

[5] See Hannah Arendt, *On Revolution* (New York: Viking Press, 1963), pp. 35–60.

[6] Ibid., p. 35.   [7] Ibid., p. 37.   [8] Ibid., p. 35.

was no longer explained as an instrumental assault on monarchical despotism, but rather as a spectacle of nature driven by forces that "had little, if anything, to do with the willful aims and purposes of men."[9]

This intuition was formulated more systematically during the nineteenth century by the theorists of historical necessity, principally Hegel and Marx. History was portrayed as an independent force in political and social life, whose power, like the motion of the stars, defied human manipulation or control. The new doctrine lent grandeur and authority to Marx's bold "materialist" theory of revolution, which, like most later theories, devoted relatively little systematic attention to problems of strategy and organization. For Marx, revolution was not the product of rational calculation or skillful political maneuvering, but the inevitable consequence of inexorable historical processes. "Modern bourgeois society," he wrote in *The Communist Manifesto*, "is like the sorcerer, who is no longer able to control the powers of the nether world whom he has called up by his spells."[10]

Such a vision of revolution allows little room for political maneuvering by the dissatisfied elements in society who long for a new social order. By logical implication, theories of historical necessity that liken revolutions to natural calamities or to the work of genies can only accommodate revolutionary activists as impotent dreamers whose efforts to bring about a cataclysm must be as futile as attempts to summon forth an earthquake. In its extreme forms, the historical pattern of explanation leads to a conception of the revolutionary as ineffectual theorist, much like the astronomers who chart the revolutions of the stars and planets. The "professional revolutionist" of the nineteenth century, writes Arendt, "was an entirely new figure on the political scene" without whom "no history of the European leisure classes would be complete."[11] Such people spent their lives "not in

---

[9] Ibid., p. 44.

[10] Marx and Engels, "Communist Manifesto," p. 340. No one can deny that a strong voluntarist strain also runs through Marx's thought, reflecting his personal involvement in organizing the proletarian movement. The arguments of Marx-the-politician and Marx-the-historian are often strikingly at odds, suggesting the discontinuities between a historical and a strategic perspective that we shall be discussing presently. The current discussion presumes only to describe Marx's reasoning as a theorist of historical necessity. This viewpoint is especially pronounced in "Wage Labour and Capital," and "Manifesto of the Communist Party."

[11] Arendt, *On Revolution*, p. 262.

revolutionary agitation for which there existed but few opportunities," but in "an essentially theoretical way . . . in the famous libraries of London and Paris, or in the coffee houses of Vienna and Zurich."[12] Nor did they bring about revolutions. Instead, they watched and waited, and were surprised like everyone else when a revolution actually happened.

> There exists hardly a revolution whose outbreak could be blamed on their activities. It usually was the other way round: revolution broke out and liberated, as it were, the professional revolutionists from wherever they happened to be—from jail, or from the coffee house, or from the library.[13]

Strategy in the Historical Explanation

THIS none too flattering portrait appears to negate the very idea of building a theory of revolutionary strategy. Let us accept the historical pattern of explanation for a moment and ask whether a theory of strategy has any justification or utility in a world where old regimes crumble not from the pressures mobilized by radical activists, but spontaneously, under the weight of history. Of course, a good theory of strategy might still be useful for understanding the lesser forms of civil disorder. Perhaps we can appreciate the relatively more humble dynamics of a rent strike or a labor dispute without calling upon an elaborate theory of historical necessity. And surely the activities of revolutionaries are to some degree interesting for their own sake, however futile or misguided they might be. But the question remains whether a theory of strategy has any place in the larger theory of revolution.

Even if we accept the bold imputations of theorists like Arendt, the answer to this question appears to be an unequivocal yes. The tendency among theorists of the historical school to dismiss or belittle the importance of revolutionary strategy rests in large part on a narrow perception of what needs to be explained about revolutions. When one relies on calamities of nature as a model of the revolutionary process, the natural inclination is to search for grand causes that explain why and when and where the calamities are likely to happen. The events that occur after the disaster strikes attract far less theoretical attention.

---

[12] Ibid., p. 263.   [13] Ibid.

As the noted historian of the French Revolution, R. R. Palmer, points out:

> For so vast an upheaval vast explanations have usually been found. It has been the habit of historians and political commentators to set the Revolution in a long context of centuries, finding for it distant origins and underlying causes.[14]

The difficulty with these accounts, as Palmer warns, is that "they explain everything but the Revolution itself."[15] While they may make it comprehensible that a great upheaval should have occurred in a particular historical era, they do little to clarify the nature or dynamics of the revolutionary struggle.

If we seek to explain the political trajectory of revolutions after they begin and the patterns of conflict that decide who wins and who loses, it becomes more difficult to ignore the strategic maneuvering of revolutionary politicians. Even Arendt admits that the "professional revolutionists" have profoundly affected the course of revolutions, despite having a role in their outbreak that is "insignificant to the point of non-existence."[16] And while we may agree with Arendt that professional revolutionaries enjoy a life before the fall that "demands no specific work whatsoever," a life spent "in study and thought, in theory and debate,"[17] it must also be recognized that these theories and debates address, for the most part anyway, problems of political strategy rather than problems of history. The preoccupation of the revolutionary activist is how to seize power in the long run, and how best to manipulate the opportunities history has presented in the short run. Moreover, the years spent in reflection, debate, and heated factional struggle about these problems are precisely the fundamental political experience upon which the professional revolutionary draws when history throws open the gates to the tyrant's palace. Thus, we cannot hope to understand how the struggle to fill the vacuum is waged, or the nature of the sequence of provisional regimes that tentatively fill the void, or what a revolutionary group does after it seizes power without understanding the components of a revolutionary strategy.

---

[14] R. R. Palmer, *The Age of the Democratic Revolution*, 2 vols. (Princeton: Princeton University Press, 1959), 1:443.
[15] Ibid.   [16] Arendt, *On Revolution*, p. 264.   [17] Ibid., p. 262.

To take a concrete example, consider the Bolshevik party after the tsarist regime finally collapsed early in 1917. Certainly no revolutionary group or party could claim direct responsibility for the demise of the Romanovs, least of all the Bolsheviks, whose leading figures were living in exile at the time. Nor should anyone dispute Arendt's description of the party's leaders as professional theorists, whose principal experience in political struggle was years of factional infighting. Still, one has to admit that Lenin, unlike Marx, was primarily a theorist of political strategy rather than a theorist of political history. He was most deeply concerned with the problems of how to build a revolutionary organization, how to create a revolutionary consciousness among the masses, how to approach the tactics of compromise and violence, and how to mobilize a revolutionary insurrection. And who would disagree that Lenin's theories of strategy had a profound effect on the Bolsheviks' activities during 1917—whether one considers the party's slogans and tactics of mass mobilization; its intransigent stance toward the provisional government; its attitudes about compromise, coalition, and violence; or its readiness to seize power by force when other socialists shrunk back.[18] To be honest, one has to consider Arendt's reasoning a bit forced when she asserts that the professional revolutionists'

> great advantage in this power struggle lies less in their theories and mental or organizational preparation than in the simple fact that their names are the only ones which are publicly known.[19]

Much more convincing are Trotsky's observations about the importance of a revolutionary theory during a revolutionary high tide. As he explains in his *History of the Russian Revolution*:

> A revolutionary conception without a revolutionary will is like a watch with a broken spring. . . . But the absence of a broad political conception condemns the most willful revolutionist to indecisiveness in the presence of vast and complicated events.[20]

---

[18] An excellent recent study that makes this point without overstating Lenin's role is Alexander Rabinowitch, *The Bolsheviks Come to Power* (New York: W. W. Norton, 1978).

[19] Arendt, *On Revolution*, p. 263.

[20] Leon Trotsky, *The History of the Russian Revolution*, trans. Max Eastman, 3 vols. (New York: Monad Press, 1980), 1:289.

In much the same way, it is difficult to understand how a revolutionary organization exercises power without attending to its prior strategy for seizing it. How can we hope to understand Lenin's party state—its organizational structure; its hostility to spontaneous, democratic bodies like the soviets;[21] its attitudes toward repression, class collaboration, and compromise; or its sense of mission as an agency of historical transformation—without understanding the theory of revolutionary strategy upon which Lenin's conception of the Bolshevik party rested. After all, his vision of the party contained, in embryonic form, all of the essential characteristics of the Soviet state.

To sum up, then, a serious shortcoming of the historical pattern of explanation is its narrow preoccupation with explaining the outbreak of revolutions, and its tendency to neglect the dynamics that determine their eventual outcomes. This unconscious bias generates theories of revolution that devote vastly more attention to the large-scale historical forces that precede revolutionary crises than to the revolutionary organizations that play them out. These historical explanations provide, as a result, very little analytical leverage for understanding the political struggles that are the essence of the revolutionary process after the crisis begins, and from which the new regime emerges.

Explaining the Onset of Revolutionary Crises

IF EXPLAINING how revolutions unfold seems to require a theory that describes the logic of revolutionary struggles, the classical attribution of revolutionary crises to historical necessity (i.e. to large-scale processes of historical change) is itself highly suspect as an explanation for why revolutions *occur*. Theorists of history have been no more (and usually far less) successful than professional revolutionaries at predicting when revolutions happen, despite their putative inevitability. The difficulties are nowhere more evident than in the Marxist tradition of explanation, which has been mistakenly predicting the imminent collapse of capitalist society for over 100 years, while, in the meantime, two socialist revolutions of historic proportions have already occurred in the precapitalist, "petty bourgeois" backwaters of peasant society that Marx described as "conservative, nay more, reactionary."[22]

---

[21] See Arendt, *On Revolution*, p. 269.
[22] Marx and Engels, "Communist Manifesto," p. 344.

Some writers of the historical persuasion attribute the unpredict-
ability of revolutionary uprisings to the essential randomness of their
precipitating events,[23] but the difficulties often seem to run deeper.
Though the Bolsheviks were surely surprised by the "spontaneous"
insurrections of 1905 and February 1917, Arendt's idea that revolutions liberate revolutionaries from coffeehouses and libraries is simply
ludicrous as a description of the revolutions that took place later
in China and Vietnam. In these instances, the historical pattern of
explanation appears to underestimate drastically the role played by
revolutionary organizations, both in mobilizing opposition against the
governing regimes and in designing the large-scale disruptions that
eventually unseated them. These revolutions seem far less spontaneous
than either the French Revolution or the Russian uprisings in 1905
and 1917, and defy explanation by theories of historical necessity that
were spawned by the French experience.

If we look more carefully at the theories of historical necessity, it
appears that two sorts of analytical shortsightedness undermine their
capacity to explain recent revolutionary experiences and to compre-
hend properly the role of political maneuvering in the development of
revolutionary crises. The first difficulty results from a pronounced
empirical tunnel vision among theorists of the "inevitabilist" persuasion. One implication of the idea that revolutions are historically
necessary, or inevitable, is that all of the revolutions that might have
happened actually have occurred. The historian's search for causes
has therefore been conducted almost exclusively in the archives of
countries where successful revolutions have taken place. This seems
only natural, for if one believes that revolutions occur by necessity, it
follows that their causes cannot be discovered and studied in other
bodies of evidence. As the historian James Joll explains:

> When a revolution succeeds, historians are concerned to trace its roots
> and unravel its origins and development, so that, very often, the whole
> chain of events leading to it over many decades is represented as an
> inevitable process, and each idea or episode is judged by the extent to
> which it helped or hindered the final result.... Revolutions which failed
> are treated as blind alleys, and the men and ideas that inspired them are
> rarely studied for their own inherent interest.[24]

---

[23] See, for example, Eckstein, "On the Etiology of Internal Wars."
[24] James Joll, *The Anarchists*, 2nd ed. (Cambridge: Harvard University Press, 1980),
p. viii.

The consequence of such tunnel vision is the simultaneous explanation of too much and too little. On one hand, the historical circumstances that precede each of the great revolutions are so tangled and complicated (not to say murky) that dozens of patterns or mechanisms can be found in them, all with more or less equal claim to being the "real" explanation. In this sense, the great revolutions are fantastically overdetermined by a list of causes, which usually seem plausible if considered individually, but which, taken together, have little or no coherence when they are not absolutely self-contradictory.

Our despair over this bewildering embarrassment of riches would dissipate quickly, however, if we considered a complete census of *all* the historical instances of economic catastrophes; rapid economic growth; military humiliations; turns past the apex of J-curves; class, ethnic, or colonial oppression; relative or absolute deprivations; population explosions; political unresponsiveness; or ruthless repression—rather than the subset of cases that happened to precede revolutions. We would find that only the tiniest fraction of the events that are said to make revolutions inevitable actually predated an uprising or insurrection, however pitiful or short-lived. Surely the first casualty of this humbling exercise would be the spurious intuitive sense of inevitability that necessarily arises when historical explanations are derived from, and tested upon, data that have been collected *just because* they preceded the events we hope to explain. Perhaps we would begin to appreciate what revolutionaries have known all along—that spark-and-tinder models vastly underestimate the difficulty of mobilizing a revolutionary insurrection, however miserable, or oppressed, or ambitious, or frustrated the population might be. As the terrorist journal *Narodnaya Volya* once declared (with considerable, though not perfect, accuracy): "No village has ever revolted merely because it was hungry."[25]

And perhaps a broader empirical perspective might generate new questions that do not implicitly assume that political maneuvering by radicals and regimes has no effect on the course of events. The truly difficult problem, it would seem, is not to explain why revolutions happen spontaneously and inevitably (without calculated planning or direction), but rather to understand why revolutions happen hardly

[25] Cited in Franco Venturi, *Roots of Revolution: A History of the Populist and Socialist Movements in Nineteenth Century Russia*, trans. Francis Haskell (London: Weidenfeld and Nicolson, 1960), p. 680.

at all in a world that abounds with misery, deprivation, injustice, and spellbindingly rapid change. When we ask why revolutions don't happen, rather than assuming that they must, the political stratagems and blunders of radical leaders and defenders of the old order are far more likely to appear consequential. The reason is simple. Once we begin to investigate all the occurrences of the historically rooted deprivations and injustices that are said to provoke insurrections, and not just the ones that are concomitant with revolutionary explosions, our estimates of other more proximate effects will necessarily be enhanced. We may well find ourselves becoming sympathetic, at least in spirit, to the conclusions drawn by Leon Trotsky about the insurrection of February 1917. In a chapter of his *History* that inquires into the leadership of this insurrection, Trotsky insists that "the mystic doctrine of spontaneousness explains nothing."[26]

> A mass insurrection is never purely spontaneous. Even when it flashes out unexpectedly to a majority of its own participants, it has been fertilized by those ideas in which the insurrectionaries see a way out of the difficulties of existence.[27]

Moreover, Trotsky continues, there are "tactical rules which if violated will make the victory of any insurrection extremely difficult if not impossible."[28] Trotsky's general conclusion that the political maneuvers of revolutionary parties had a decisive effect on the Russian Revolution is, a priori, no more or less plausible than a host of other explanations that identify diverse occurrences that may have aroused the workers and peasants and dispirited the defenders of the old order. Nevertheless, we are far more likely to take it seriously if we consider all of the available evidence about purported causal factors, and not just those instances that precede successful uprisings.

Historical Inevitability and the Revolutionary Initiative

TROTSKY regards his account of the Russian Revolution as the work of a historian, but his outlook remains very much that of a political strategist. Let us adopt this perspective ourselves and reconsider the doctrine of historical necessity from the vantage point of the professional revolutionary. Doing so will help us to understand a second and

[26] Leon Trotsky, *History*, 1:150.
[27] Ibid., 3:168.   [28] Ibid., 3:170.

possibly more fundamental weakness in theories that ignore the initiatives of radical politicians.

While it may be reassuring to believe that the forces of history are on one's side, the notion that revolutions happen inevitably is basically alien to the mentality of a professional politician. If one accepts the doctrine of necessity in its strong form, embracing the view that the forces of history are *irresistible* like the motion of the stars, then it follows that revolutions happen inevitably *at a specific historical moment*, just as eclipses and occultations do. But why, then, pursue a career as an insurrectionist? One might just as well sit back and enjoy the interim period, knowing full well that efforts to hasten the revolution's arrival can be no more fruitful than the regime's efforts to forestall it. In this strong sense, historical necessity negates action by rendering it futile and meaningless.

Such a doctrine is repugnant to the political activist whose calling rests upon a conviction that strategy matters, that some strategies are better than others, that amateurish mistakes are costly, that political opportunities should be exploited, and that insurrection is an art. If he accepts the doctrine of historical necessity at all, the professional revolutionary is likely to prefer a weakened form. Revolutions may be historically inevitable, he might argue, but their timing can be affected by political maneuvering. This is Mao's position in an early essay entitled "A Single Spark Can Start a Prairie Fire."[29] There he argues against the pessimism of his comrades who believed that the historical situation in China was not ripe for revolution.

> Some comrades in our Party still do not know how to appraise the current situation correctly.... Though they believe that a revolutionary high tide is inevitable, they do not believe it to be imminent.... They seem to think that, since the revolutionary high tide is still remote, it will be labour lost to attempt to establish political power by hard work.... They do not have a deep understanding of the idea of accelerating the nation-wide revolutionary high tide through the consolidation and expansion of Red political power.[30]

This might seem like a modest amendment to the doctrine of historical necessity, but it can lead to dramatically different conclusions

---

[29] Mao Tse-tung, "A Single Spark Can Start a Prairie Fire," *Selected Military Writings of Mao Tse-tung* (Peking: Foreign Languages Press, 1972) pp. 65–76.
[30] Ibid., p. 65.

about the importance of revolutionary initiatives, depending on one's suppositions about the length of the temporal span in which the revolution can be hastened or delayed and the location of the span in the future. Presumably, the incentive to devote a lifetime to arduous political struggle diminishes as the length of this span approaches zero or as the near edge of the span recedes into the future. In the first case, one has to ask whether accelerating the revolution by a short interval (a week? a month? a year?) justifies the personal sacrifice required to be a revolutionary. In the second case, the question is whether accelerating the revolution by even a large amount (a decade? five decades?) is worthwhile when the outcome lies far in the future. Under either assumption, the implications of the weakened doctrine of necessity are not significantly different from those of the strong version (where the span collapses to a point). Using the human life span as a frame of reference, both imply that a revolutionary career is essentially futile.

The notion of necessity becomes vacuous, however, as one's temporal assumptions become more optimistic. Suppose, as Mao does, that the timing of the revolution can be affected substantially by "each side's subjective ability in directing the war,"[31] and furthermore that the near edge of the span lies close by in the future. "When I say that there will soon be a high tide of revolution in China," Mao writes, "I am emphatically not speaking of something which in the words of some people 'is possibly coming,' something illusory, unattainable and devoid of significance for action."[32] Then surely the political imperative is to find the strategy that leads to the earliest possible uprising. The presumption of necessity becomes irrelevant under these assumptions, because using bad strategy has manifestly unfavorable consequences (again adopting the adult life span as a frame of reference). History having thus far unfolded, it is as though the revolutionaries control their own destiny.

And so it is that professional revolutionaries have become a principal source of resistance to theories of historical necessity (at least in their undiluted, strong forms). Consider the Marxist tradition, for example, where the most important strategic thinkers have launched determined revisionist attacks on the sacred texts of the founding fathers. While Bernstein argued strenuously against Marx's fundamental

[31] Mao Tse-tung, "Problems of Strategy in China's Revolutionary War," *Selected Military Writings*, p. 88.
[32] Mao Tse-tung, "A Single Spark," p. 75.

precept that the capitalist economic system was inherently unstable and doomed to inevitable collapse, Lenin insisted that the proletariat could never develop a sufficiently revolutionary outlook on its own to revolt spontaneously. Why Lenin and Bernstein favored such different political programs is a problem we shall consider later, but the crucial point to understand here is that both were driven by the same imperatives. Both men sought to devise strategies that could hasten the revolution's arrival, and both were obliged to revise the master's theory of necessity in order to place their strategic precepts on logically sound footing. Here, then, is a second and more basic weakness in theories of revolution based on large-scale and uncontrollable processes of historical change—they are repugnant to the very people whose behavior they would explain. People who take such theories seriously become historians, not revolutionaries, while people who become revolutionaries direct all their energies to rendering the theories false.

Accelerating History: The Evolution of Revolutions

THE DEVELOPMENT of revolutions reflects the ongoing search by radical politicians for new strategies to accelerate the glacial flow of history. This quest has transformed the revolutionary process in such basic ways that modern revolutions often bear little resemblance to their historical antecedents. The evolution of revolutions is marked by fundamental changes in the dynamics of mass mobilization, in the methods of struggle adopted by the revolutionary forces, and in the organization of the radical leadership. These changes are a consequence of strategic innovations that have elevated the insurrectionary arts from primitive beginnings to a high level of sophistication and have greatly enhanced the role of the professional revolutionary.

Among the most basic of these innovations has been the emergence of increasingly durable and coherent revolutionary organizations. Such organizations were unknown to the amateur politicians of the eighteenth century who shaped the course of the French Revolution. Their hastily arranged and chaotically unstable coalitions gave way in the nineteenth century to systematically organized political parties whose sole objective was to make revolutions happen. These parties were the political step-children of Arendt's "professional revolutionists," who had grown dissatisfied with a theoretical life spent in

historical speculation and endless coffeehouse debates. Their revolutionary parties evolved from tiny underground circles, resting, in
Lenin's words, upon "personal friendship or an instinctive confidence
for which no reason was given," into complex organizations, governed
by "formal, bureaucratically worded rules."[33] The revolutionary parties gradually became more specialized and structurally elaborate as
they adapted themselves to perform the very tasks that were regarded
as the province of history by the theorists of historical necessity. On
one hand, they became agencies of revolutionary agitation, ideological mobilization, and strategic direction, while on the other, they pro-
tected the revolutionary impulse from counterrevolutionary repression.
As radical politicians became more sophisticated about the ways in
which a well-designed organization could be used to galvanize latent
discontent into open political opposition, and as their revolutionary
parties became enduring fixtures of the modern political landscape,
revolutionary uprisings became less spontaneous and undirected.

The development of this organizational and strategic awareness is
readily apparent in the writings of the Marxist theorists of revolution.
The master himself was, of course, the theorist of historical necessity
par excellence. Marx devotes hardly any systematic attention to the
design of revolutionary organizations or to their strategies. The theory
of revolution set forth in *The Communist Manifesto*, for example, assigns most of the responsibility for organizing the proletarian revolution to the inner workings of the capitalist economic system. "With
the development of industry," Marx writes, "the proletariat not only
increases in number; it becomes concentrated in greater masses, its
strength grows, and it feels that strength more."[34] Meanwhile, commercial crises caused by epidemics of overproduction regularly reduce
capitalist society to "a state of momentary barbarism."[35] These crises, according to Marx, "put on its trial, each time more threateningly,
the existence of the entire bourgeois society."[36] Thus, the steady im-
miseration and growth of the proletariat lay the groundwork for the
revolutionary cataclysm, while the explosive oscillation of the business
cycle plays the role of agitator and mobilizer until the bourgeois order
finally crumbles.

---

[33] V. I. Lenin, *Selected Works*, Vol. 1: *One Step Forward, Two Steps Back* (New York:
International Publishers, 1967), p. 421.
[34] Marx and Engels, "Communist Manifesto," p. 342.
[35] Ibid., p. 340.   [36] Ibid.

In Lenin's analysis of the revolutionary process, the emergence of a revolutionary consciousness among the proletariat becomes the work of a highly organized vanguard party, rather than a spontaneous reaction to economic instability and decay. "The working class, exclusively by its own effort, is able to develop only a trade-union consciousness," Lenin insists in *What Is To Be Done?*. "The workers were not, and could not be, conscious of the irreconcilable antagonism of their interests to the whole of the modern political and social system." Instead, such a revolutionary awareness must "be brought to them from without."[37] Here Lenin quietly appropriates for his revolutionary party the role played by large-scale processes of economic development in Marx's theory. Rather than waiting for a revolutionary explosion to occur spontaneously, the Bolsheviks set out themselves to create the conditions for an insurrection. *What Is To Be Done?* contains not a single word about catastrophic depressions or other uncontrollable processes that might mobilize an uprising against the tsarist state. The initiative goes instead to the "organization of revolutionaries," without whom, Lenin says, "no class in modern society can wage a determined struggle."[38]

Whether the Russian revolutions of 1905 and February 1917 were in fact "spontaneous" is a question that has excited controversy among scholars and revolutionaries alike. Everyone agrees that the uprisings were not mobilized according to some premeditated plan by a revolutionary political organization. Nonetheless, the amount of systematic and consciously revolutionary agitation that took place before the insurrections raises doubts about explanations that ignore the revolutionaries. The question of spontaneity becomes less controversial, however, as we pass from the transitional Russian case to the Chinese and Vietnamese revolutions. The protracted campaigns of encirclement and gradual strangulation that brought the Chinese and Vietnamese Communists to power barely resemble the explosive mass insurrections that occurred in earlier revolutions. To an unprecedented degree, though by no means completely, the victors in China and Vietnam relied on strategies that brought both central elements of the revolutionary process—ideological mobilization and collective struggle—under the direct control of their revolutionary organizations. Mao Tse-tung and Ho Chi Minh used their organizations to

[37] V. I. Lenin, *Selected Works*, Vol. 1: *What Is To Be Done?*, p. 122.
[38] Ibid., p. 197.

build armies that became simultaneously the principal revolutionary agent for mobilizing the masses ideologically and the principal destructive instrument for assaulting the forces of the state.

This political fusion represented a fairly ambitious departure from the Bolsheviks' transitional concept of the revolutionary process, just as Lenin's ideas marked a bold advance from Marx's largely spontaneous conception. The Leninists regarded their party organization as an instrument for arousing the revolutionary aspirations of the masses, but not as a combat organization with which to bludgeon the old order. The Bolsheviks tried to lay the political groundwork for a mass uprising, and then to tap its destructive energy for their own political purposes. As Trotsky explains in his *History*:

> Without a guiding organization, the energy of the masses would dissipate like steam not enclosed in a piston-box. But nevertheless what moves things is not the piston or the box, but the steam.[39]

Thus, the Leninists' conception of revolutionary strategy revolved around the process of ideological mobilization rather than collective struggle. An explosive mass insurrection of the French type was still regarded as the only conceivable means to destroy the tsarist state, and the Bolsheviks understood their main task to be the creation of a favorable political climate for such an uprising. They did not believe that a revolutionary organization could, by itself, overturn the state, nor did they imagine that a mass insurrection could be summoned forth and controlled at will. Instead, they shared the basic perceptions of the theorists of necessity, regarding the mass insurrection as an elemental force of nature that could be exploited but not directed. "To be successful," Lenin wrote,

> insurrection must rely not upon conspiracy and not upon a party, but upon the advanced class. That is the first point. Insurrection must rely upon a *revolutionary upsurge of the people*. That is the second point. Insurrection must rely upon that *turning-point* in the history of the growing revolution when the activity of the advanced ranks . . . is at its height, and when the *vacillations* in the ranks of the enemy . . . are strongest.[40]

According to this view, the problem of collective struggle was basically not a question of direction and control but one of timing. The culminating task in the revolutionary process was "to feel out the growing insurrection in good season" and to have ready a suitable plan for

[39] Leon Trotsky, *History*, 1:xix.
[40] V. I. Lenin, *Selected Works*, Vol. 2: "Marxism and Insurrection," p. 365.

seizing power when the old regime collapsed.[41] "The most responsible task of the revolutionary leaders," Trotsky writes in his famous chapter on the art of insurrection, is to discriminate the short period between "the moment when an attempt to summon an insurrection must inevitably prove premature ... and the moment when a favorable situation must be considered hopelessly missed."[42] Thus, the Bolsheviks' theory of strategy can justly be called transitional in the sense that it subsumes one facet of the revolutionary process, ideological preparation, while it regards the process of collective struggle as largely spontaneous and autonomous.

The strategy of rebellion that Mao developed in the hinterlands of Kiangsi province deployed a revolutionary army to unseat the incumbent regime, rather than relying upon the fickle, if powerful, winds of a mass insurrection. In order to exploit the revolutionary energies of the masses to their fullest potential, Mao sought to fuse the process of ideological mobilization to a highly rationalized method of violent struggle based on rigorous military reasoning. Drawing upon the systematic insights about force and violence that had been accumulated by theorists of military strategy, Mao devised new strategies of revolutionary political violence that went far beyond the Bolsheviks' vision of an armed insurrection. While the Russians had relied primarily on political agitation to hasten the revolution's arrival, Mao sought to accelerate events even further by harnessing the masses' revolutionary energies to a powerful and efficient engine of destruction. "A special characteristic of the revolution in China," he writes, "is the use of military action to develop insurrection."[43] The essence of Mao's highly original strategic conception was to develop a close symbiotic relationship between the political and the military aspects of the revolutionary struggle and, by so doing, to create possibilities for a socialist revolution in a situation that was not even remotely like the one described by Marx's theory.

Mao built his Red Army virtually from scratch, using a political organization to instill revolutionary commitment in a ragtag following that included bandits, adventurers, "lumpen-proletarians," mercenaries, and soldiers captured in battle.[44] These were not the politically

---

[41] Leon Trotsky, *History*, 3:172.

[42] Ibid., 3:173.

[43] Mao Tse-tung, "Struggle in the Chingkang Mountains," *Selected Military Writings*, p. 47.

[44] For a description of Mao's early recruits, see ibid., pp. 28–35.

sophisticated ideologues from which Lenin's party was fashioned. Instead, they were among the least educated and politically most backward elements in China, lacking, for the most part, any systematic ideological orientation at all. The Red Army therefore had to fashion new political men from these unlikely socialists after they were recruited into its closed organizational environment. "The majority of the Red Army come from the mercenary armies," Mao wrote in 1928, "but their character changes once they are in the Red Army.... After receiving political education, the Red Army soldiers have become class-conscious ... and they know they are fighting for themselves, for the working class and the peasantry. Hence they can endure the hardships of bitter struggle without complaint."[45] Later, he notes, "The Red Army is like a furnace in which all captured soldiers are transmuted the moment they come over."[46]

As it grew larger, the Red Army attempted to carve out a secure territorial base, remote from urban centers, where it could erect a model regime and exploit the advantages of state power to develop even further. Within the base area, the revolutionary army could collect taxes and conscript recruits, while it assiduously nurtured its legitimacy and authority among the masses. By enfolding its recruits in a carefully designed organizational environment, by exploiting its quasi-governmental status in the base area, and by deploying its raw military might, the Red Army introduced a host of new incentives in the process of revolutionary mobilization. Unlike a spontaneous mass uprising where acute feelings of injustice or political outrage are the principal spurs to participation, most of Mao's followers only became revolutionary *after* they joined the movement. The Maoist approach to ideological mobilization evolved from the Bolsheviks' principles of agitation and propaganda into an organizational system of ideological transformation. It allowed the Chinese Communists to develop support for "advanced" socialist principles in what could fairly be called an ideological vacuum.[47]

The base area was more than a source of manpower, however. It also became the cornerstone of a military strategy that allowed militarily

[45] Ibid., p. 29.
[46] Ibid., p. 30.
[47] Information about the early Red Army is sparse, but an excellent description of the Vietnamese NLF's organizational "furnace" of ideological transformation, based on a careful analysis of interview data, can be found in Paul Berman, *Revolutionary Organization* (Lexington, Mass.: D. C. Heath, 1974).

inferior forces to engage and defeat the larger and better equipped armies of the regime. Here the fundamental principle was to "lure the enemy in deep" where his forces could be annihilated piece by piece in brief guerrilla encounters. The success of this strategy depended entirely upon exploiting the military advantages offered by a friendly political sanctuary. Only by using the larger population to provide intelligence, camouflage, and logistical support could the Red Army, and its later imitators, achieve sufficient mobility and surprise to secure local superiority against the enemy, and to maintain the military initiative despite an unfavorable balance of forces.

Mao's conception of the revolutionary process therefore assumed the form of a protracted military and political struggle unlike an explosive mass uprising of the French model. The idea was to advance in waves, establishing base areas and consolidating political power within them, luring the enemy in deep and wearing him down with surprise attacks, forcing the enemy to withdraw toward his urban enclaves, extending the base area into the resulting vacuum, drawing upon the larger base to fortify the revolutionary army, and renewing the struggle on a larger scale. Gradually, the struggle assumes the character of a conventional war as the revolutionaries undertake a strategic counter-offensive and the regime falls back in strategic retreat. The revolutionary forces occupy the countryside and eventually encircle the regime's urban strongholds, suffocating the helpless cities until the capital finally falls. This was roughly the pattern of the Chinese Revolution and precisely the pattern of the Vietnamese Revolution. "Only thus," Mao concluded in 1930, would it be possible "to arouse the masses on a broad scale" and "to hasten the revolutionary high tide."[48]

A Modern Theory of Revolution Requires a Theory of Strategy

DESPITE evident and widely noted changes in the nature of revolutionary struggles, many theorists nevertheless seem reluctant to elevate the theoretical standing of radical politicians and their strategies from their present lowly status as precipitants or catalysts to a more central position in the revolutionary process.[49] Strictly historical or

---

[48] Mao Tse-tung, "A Single Spark," p. 67.

[49] The "resource mobilization" theorists of revolution in sociology are notable exceptions. For example, Charles Tilly's *From Mobilization to Revolution* (Reading, Mass.: Addison-Wesley, 1978) shares many of the concerns expressed here and develops a theory that focuses on the behavior of radical organizations.

"structural" modes of explanation still retain a wide following, despite their shortsightedness about the growing capacity of radical organizations to exploit unfavorable situations and to influence the course of revolutionary developments. This hesitancy can be traced to persistent misconceptions about how a revolutionary strategy should be explained and how the independent impact of a strategy should be assessed.

Surely no one would argue that radical movements can, by using good strategy, accomplish any political objective in any situation. Strategies are constrained by political circumstances, and a fundamental problem in a theory of strategy is to understand the interaction between strategic choice and the political environment. The real question is whether good strategy allows the revolutionaries to accomplish their objectives in a broader range of circumstances than otherwise would be possible. One must be careful, therefore, about drawing hasty conclusions from the observation that revolutionary leaders sometimes tailor their strategies to exploit existing circumstances. When a strategy succeeds, there is a tendency among theorists of the historical persuasion to assert that the political situation *determined* the strategy and hence the larger outcome.

This, for example, is Theda Skocpol's interpretation of the Chinese Revolution in her recent study, *States and Social Revolutions*.[50] Skocpol readily admits that the Chinese Revolution bears little resemblance to the spontaneous eruptions of the peasantry that occurred in Russia and France. "The peasant contribution to the Chinese Revolution," she writes, "resembled much more a mobilized response to a revolutionary elite's initiatives than did the peasant contributions in France and Russia."[51] Nonetheless, she argues that the lack of spontaneity in the Chinese Revolution "had little to do with revolutionary ideology and everything to do with the 'peculiarities' ... of the Chinese agrarian sociopolitical structure."[52]

Skocpol rests her case on two basic arguments. First, she asserts that the Chinese peasantry was so dominated by the local gentry class that it was "not in a structural position to revolt collectively and autonomously."[53] The Chinese peasants, in her opinion,

---

[50] Theda Skocpol, *States and Social Revolutions* (Cambridge: Cambridge University Press, 1979).
[51] Ibid., p. 154.   [52] Ibid.   [53] Ibid., p. 239.

lacked the kind of structurally preexisting solidarity and autonomy that allowed the agrarian revolutions in France and Russia to emerge quickly and spontaneously.[54]

Moreover, the strategy of guerrilla warfare pursued by the Red Army was "the only one possible in the circumstances,"[55] or more precisely, "the only really viable possibility open to the Communists."[56] On one hand, the "decentralized mode of fighting" in guerrilla warfare suited the peasants' "localistic proclivities,"[57] while the agrarian socio-political structure generated large numbers of "marginal poor-peasant outcasts" during times of crises. Thus, "fortunately for the Chinese Communists but not incidentally," large numbers of displaced peasant recruits were available when they were needed during the era of war-lordism after 1911.[58] And finally, the forces of repression were much weaker in the countryside than they were in the cities. Skocpol concludes, therefore, that the Chinese Revolution was "structurally" determined in the same way that earlier and more spontaneous revolutions were.

> Organized revolutionary vanguards have with time become increasingly self-conscious and vociferous about their indispensable role in "making" revolutions. It nevertheless seems to me that recent revolutionary crises, just as surely as those that launched the classic social revolutions, have come about only through inter- and intranational structural contra-dictions and conjunctural occurrences beyond the deliberate control of avowed revolutionaries.[59]

Now it should be noted at once that Skocpol's account of the Chinese Revolution differs from older theories of necessity, which suggest that the same outcome results *regardless* of what strategy the revolutionaries follow. Skocpol openly admits that the Chinese Communists had a decisive effect on the course of events. Still, she tries to rescue a semblance of historical necessity by claiming that the revolution could *only* have happened as it did given the sociopolitical structure in agrarian China. In other words, the revolution was structurally or historically determined, despite the role played by a revolutionary organization.

In the game of chess, it is obvious that the structure of the board and the configuration of pieces constrain the players' choices, but when

---

[54] Ibid., p. 148.   [55] Ibid., p. 252.   [56] Ibid., p. 253.   [57] Ibid., p. 252.
[58] Ibid., p. 254.   [59] Ibid., p. 291.

can it be said that a situation *determines* the subsequent course of the game and its outcome? Such a conclusion clearly requires a stronger argument than simply asserting that the arrangement of the board affects the players' moves. The same can be said about revolutionary politics, which is no less complex than chess. Skocpol's basic conclusion depends on three crucial propositions, all highly dubious, that she defends with only a minimum of evidence.

The first is that a winning strategy was unique in the Chinese Communists' political environment, i.e. that no other strategy would have allowed the Communists to seize power or otherwise to accomplish their objectives. But here Skocpol presents neither an exhaustive review of alternative strategies nor convincing evidence to show that all of them would have failed. Surely her brief summary of the Communists' difficulties in the cities[60] only scratches the surface. More fundamentally, however, Skocpol's theory of revolution does not even begin to define the set of strategies that radical organizations have at their disposal. In this respect, her work suffers from a common shortcoming among modern theories of revolution generally.

Secondly, Skocpol's conclusion assumes that the optimal strategy will inevitably be identified and implemented, even when it is unique. Otherwise, the outcome of revolutions would depend on the political sophistication and skill of radical strategists and their system of reckoning in a complicated political environment (just as chess games depend on the strategic sensibilities of the players). Skocpol's analysis of the Chinese experience says not a word about the dynamics of decision making in radical organizations that would justify this expectation, however, while it leaves a host of questions unanswered. Why, for example, do revolutionary movements pursue ineffective and even counterproductive strategies? Why did Mao's strategy provoke bitter factional controversy within his party, if it was the only one possible? Why did the Chinese Communists collaborate with the Kuomintang if the disastrous purge that decimated their party in 1926 resulted from a choice that "could not have gone differently?"[61] And why, indeed, did the KMT not adopt the Communists' strategy when it proved to be an effective one?

Skocpol's argument betrays the same spurious sense of inevitability that typifies an entire tradition of explanations, built by observing

---

[60] Ibid., pp. 252–53.   [61] Ibid., p. 246.

successful revolutions after the fact. To say that the winner's strategy in a game of chess depended on an earlier configuration of pieces, while true in a trivial sense, hardly implies that either player's choices were *determined* by the situation at some earlier point in the game. In chess, as in politics, a host of alternative moves usually seem plausible, and different players rarely react to a particular situation with the same response. Nor do we expect players who differ in strategic skill to find equally effective moves, especially as the set of winning strategies shrinks in size (recalling Skocpol's first principle).

And finally Skocpol's conclusion seems to imply that the success of Mao's strategy depended completely on the "peculiarities" of the Chinese sociopolitical context. Otherwise, it would be illogical to assert that the Chinese Revolution was possible only because of the "structural contradictions and conjunctural occurrences" she describes. But how, then, are we to understand the success of the Vietnamese Communists who followed Mao's strategy virtually to the letter despite the absence of roving mercenary bands in the Vietnamese countryside, despite the absence of a warlord system, despite the smaller geographic scale of the revolution, and despite the technologically more sophisticated and vastly better equipped armies of the comprador regimes? Two possible accounts of this evidence come to mind, both damaging to Skocpol's thesis. Either Mao's strategy succeeded in a basically different situation, undermining her conclusion directly, or the success of the strategy depended not on the fine details of Chinese agrarian society that Skocpol emphasizes in her account but only on the more general features of the landholding and tenancy system that were also present in Vietnam. But why, then, have there been no successful socialist revolutions in the other East Asian countries, which have essentially similar agrarian arrangements? Again, it is impossible to claim that the social structure determines the revolution, if the same structure yields a revolution in some cases but not others.

These shortcomings in Skocpol's reasoning are symptomatic of the difficulties that arise when recent revolutions are analyzed from the outmoded theoretical perspective of historical necessity—a perspective that was developed more than a hundred years ago to understand the more primitive and spontaneous uprisings of an earlier era. A theory of revolution that disregards the problem of strategy is analogous to a theory of warfare that ignores developments in military technology since the Napoleonic era. Through their efforts to broaden the range of political circumstances in which their objectives can be realized, revolutionaries have become increasingly resourceful at mobilizing a following and exploiting sophisticated forms of political violence and disruption. This book presents a theory to explain the political logic, rather than the operational details, of this endeavor. It seeks to understand in a general way how dissident organizations and parties go about choosing their strategies and refining them when they prove to be ineffective. To answer these questions, a good theory must:

1. Describe the nature of conflicts between dissidents and regimes

2. Elaborate systematically the range of strategic alternatives available to *both* sides

3. Establish what characteristics of the political situation govern the outcomes of strategies, and determine which strategies are therefore better suited to particular situations

4. Describe the process of decision making by which one strategy is selected from a larger set of alternatives

Those who have been conditioned by theorists of necessity to regard these problems as matters of common sense will no doubt be surprised at how complicated and subtle they can become. In fact, the schematic and highly tentative theory that follows only begins to reflect their true complexity.

CHAPTER TWO

A Formal Model of Protest
and Rebellion

IN ORDER to build a rigorous theory of strategy in protest and rebellion, the elements of the political situation facing radical movements must now be defined systematically. This delicate operation requires a judicious balancing of competing objectives, including generality, abstraction, and tractability on one hand, and political richness, realism, and relevance on the other.

Stakes of the Game

WE SUPPOSE, in our theory, that protesters and rebels seek ultimately to displace the policies of their governments by creating disruption in the streets. Since governments sometimes make it their policy to restructure society, this conception of the dissidents' purpose is general enough to accommodate even revolutionary aspirations. We use the term *government* here in a general way to denote the institutional arrangement of power in a ruling organization. The incumbent administration occupying those institutions will be called a *regime*. Taken in this broad sense, the terms might describe a military command, a clerical body, or a university administration, as well as civil governments in the usual sense.

We shall represent the policies of the government and the dissidents' demands as points along a one-dimensional "ideological spectrum," defined mathematically as a finite interval on the real number line.[1]

---

[1] The spatial analogy has a number of fruitful applications in politics and economics, including spatial theories of electoral competition. The seminal work in the latter literature is Anthony Downs, *An Economic Theory of Democracy* (New York: Harper and Row, 1957). Readable reviews of Downs' work and subsequent developments can be found in William H. Riker and Peter C. Ordeshook, *An Introduction to Positive Political Theory* (Englewood Cliffs, N.J.: Prentice-Hall, 1973); Brian Barry, *Sociologists, Economists, and Democracy* (London: Collier-Macmillan, 1970); Gerald H. Kramer and Joseph E. Hertzberg, "Formal Theory," in *Handbook of Political Science*, ed. Fred I. Greenstein and Nelson W. Polsby (Reading, Mass.: Addison-Wesley, 1975); and Dennis C. Mueller, *Public Choice* (Cambridge: Cambridge University Press, 1979).

Implicit in this approach is the idea that every policy alternative can be placed in one-to-one correspondence with a position on the number line. This correspondence is frequently natural and straightforward, the core issue in many protests being the level at which some quantitative social policy instrument should be set. Depending on the situation, the policy space might be interpreted as the length of the working day, the rate of taxation on some good or service, the number of troops deployed overseas, the percentage of employees to be hired from minority groups, the level of wages, the size of a budget, or the distribution of land. As a matter of fact, it is quite difficult to think of important political issues that do not involve quantitative considerations of some kind.

More generally, the policy space can be interpreted as a left-to-right ideological spectrum, in which case the number line models the vaguer notions of ideological direction and distance[2] implicit in ordinal taxonomies of political groups and programs. Descriptive terms like left-wing extremist, moderate socialist, left-liberal, centrist, and ultra-conservative all reflect an essentially geometric perspective, which, by the way, plays a central role in the literature of radical politics. While such terms are notoriously difficult to define precisely, the important question for our purposes is whether, in a particular society, a common perception exists of how the various groups are arrayed across the political spectrum. If everyone orders the groups in the same way, we can build a very acceptable theory of protest without ever specifying what it means to be a "liberal" or a "conservative" in some absolute sense.

Political Preferences

WE SHALL assume that each party to the conflict, including the dissident leadership, the members of the population, and the regime, prefers some position along the ideological spectrum above all others and ranks the rest strictly according to their distance from the ideal point. An individual prefers one policy P_X to another P_Y if, and only if, P_X lies closer to his ideal point than P_Y does. If the distances are equal, the individual is indifferent between the two alternatives. Thus, the liberal prefers a centrist policy to a conservative one, and a conservative policy to an ultraconservative. While the liberal and the centrist

---

[2] Where ordinary Euclidean distances measure the difference between policy positions.

disagree about the ideal state of affairs, note that they still share a common system of political reference, reflected in their agreement that a conservative policy is preferable to an ultraconservative policy. Everyone's preferences therefore satisfy Black's condition of single-peakedness.[3] Under these conditions, we can represent each person's political preferences by a quasi-concave utility function of the ordinal type, defined over the ideological spectrum.[4]

The Responsiveness of the Regime

THE EFFECTIVENESS of demonstrations depends ultimately on the responsiveness of the regime to disruption in the streets. Roughly speaking, we mean by *responsiveness* the regime's willingness to trade concessions for tranquility. Our theoretical interpretation of responsiveness therefore depends critically on the sense we give to the notion of disruption.

Disruption is a difficult concept to capture mathematically because tranquility can be disrupted in so many different ways, and because regimes differ markedly in their capacity to endure various kinds of disruption. These differences arise from variability in the way governments are constituted institutionally, in the social foundations of each regime's political power, in the level of technological development, and many other factors. We need an abstract representation for this complicated amalgam of forces that is general enough to capture the common dynamics underlying the diverse forms of disruption without being politically vacuous.

Despite their great diversity in form and purpose, oppositional movements appear to share at least one thing in common. Regardless of the political context, there always seems to be power in numbers. No less an authority than Mao Tse-tung insists that "the richest source of power lies in the masses of the people,"[5] and it is nearly impossible to imagine political circumstances where the disruptiveness of dissident activity would diminish as its scope increased (other things,

[3] Duncan Black, *The Theory of Committees and Elections* (Cambridge: Cambridge University Press, 1958).

[4] See Michael D. Intriligator, *Mathematical Optimization and Economic Theory* (Englewood Cliffs, N.J.: Prentice-Hall, 1971), Chapter 7.

[5] Mao Tse-tung, "On Protracted War," *Selected Military Writings of Mao Tse-tung* (Peking: Foreign Languages Press, 1972), p. 260.

soon to be named, being equal of course). Accordingly, we take the disruptiveness of protests, demonstrations, and uprisings to be first and foremost a question of numbers.

The size of the dissidents' demonstrations affects the regime both directly and indirectly. Naturally the disruption of daily routines increases with numbers, and the regime's ability to control crowds inevitably suffers as they grow larger. In addition to the immediate disruption they cause, demonstrations (by their size) also give the regime an indication of how much support the dissidents enjoy. The broader the movement's appeal, the easier it is to enlist the support of people with organizational skill, courage and determination, and all the other attributes needed to absorb repression and sustain the struggle. Thus the demonstrations become more ominous as they grow larger, because the implicit threat of continued disruption becomes more credible.

The tactics used by the demonstrators also influence the disruptiveness of their protests. Small groups of terrorists can sometimes disrupt a nation's domestic tranquility just as much as large movements can by demonstrating peacefully. Our second fundamental assumption is simply that demonstrations become more disruptive as they grow more violent, other things being equal. Of course, the perception of violence is colored by cultural norms and traditions, and the disruptiveness of specific activities varies considerably from one political setting to the next. Our definition of tactics must therefore be abstract. Let the violence of particular tactics be indexed, then, by values in the closed interval of the real number line between zero and one. Zero represents peaceful demonstrations, and larger numbers correspond to more violent or aggressive events. We reserve a value of one for the most horrendously violent tactic conceivable in the political domain under study. Perhaps only the detonation of nuclear weapons would attain a value of one in our horrendously violent world. In any event, the usefulness of this approach clearly depends on our ability to rank the different tactics radical groups might use according to how violent they seem in a particular political culture. This task no doubt requires expertise and political sensitivity, but it is surely feasible in principle.

Armed with our twofold characterization of disruption, we can now represent the entire universe of possible demonstrations as points in a three-dimensional space whose coordinate axes describe the targets of the protests as well as their disruptiveness. Each point corresponds to an ordered triple of the form (P, M, V), where

P = the position of the government's policy along the ideological spectrum

M = the percentage of the population mobilized against P

V = the level of violence used by the demonstrators.

Naturally, the political situations described by these points vary considerably in their attractiveness to the regime. Ideally, it would like to adopt its most preferred policy without suffering any disruption in the streets. If we denote the ideal policy by P_G, the most favorable position in the three-dimensional space from the regime's perspective is the point $(P_G, 0, 0)$. If the dissident elements become disruptive, however, the regime faces the question of whether to shift its policy away from P_G in an effort to restore tranquility. Such a propensity to barter political concessions for tranquility we call responsiveness. The responsiveness of any regime can be represented formally, as in Figure 2.1, by indifference surfaces in the three-dimensional space. Each surface connects points in the space among which the regime is indifferent (i.e. which yield a constant level of utility). The responsiveness map as a whole consists of nested surfaces, each corresponding to a different level of preference. The inner surfaces, which converge toward the point $(P_G, 0, 0)$, represent more favorable situations, while the higher surfaces are less favorable. This is only to say that the regime prefers neither to move away from its ideal policy nor to cope with demonstrations that are larger or more violent (or both). The architecture of the individual indifference surfaces also conforms to these assumptions. Consider the outermost surface in Figure 2.1, for example. As the regime's policy drifts away from P_G, note how the demonstrations against the new policies become smaller or less violent. Such compensation is necessary if the regime is to remain indifferent after it adopts a less attractive policy.

The slopes of the indifference surfaces[6] provide a quantitative measure of the regime's willingness to trade concessions for reductions in disruption. Generally speaking, the steeper the slopes, the more disruption the dissidents must create in order to interest the regime in a particular concession (i.e. the less responsive the regime is). Of course,

---

[6] In the parlance of economic theory, the slopes are called marginal rates of substitution.

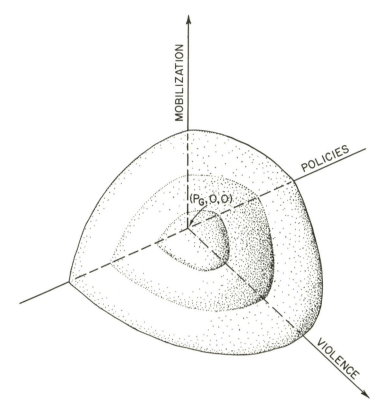

FIG. 2.1
A Typical Regime's Responsiveness Map

the interpretation of the slopes varies according to the direction in which they are measured. If we hold the level of violence constant, the slope of the surface indicates the rate at which the regime is willing to substitute concessions for a reduction in the size of protests, given its policy and the particular tactic. When the level of mobilization is fixed, the slopes measure the regime's willingness to make concessions in return for less violence. And when the slopes are measured on a tack parallel to the violence axis, they indicate the regime's relative aversion to violence and mobilization. Note that the government cannot be indifferent between two demonstrations against a particular policy unless the more violent one is smaller in size.

The responsiveness map is a compact and flexible way to summarize the complicated array of social forces that influence the regime's attitudes and responses to disruption in the streets. These forces might include legal or constitutional constraints, the interests of groups that sponsor the regime, the whims of a dictator, the loyalty of the armed forces, or institutional arrangements for succession. By varying the slopes of our responsiveness map in one or several respects, we can portray a wide variety of regimes with distinct political personalities. The responsiveness maps of particular regimes are not, of course, directly observable, and there is no well-developed theory that allows us to predict them from a configuration of variables like the ones mentioned above. The shape of the responsiveness map can be surmised, however, by observing the regime's reactions to demonstrations. This method is precisely how most dissident groups go about estimating the responsiveness of their opponents and the amount of support they need to reach their goal. In no sense, then, is the responsiveness map an empty theoretical abstraction devoid of operational significance.

Additional Notes on Responsiveness

SOMETIMES we shall be able to confine our attention to limited sections of the responsiveness map, without elaborating the entire structure. In the theory of peaceful protest, for example, only the front edges of the indifference surfaces are relevant to the story. When the dissidents rely on peaceful tactics, the disruption of tranquility boils down essentially to a question of numbers. The regime's responsiveness to this kind of protest can then be summarized by a set of nested indifference *curves*, lying in the two-dimensional space defined by the ideological spectrum and the mobilization axis. Figure 2.2 shows how responsiveness to peaceful protest is represented by our model.

The same kind of simplification is possible in the study of terrorism. In this theory, terrorist activities are understood to be demonstrations of pure violence. The terrorists explode their bombs and issue demands from the underground without mobilizing anyone in public demonstrations. (The same logic pertains to kidnapping, assassination, and hijacking.) The class of terrorist strategies therefore defines outcomes in the two-dimensional plane formed by the ideological spectrum and the violence axis, where mobilization equals zero. The bottom edges of the full indifference surfaces describe the regime's responsiveness to these events.

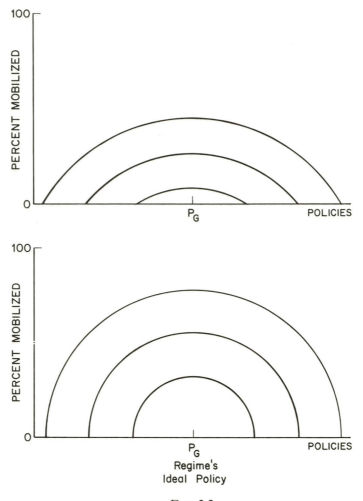

FIG. 2.2
Responsive and Unresponsive Regimes

At this point, the reader might pause to verify that the indifference curves and surfaces can never intersect without violating one of our basic assumptions.

The Dissidents' Strategy

POPULAR support is the cornerstone of a movement's power to influence public policy. How people are mobilized into the radical cause and how the movement's support varies with its choice of strategy are therefore theoretical issues of paramount importance. Coming to grips with them requires first that we define carefully what it means to pursue a strategy.

We shall use the word *strategy* to mean a comprehensive political plan, prescribing the kind of demonstration the movement shall mobilize against every conceivable policy the regime might adopt.[7] The leaders of the movement must decide what policies to oppose and the demands and tactics to use in demonstrations against them. A natural and useful mathematical model for such a plan is a function defined over the policy space that assigns a demand and a tactic (i.e. an ordered pair) to each position along the ideological spectrum.[8] This definition provides a flexible analytical tool for studying particular plans of attack as well as general classes of strategy.

The first decision to be made in designing a strategy is which policies of the government to oppose. A decision not to mobilize a demonstration against a particular policy can be modeled by assigning to that policy an identical demand. When the dissident movement does not call for a new policy, there is no occasion for a demonstration. This formalism may seem a bit unnatural, resting as it does on fictional "nondemands," but it is a convenient device for studying the political logic of withdrawing from the streets. Given this analytical approach, it is important to remember that assigning a demand to a policy does not, in a formal sense, mean the same thing as mobilizing a protest against it. Only "genuine" demands, those which differ from the government's policy, bring people into the streets. To avoid tedious terminological qualifications in the discussion to follow, general references to demands will be limited to the genuine (i.e. dissimilar) variety.

We can define the set of policies that are targets for disruption, called the *target set*, as those policies to which dissimilar demands are assigned. Having first determined the targets for disruption, the dissident strategists must next decide what demands to lodge against them. We

---

[7] This definition conforms to the game-theoretical notion of strategy. See R. D. Luce and H. Raiffa, *Games and Decisions* (New York: John Wiley, 1957).

[8] Let $I \in \mathbf{R}^1$ be the ideological spectrum. Then a strategy S is a mapping from I into a rectangle in $\mathbf{R}^2$:

$$S:I \rightarrow \mathbf{R}^2$$

If P_G is a point in I, $S(P_G) = (D(P_G), T(P_G))$ where $D(P_G) \in I$ is the dissidents' demand against P_G and $T(P_G) \in [0, 1]$ is their tactic.

shall call a strategy *steadfast* if it lodges the same demand against all the policies in the target set. In other words, the dissidents cling steadfastly to a single demand. A strategy whose demands vary inside the target set will be called *flexible*. The demands of a flexible strategy change with the policy chosen by the government. A *sincere strategy* steadfastly demands the ideal policy of the strategy maker. Flexible strategies cannot be sincere, since they lodge demands for more than one policy. It is also possible to distinguish between *peaceful* and *violent* strategies, according to whether the tactics assigned to the target set are always peaceful or not.[9]

Strategy and Spontaneity

THE DEFINITION we have chosen for strategy follows from our interest in explaining the calculated use of mass demonstrations and political violence for securing political change. No one who reads the political writings of the great strategists of protest and rebellion[10] can doubt that radical movements have achieved momentous historical transformations by proceeding in a strategic way—i.e. by considering contingencies in the political situation and reacting with calculated plans. This is not to say that political violence is always cool and calculated rather than hot and spontaneous. Nor does our theory pretend to explain the dynamics of violence that erupts in the heat of the moment. Our goal is to understand an important class of political activity, undertaken by dissident leaders who, in Michael Walzer's words, are

---

[9] More formally then:
Let I be the ideological spectrum. The *target set*, T, is the subset of I which the dissidents target for disruption

$$T = \{P_G \in I \mid D(P_G) \neq P_G\}$$

where P_G is an arbitrary policy of the government and $D(P_G)$ is the demand assigned to it by the dissidents' strategy.

A *steadfast strategy* is a mapping, S, such that $D(P_G) = K$ for all $P_G \in T$.

A *flexible strategy* is a mapping, S, such that for at least two policies P_G, $P_{G'} \in T$, $D(P_G) \neq D(P_{G'})$.

A *sincere strategy* is a mapping, S, such that $D(P_G) = P_S$ for all $P_G \in T$, where P_S is the ideal policy of the strategy maker.

A *peaceful strategy* is a mapping, S, such that $T(P_G) = 0$ for all $P_G \in T$, where $T(P_G)$ is the tactic assigned to the arbitrary policy P_G.

A *violent strategy* is a mapping, S, such that there exists some $P_G \in T$ for which $T(P_G) \neq 0$.

[10] V. I. Lenin, Leon Trotsky, Mao Tse-tung, Eduard Bernstein, Rosa Luxemburg, Mahatma Gandhi, Marx, Engels, Saul Alinsky, and Martin Luther King are outstanding examples whose strategies we shall have occasion to consider.

"systematically active, imaginatively responsive to opportunity, seeking victory."[11] It is a class of activity about which theories of political rage and frustration-aggression reactions have remarkably little to say.

Mobilizing Support

THE DISSIDENTS' technique for recruiting support ultimately determines the connection between their choice of strategy and the number of people in the streets. The recruiting process can be described formally by a function that assigns to partisans of each policy along the ideological spectrum the conditional probability of joining a particular protest. Given the government's prevailing policy, P_G, and the movement's strategy (i.e. the demand and tactic lodged against P_G), the recruiting function assigns a number between zero and one to each location along the ideological spectrum. Two simple examples illustrate how such a function can be defined to capture the salient features of very different approaches to mobilizing support.

To keep things manageable until the framework becomes more familiar, let us confine our attention to movements that rely on peaceful strategies. Their recruiting techniques can be represented fairly straightforwardly without attending to all the complications surrounding the use of violence.

Ideological Recruiting

ONE WAY to mobilize a protest is simply by advertising a demand along with the time and place where people should gather to demonstrate on its behalf. Those people who support the demand in preference to the government's policy arrive at the appointed hour, while the people who are indifferent or who favor the government's cause stay home. We shall call this technique of organizing protests *ideological recruiting*. Its simplest form involves nothing more complicated than comparing the political stances adopted by the two contending sides. In our model, everybody's political preferences are governed by relative distances from their ideal points. People whose political aspirations lie closer to the dissidents' demand than to the government's current policy therefore prefer the demand and join the protest. Others stay

[11] Michael Walzer, *The Revolution of the Saints* (Cambridge: Harvard University Press, 1965), p. 17.

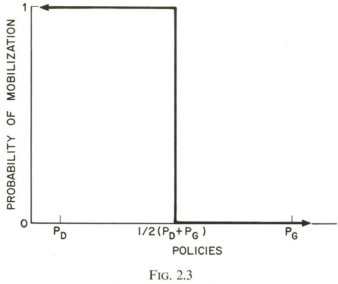

FIG. 2.3
Ideological Recruiting

home. In this system of mobilization, then, the recruiting function takes the form of a step function, assigning a probability value of one to people on the movement's side of the boundary point which is halfway between the movement's demand and the regime's policy, and zero to the people on the government's side (as in Figure 2.3).[12]

This idealized model of recruiting captures the essence of many classical accounts of protest and rebellion, which assume that people are mobilized by substantive political grievances. Such is the flavor of a large and distinguished literature that calls upon class interests, economic disasters, political injustices, or relative deprivations to explain why men rebel. Our very simple recruiting function captures the idea that movements sacrifice support as their demands become extreme and gain support as the regime drifts away from the political main-

---

[12] The system of ideological recruiting for peaceful strategies is formally described by a function of the following form:

$$Pr(\text{Participation}\,|\,P_G, P_I, S) = \begin{cases} 1 & \text{if } d(P_I, P_G) > d(P_I, D(P_G)) \\ 0 & \text{if } d(P_I, P_G) \leq d(P_I, D(P_G)) \end{cases}$$

where P_I is the individual's ideal policy and S is the dissidents' strategy. Note that under the single-peaked preference ordering:

$$U(P_G) \geq U(D(P_G)) \Leftrightarrow d(P_I, P_G) \leq d(P_I, D(P_G))$$

where d is the ordinary Euclidean metric.

stream. It is not rich enough to help us unravel every problem, but it takes us surprisingly far into a host of interesting questions. And it provides a point of departure for all kinds of more complicated refinements.

Organizational Recruiting

MUCH of the recent literature on social protest, peasant revolutions, and guerrilla war rejects the classical emphasis on ideological motives in the recruiting process. It focuses instead on the personal, nonpolitical appeals exploited by dissident organizations to recruit people who do not harbor deep-seated grievances against the regime. Paul Berman's conclusions about the National Liberation Front in South Vietnam have this flavor, for example:

> Were peasants who accepted membership rebelling? To be sure grievances existed, but a general sense of oppression did not. . . . Feelings of "relative deprivation" did not activate villagers. Peasants were mobilized by an organization. . . . The Front was the active agent; it sought out the peasant, not vice versa.[13]

Eric Hoffer's explanation for why people join mass movements has the same tone, though the particulars differ:

> A rising mass movement attracts and holds a following not by its doctrine and promises but by the refuge it offers from the anxieties, barrenness, and meaninglessness of an individual existence. It cures the poignantly frustrated not by . . . remedying the difficulties and abuses which made their lives miserable, but by . . . enfolding them into a closely knit and exultant corporate whole.[14]

The writers who focus on the organizational dynamics of rebellion generally concur that recruits are not necessarily pushed into dissident movements by substantive political grievances, but rather are frequently pulled in through influential contact with members of the rebel organization. The appeals used by the rebel organizers seem not to have much political content in many instances, nor any direct connection to the movement's larger goals. Instead, they include incentives like bonds of friendship, a means to support one's family, threats and coercion, or the call to adventure. Participation in some movements,

---

[13] Paul Berman, *Revolutionary Organization* (Lexington, Mass.: D. C. Heath, 1974), pp. 76–77.
[14] Eric Hoffer, *The True Believer* (New York: Harper and Row, 1951), p. 44.

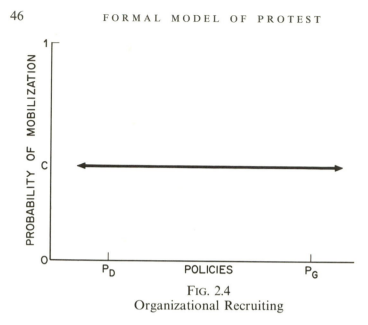

FIG. 2.4
Organizational Recruiting

then, appears to be quite unaffected by political preferences. When this is the case, we can deploy a recruiting function like the one in Figure 2.4 to represent the process of "organizational recruiting." Here the probability of mobilization is unaffected by the movement's demands, the government's policy, or the individual's personal political ideals. It remains constant across the entire political spectrum, depending only on the "vigor" of the organization.

Evaluating schematic representations of political reality like the ideological and organizational models of recruiting is tricky business requiring far more effort than simply appealing to reasonableness or literalness. Ultimately, the utility of these models depends on their capacity to clarify the important features of complicated political processes, and the ease with which they can be generalized after the simplest cases are understood. In the chapters to follow, we shall devote considerable attention to these questions. At this point, let us simply reemphasize the pivotal importance of the recruiting function in the theory, whatever form it assumes.

The Mobilization Curve

THE ANALYTICAL machinery developed so far allows us now to determine how many people will join the protests defined by the dissidents' strategy. We can then describe the kind of demonstrations that will occur in response to whatever policy the government adopts. The requisite information is summarized by three functions, all of which can be adjusted to model different political situations. Taking the government's policy as given, the *dissidents' strategy* assigns to it a demand and a tactic. The *recruiting function*, using this information, then specifies what fraction of the population will join the protest from each interval along the ideological spectrum. Finally, a *cumulative distribution function* describes how the ideal points of the population are distributed across the policy space. We need only sum up the number of supporters the demonstration attracts in each political neighborhood to ascertain its total size. Repeating this process for every potential governmental policy defines the *mobilization curve* associated with the strategy. For each policy alternative available to the government, the mobilization curve describes the level of disruption resulting from the dissidents' political plan (i.e. the size and violence of its protests).

Equilibrium Outcomes

THIS LEADS to the most basic question of all: What concession can be won by pursuing a particular strategy? The answer depends on the amount of disruption it creates (described by the mobilization curve associated with the strategy) and the responsiveness of the regime (summarized by its responsiveness map). The regime is interested in finding the policy that yields the most palatable combination of programmatic substance and disruption in the streets. Given the dissidents' plan of attack, this policy is located where the mobilization curve reaches its lowest tangency on the responsiveness map. At such an *equilibrium outcome* (or outcomes, there may be several), the regime achieves a more satisfactory result, according to its own preferences, than it can from adopting any other policy (where the mobilization curve lies on higher, less attractive indifference surfaces). As long as the dissidents sustain their strategy, the regime can never improve its situation unilaterally by shifting away from an equilibrium point. These policies therefore represent genuine or stable concessions, compelled by the disruption in the streets. For this reason, equilibrium outcomes will be our basic analytical tool for assessing what strategies are likely to ensue in various political circumstances.

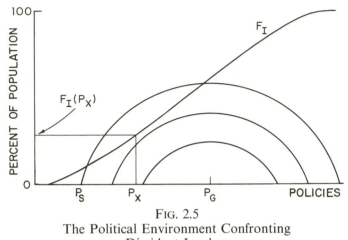

FIG. 2.5
The Political Environment Confronting
Dissident Leaders

A Simple Example

LET US review our approach by studying a simple example that nevertheless captures the essence of a basic dilemma facing many radical groups. Suppose our movement relies on ideological recruiting and nonviolent tactics in a struggle to achieve its ideal policy, P_S. Figure 2.5 contains a compact summary of the political environment confronting the movement's leaders.

The curve labeled F_I is the cumulative distribution of popular preferences. At each point P_X along the ideological spectrum, $F_I(P_X)$ describes the percentage of the population with ideal policies at P_X or to its left. Note that only a small percentage of the population holds views to the left of the movement's leaders at P_S. The intersection of F_I and the policy axis defines the leftward limit of public opinion, while the rightward limit lies at the policy where F_I first attains a value of 100 percent. The quantity $F_I(P_A) - F_I(P_B)$ defines the percentage of the population with ideal points between two arbitrary policies P_A and P_B. The cumulative distribution therefore provides a complete description of how public opinion is distributed across the ideological spectrum.

The regime's responsiveness to peaceful protest is described by the indifference curves located over its ideal policy, P_G. The indifference curves are simply the front edges of the full indifference surfaces illustrated in Figure 2.1. Note that the indifference curve passing through the point (P_S, 0) establishes the minimum level of disruption the dissidents must generate against all the policies to the right of P_S if they

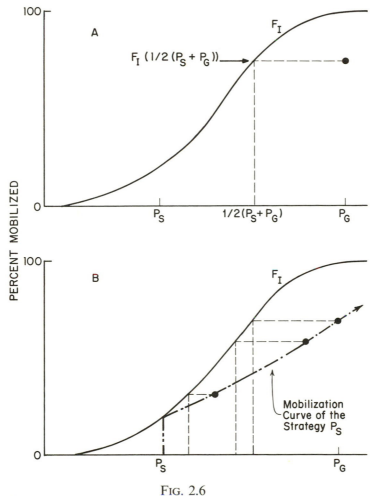

FIG. 2.6
Construction of Mobilization Curves

are to achieve their objective. Should they mobilize fewer people than the indicated minimum against any policy in this interval, P_S will never become the regime's most attractive alternative, even if it can secure complete tranquility by granting the dissidents' demand.

Now suppose the radical leaders decide to pursue a sincere strategy, despite the extremeness of their views. In particular, they agree to lodge the demand P_S against all the policies to its right.[15] Figure 2.6 shows

---

[15] Note that other sincere strategies might also be chosen. They would oppose different intervals of policies.

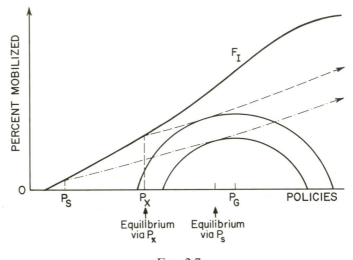

FIG. 2.7
Outcomes under Sincere and Compromising Strategies

how we can calculate the amount of support this strategy attracts as the government varies its policy (i.e. the mobilization curve for the strategy). When recruiting is ideological, mobilization curves can be derived straightforwardly from the cumulative distribution. Ideological recruiting draws support from individuals whose ideal policies lie closer to the radicals' demand than to the government's position. This group holds views to the left of the point halfway between the two sides' positions. To find the number of people supporting the demand P_S against the policy P_G, for example, we simply locate the policy halfway between P_S and P_G and read the value of the cumulative distribution at that midpoint. The lower panel of Figure 2.6 shows how an entire mobilization curve can be constructed by this procedure. Note that when the government moves from left to right, the critical halfway point trails along after it. As this happens, the cumulative distribution is translated to the right and stretched by a factor of two. The mobilization curves for steadfast strategies, then, are simple transformations of the cumulative distribution.

In Figure 2.7, we see at last how the movement fares with its sincere strategy. Here the equilibrium outcome lies only slightly to the left of the regime's ideal policy. Note that the regime would be forced to higher indifference curves (less satisfactory outcomes) if it shifted its policy in either direction away from the equilibrium point. The equilibrium is therefore a stable outcome as long as the radicals maintain their sincere strategy.

In view of the extremeness of their demand and the meager concession it secures, the radical leaders might well consider a compromise demand in hopes of generating more pressure on the government. The demand P_X is one possibility that accomplishes this purpose. The higher mobilization curve in Figure 2.7 results from pursuing this demand steadfastly, against all the policies to its right. Unlike the sincere strategy, the new strategy is *successful*; that is, it establishes equilibrium at its demand. The regime finds it more advantageous to adopt the policy P_X in return for complete tranquility than to suffer the disruption in the streets that the radicals foment against the policies closer to its ideal point.

Thus the political situation portrayed in Figure 2.7 confronts the dissident leaders at P_S with a real dilemma, forcing them to choose between ideological purity (the sincere strategy) and the additional concessions that the political environment makes available to less extreme demands. How a movement's leaders should address this kind of dilemma is a fundamental problem in radical politics.

MANCUR Olson's *The Logic of Collective Action*[16] created a great stir by calling into question widely held assumptions about the motivations of participants in collective actions (like elections, protests, and revolutions) whose outcomes involve public goods. The defining feature of such goods is that they cannot be divided up and parceled out to those who contribute in their creation, but rather are shared commonly by entire communities. The national defense, public highways, and collective bargaining agreements are frequently cited examples.

Because single individuals typically have a negligible impact on the outcome of large-scale collective activities, and because public goods cannot be withheld from those who do not join in their creation, it is argued that participation in strikes, elections, and revolutions is "irrational" whenever personal sacrifice is required. Instead, the "rational" person will take a free ride, first allowing others to absorb the costs and then sharing freely in the benefits. Thus, the rational person will never vote in national elections, however much he prefers one candidate's platform to the other's, because one vote out of millions cannot decide the election, registration and voting require time and effort, and the winner's policies will affect voters and nonvoters equally in any event. Similarly, the rational person will never participate in a civil-rights demonstration, however much he hates the apartheid policy of the government, because one extra person will not affect the outcome of the demonstration, participating may well be dangerous, and nonparticipants will fully enjoy the benefits if the apartheid policy is changed.

This reasoning raises disturbing questions about our model of ideological recruiting. To understand its implications more clearly, let us reconstruct the argument in a more formal model of the decision to join a protest. Suppose that each individual has well-defined preferences over the set of contested policies as summarized by a utility function U. Let $U(P_M)$ denote the utility of the policy advocated by the movement, and $U(P_G)$ denote the utility of the government's policy. If the dispute involves a public good, and many protests do, then every-

---

[16] See Mancur Olson, Jr., *The Logic of Collective Action* (Cambridge: Harvard University Press, 1965).

TABLE 2.1. Payoffs and Probabilities in the Decision to Join a Protest

Actions		Outcomes	
		S Movement Succeeds	S' Movement Fails
A Join Protest	Payoff Probability Expected Payoff	$U(P_M) + U(A)$ $P(S\|A)$ $[U(P_M) + U(A)] \cdot$ $P(S\|A)$	$U(P_G) + U(A)$ $1 - P(S\|A)$ $[U(P_G) + U(A)] \cdot$ $[1 - P(S\|A)]$
A' Stay Home	Payoff Probability Expected Payoff	$U(P_M)$ $P(S\|A')$ $U(P_M) \cdot P(S\|A')$	$U(P_G)$ $1 - P(S\|A')$ $U(P_G) \cdot [1 - P(S\|A')]$

one will experience the effects of a change in policy from P_G to P_M, regardless of whether they join the protest or not. Participants will also experience the costs and benefits of taking to the streets—camaraderie, repression, lost income, and the like. Denote the net utility of these costs and benefits by $U(A)$, the utility of action. It is convenient to assume here that the payoffs associated with actions and policies are additively separable. The free-rider argument assumes that individuals calculate the subjective expected utility associated with each possible course of action and then choose the one that yields the highest expected value.

We can denote possible actions and outcomes as follows:

OUTCOMES

S: the movement succeeds in winning its demand, P_M
S': the government's policy remains at P_G

ACTIONS

A: the individual joins the protest (acts)
A': the individual stays home (does not act)

In order to calculate the expected utility associated with protesting and staying home, prospective recruits must make a subjective assessment of the conditional probability of each outcome, given one course of action and then the other. Using standard notation, we can denote the conditional probability that the movement succeeds given the individual's support by $P(S|A)$. And so forth. Table 2.1 summarizes the relevant payoffs and probabilities.

In this decision problem, the expected value maximizer will participate if, and only if, the expected utility of participation exceeds the
expected utility of inaction. It can easily be verified that the expected
utility of participation equals

$$EU(A) = [U(P_M) - U(P_G)] \cdot P(S|A) + U(P_G) + U(A)$$

while the expected utility of not participating equals

$$EU(A') = [U(P_M) - U(P_G)] \cdot P(S|A') + U(P_G)$$

The requirement for participation that $EU(A) > EU(A')$ therefore ne-
cessitates that

$$[U(P_M) - U(P_G)] \cdot [P(S|A) - P(S|A')] + U(A) > 0$$

This expression reveals the so-called paradox of participation in its
full glory. The quantity $[P(S|A) - P(S|A')]$ is a measure of the in-
dividual's sense of personal effectiveness. It represents an assessment
of one's own impact on the movement's probability of success. When
people realistically perceive that the participation of one individual
is unlikely to affect the outcome of a civil disturbance, this quantity
approaches zero. As it does, all consideration of the relative attractiveness of the movement's demand and the government's policy drops
out of the decision (i.e. the entire term $[U(P_M) - U(P_G)] \cdot [P(S|A) -
P(S|A')]$ goes to zero). This leads to the conclusion that political pref-
erences about the issue in question have no impact on the decision
to join a protest. Instead, the personal costs and benefits associated
with spending a day in the streets, and $U(A)$ term, come to the fore.
When they are negative, as for example when repression is heavy, the
rational person will not participate. Of course, if everyone is rational
in this sense, no one will be mobilized into collective action despite the
existence of a common interest in securing the public good.

The trouble with this definition of rational behavior is that a theory
based upon it appears to predict that no one ever votes, and that
strikes, protests, and revolutions never occur! Because these predictions
are patently false, two options must then be considered. Either the expected utility calculations can be respecified (in an effort to rescue the
theory), or another definition of rational behavior can be adopted.

Those who somehow believe that subjective expected utility maxi-
mization is *the* definition of rationality naturally prefer the first option.
Their rescue attempts have essentially followed two paths. The first is
to claim that individuals overestimate their own importance by as-

suming falsely that a single person's efforts can significantly alter the probability of success and failure in collective actions. The purpose of this *deus ex machina* is to make the benefit side of an expected utility cost-benefit calculation positive again, rather than zero. The expected benefits in such models are defined by the individual's personal evaluation of the substantive political alternatives at issue (Goldwater versus Johnson, or apartheid versus racial equality, for instance) multiplied by the probability that participation will influence the outcome. If the probability term is mistakenly perceived to be significantly greater than zero, the expected benefit of participation can then become positive and participation may under some circumstances be "rational."[17]

There are three basic difficulties with this stratagem for rescuing an expected utility theory. First, its defenders present no evidence that people actually do overestimate their own importance (or even consider it in the first place). Instead, the proponents of this view simply assert that such miscalculation must occur, otherwise people would not behave as they do. Second, the idea behind the stratagem is completely out of character with the general approach to explanation. We are asked to believe that people are sophisticated enough to enumerate costs and benefits in a reasonably comprehensive and consistent way (which seems plausible enough), and then we are told that they are incapable of rudimentary calculations that any schoolboy could make. It certainly doesn't require very deep reflection on the part of the ordinary person, for example, to realize that the odds against one vote swinging a national election are astronomically large. Finally, a theory based on such misperceptions doesn't lead anywhere. Expected utility theory doesn't say anything about the origin and magnitude of misperceptions, and therefore all predictions must rest upon considerations that live outside the theory. But why, then, adopt a rationalist theory in the first place?

In view of these difficulties with the misperception approach, most expected utility theorists, including Olson himself, have adopted a somewhat different line. Maybe we should reconsider the cost side of the model, they say, and leave the benefit side alone. The cost side of the ledger includes all of the immediate consequences of participation

---

[17] For an exposition of this view, see Riker and Ordeshook, *An Introduction to Positive Political Theory*, Chapter 3.

that are independent of how the collective action turns out, consequences such as repression inflicted upon demonstrators and time lost in registering to vote and then going to the polls. But wait a moment. Might not some of the immediate consequences of participation be positive? After all, don't political organizations sometimes provide "selective incentives" to those who participate in collective actions, while withholding them from those who do not (e.g. unions who provide supplementary income to workers on strike)? And don't people experience a sense of gratification from the act of voting itself, regardless of how the election turns out? If so, then the terms in the expected utility model describing the utility of action per se need not be negative, and participation can be rational even though the substantive political evaluation of the underlying issues is weighted down to zero by the probability term. Using this reasoning, Tullock concludes that "the public goods aspects of a revolution are of relatively little importance in the decision to participate. . . . The important variables are the rewards and punishments offered by the two sides and the risk of injury during the fighting."[18]

The trouble with this line of argument, as Brian Barry[19] and others have pointed out, is that the motivation for participation no longer has anything to do with the political issues at stake in the election or revolution. If taken seriously, the revised theory implies that socialists will gladly participate in fascist demonstrations, and vice versa, if the organizers simply provide coffee and doughnuts to the marchers. After all, why not enjoy the selective incentives when it is obvious that one extra person will not affect the outcome of the demonstration?

These considerations demonstrate very clearly, I hope, that every expected utility theory of political participation, however formulated, has manifestly absurd political implications. The absurdity does not stem from the particular factors included in the theory, but rather from the recipe by which their relative importance is calculated. The obvious solution to the free-rider "problem" is therefore to abandon the expected utility definition of rationality, which creates all the difficulties in the first place. This is exactly what the leading formal theorists of electoral competition have done, and what I have done in my theory

---

[18] Gordon Tullock, "The Paradox of Revolution," *Public Choice* 11 (Fall, 1971).
[19] Barry, *Sociologists, Economists, and Democracy.*

as well. It should be noted that game theorists, economists, decision theorists, and operations researchers routinely employ many quite different definitions of rationality (including the minimax principle, quadratic loss, the Pareto principle, satisficing, and expected utility maximizing) whose usefulness varies considerably from one substantive application to the next. Difficulties associated with one definition in no way impeach the usefulness of others, or of a rational choice approach generally.

CHAPTER THREE

The Logic of Peaceful Protest

Introduction

ALTHOUGH radical politics are notoriously violent, one should not forget the crucial role played by nonviolent modes of disruption in many of history's most stirring episodes of political dissent and opposition to authority. The overthrow of British colonial rule in India, the American civil-rights reform legislation of the 1960s, and even the historic October Revolution in Russia were largely accomplished, and quite amazingly so, without recourse to violence. How this could happen is only one of the fascinating political questions raised by this important class of strategies. Studying their dynamics provides an excellent introduction to our theoretical system and many valuable insights about fundamental processes in the life of radical movements.

Nonviolent strategies tend to be theoretically more tractable than others because they involve simpler choices, both for the people who design them and for the people who join them. In our theory, the radical leaders develop a strategy by first considering the policies available to the regime, and then selecting demands and tactics to use in demonstrations against them. When a movement commits itself to nonviolent tactics (for whatever reasons, moral or practical), the problem of designing a strategy boils down to choosing demands. Finding the most effective demands is not a trivial problem, but neither is it as difficult as selecting demands and tactics simultaneously.

At the same time, joining a peaceful protest usually requires less soul-searching than joining a violent one. Violent methods raise troublesome questions about whether the ends justify the means, and generally force the people who use them to take substantial risks. In peaceful protests, these dilemmas tend to be less acute, if they arise at all. When qualms about tactics are minimal, the political dynamics of bringing a following into the streets are far simpler than they would be otherwise. Relatively uncomplicated models of recruiting can then be used to capture the main elements of strategy making.

Despite their comparative simplicity, peaceful strategies of protest nevertheless raise questions of fundamental political importance. In trying to understand how dissident groups select their demands, we shall have to consider why some groups hold fast to their principles while others compromise them, how factional tensions arise in radical circles and when they are likely to become explosive, how the impulse to escalate tactics arises, and how the programs of radical groups reflect the political climate in which they develop. Naturally, these questions cannot be answered with complete generality by considering only the special circumstances of peaceful protest. Nonetheless, it is much easier to set ourselves on a fruitful course by studying the simplest situations first.

Setting the Stage

SUPPOSE a leftist[1] movement decides to resist the policies of a distasteful, but law-abiding, regime by exercising its "constitutional" right to demonstrate peacefully, without suffering harassment or official retaliation of any kind. From our theoretical point of view, this political setting is about the least complicated imaginable. The dissident leaders must decide which demands to lodge against the government's policies, and the government must decide which policy to adopt. Presumably, each side wants to use its resources to the greatest political advantage. The problem is to describe, in a general way, how this can be done.

The answer depends, of course, on the methods used by the movement to recruit people into its demonstrations. Suppose the dissidents simply advertise their demand and announce where their protest rally will be held. If no attempt is made to canvass support by making face-to-face appeals, if there is no prospect of violence occurring during the rally, and if the risk of injury or arrest is negligible, then the principal grounds left for deciding whether or not to attend are the political positions adopted by the two sides. Those who support the radicals' demand take to the streets. Others stay home. This is the system of ideological recruiting described in the last chapter. Other methods of recruiting play an important role in radical politics, but for now, we

---

[1] We develop the theory from the viewpoint of leftist groups without any loss of generality. The same reasoning applies to movements of the right.

want to study this one in some detail. It is simple and highly idealized, but it captures the flavor of what happens when substantive political grievances generate public expressions of dissent.

Another important feature of the political landscape is the distribution of opinion across the ideological spectrum. Of course, any number of distinct distributions are conceivable, and as the historians like to point out, each one is unique. We need not worry about the particular details of each distribution, however, to understand the political logic of waging protests. Our concern is with general characteristics of these distributions, especially *continuity*. Is the population clustered in discrete ideological groups or factions, or is it arrayed more or less continuously across the political spectrum (that is, without gaps)? Let us consider the latter possibility first by studying a population sufficiently large and diverse that virtually every ideological alternative within the bounds of popular opinion lies close to somebody's ideal point. A cumulative distribution of preferences that is strictly increasing in the range between zero and 100 percent provides an acceptable approximation to this reality. The cumulative distribution describing a factionally divided society has "flats," a feature whose political significance we shall take up later.

Finally, let us confine our attention to movements and regimes whose demands and policies fall within the boundaries of political opinion defined by the cumulative distribution. This assumption is wholly inconsequential and is adopted only for convenience. All we require is that each side's political program remain within the limits defined by the most wild-eyed fringes of political opinion. When preferences are distributed continuously, it means that each side's position must be considered ideal by at least one person. Parties that adopt truly extreme positions (those without any adherents) are theoretical nuisances, as well as being historical oddities (if they exist at all). They clutter the story with tedious and trivial complications, and surely defy explanation by a theory like ours anyway. We leave it to others to make sense of their activity.

Our plan, then, is to undertake the construction of a theory of protest by considering first the simplest situations imaginable. If our hypothetical radical movement relies upon peaceful tactics and ideological recruiting, if repression is negligible, if the population is distributed continuously across the ideological spectrum, and if the parties on both sides avoid truly extreme positions, we can pose the following problem: Does some strategy yield a bigger concession from the regime than others, and if so, can it be described in a general way, without reference to particular details of the political situation?

Characteristics of Strategies

To answer these questions, we need a richer political vocabulary. In our theory, the term *strategy* means a function or schedule that assigns demands and tactics (here peaceful) to the policies of the government. One way to characterize strategies is by the demands they lodge— steadfast, flexible, sincere, or insincere, for example. Equally important is the set of policies against which a strategy mobilizes disruption. We call these policies the target set.

DEFINITION: The Target Set[2]
If the level of mobilization against an arbitrary policy of the government, P_X, is denoted by $M(P_X)$, then the target set is the set of policies for which $M(P_X)$ is greater than zero: $T = \{P_X | M(P_X) > 0\}$.

This definition captures directly the idea that the target set contains those policies that are targets for disruption. In the special circumstances of peaceful protests, mobilized by ideological recruiting and demands that are not (truly) extreme, the new definition is equivalent to the one set forth earlier. Under these conditions, demands that differ from the government's policy always mobilize a disturbance. The concept of the target set allows us to study decisions to pull out of the streets and, more generally, the logic of choosing which policies to oppose.

RULE 1: The target set is a continuous interval along the political spectrum. Therefore we can use the names *target set* and *target interval* interchangeably.

This rule follows directly from the definition of responsiveness set forth in the last chapter. No regime ever has any incentive to move further away from its ideal point than a policy that attracts no opposition. If a dissident group does not mobilize a demonstration against one policy, there is simply no opportunity to create disruption against more extreme policies. Thus, there can be no gaps between the policies

---

[2] Compare the definition of the target set given in Chapter 2.

in the target set. Wherever the movement first demobilizes along the political spectrum defines the boundary of the set. For leftist movements, the interesting question is where to locate the leftward boundary of the target set (there need not be a boundary on the right).

DEFINITION: Stubborn Strategy
When the target set extends to the radicals' most extreme demand, their strategy is called stubborn.

This definition perhaps appears a bit roundabout, but the idea behind it is simple. The term *stubborn* refers here to an unwillingness to accept partial concessions without a struggle. If the dissidents target for disruption *all* the policies that fall short of their (most extreme) demand, their strategy is stubborn. Recall that flexible strategies lodge more than one demand inside the target set. Hence the stipulation that the *most extreme* demand defines the boundary of the target set. Note that sincere strategies need not be stubborn and that stubborn strategies need not be sincere. The two concepts are logically distinct.

DEFINITION: Abbreviated Strategy
A strategy is abbreviated by shortening the interval of policies it targets for disruption without otherwise changing its demands.

Any strategy has an unlimited number of abbreviated versions, no two of which mobilize disruption against exactly the same interval of policies. The demands of an initial strategy and its abbreviated cousins are identical where their target intervals overlap, however. The original mobilization curve is therefore unaffected in these intervals. The definition raises the question of when it makes more sense to cut short a series of demonstrations, that is, to accept without protest a compromise policy from the regime, rather than to punish the regime with further disruption.

DEFINITION: Successful Strategy
A successful strategy establishes equilibrium at its (most extreme) demand.

Every dissident strategy defines at least one equilibrium policy. Given the level of disruption resulting from the strategy, an equilibrium policy is one that the regime finds at least as preferable as any other policy it might adopt. In other words, no policy is more attractive to the regime, given the dissidents' protests, than an equilibrium policy. Several equilibriums may exist simultaneously. A successful strategy creates an equilibrium at its (most extreme) demand. Thus, the regime can do no better for itself than to accede to the demand (or, in the case of flexible strategies, to the most extreme demand). Note that the word successful refers here to strategies, rather than to the people who use them. When a strategy is successful, we cannot infer that the dissidents got what they *wanted*, because not all strategies are sincere. Rather, we can only infer that they got what they demanded,[3] that is, that their strategy was successful.

RULE 2: All successful strategies are stubborn.

If the dissidents' (most extreme) demand is to appear no less attractive to the regime than the policies closer to its ideal point, all of those policies must be made targets of disruption. In other words, the dissidents' most extreme demand cannot become an equilibrium policy unless the target set extends to that demand.

The Logic of Withdrawing from the Streets

SUPPOSE, after experiencing a series of protests, a regime considers it more advantageous to adopt a policy that entails a certain measure of disruption than to offer a bigger concession in return for complete tranquility. In other words, the equilibrium policy associated with the dissidents' strategy falls inside the interval targeted for disruption. This eventuality is illustrated by the upper panel of Figure 3.1, where the stubborn strategy demanding P_X establishes an equilibrium at the policy P_E. What are the movement's political options if the compromise policy adopted by the regime seems unsatisfactory?

In the short run, two possibilities present themselves—either the demands of the original strategy can be changed, or the strategy can be abbreviated. The middle panel of Figure 3.1 illustrates the logic of the second approach. The movement wins a bigger concession by suspending its demonstrations anywhere in the shaded interval between P_E (the initial equilibrium) and P_B (where the equilibrium-defining indifference curve intersects the policy axis) than it does by stubbornly resisting all the policies that fall short of the demand P_X.

---

[3] We shall learn presently why this statement is true, at least to infinitesimal tolerances, even if multiple equilibriums exist.

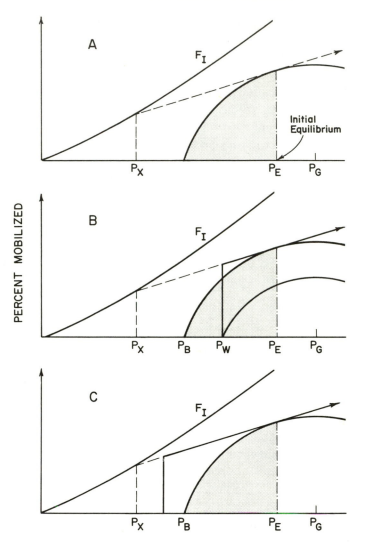

FIG. 3.1
The Logic of Withdrawing from the Streets

The reasoning is simple. Suppose the dissidents abbreviate the original strategy by withdrawing from the streets somewhere in the shaded interval, say at P_W. This maneuver immediately makes P_W more attractive than all the policies to its left, including P_B. Among the policies more moderate than P_W, P_E remains the most attractive (abbreviating the original strategy does not affect the mobilization curve where the new target interval overlaps the old). But the regime is indifferent between P_E and P_B (by construction), while it strictly prefers P_W to P_B. P_W therefore becomes the new equilibrium outcome, being preferable in the regime's eyes to all the policies on its right and left.

The reasoning about P_W applies to the other policies between P_E and P_B, as well. Clearly, the movement wins the biggest concession by demobilizing infinitesimally to the right of P_B.[4]

The lower panel of Figure 3.1 shows why not all abbreviated versions of the original strategy win bigger concessions.

These considerations lead to another rule and a further extension of our vocabulary.

RULE 3: If the equilibrium policy associated with a strategy lies inside its target interval, then some abbreviated version of the strategy yields a bigger concession.

In other words, when a strategy fails to make *all* the policies it opposes too uncomfortable to adopt, it sacrifices potential concessions by trying to do too much. A better outcome can always be achieved with the same demands simply by shortening the target interval.

DEFINITION: The Efficient Version of a Strategy
The version of a strategy (either original or abbreviated) that attains the largest concession is called efficient.

This concept provides a useful way to summarize the political effectiveness of essentially similar strategies. For example, we might be interested in a family of sincere strategies that lodge the same demand against various spans of policies. The stubborn version is a natural base line for comparison, and if it proves to be unsuccessful we can

---

[4] Withdrawing exactly at P_B creates dual equilibriums, and the government might then choose the more moderate of the two at P_E. The equilibrium attained by suspending operations at the policy adjacent to P_B is unique, and therefore a sure thing. The same reasoning applies to successful strategies that have multiple equilibriums. In these cases, the movement can always force the regime arbitrarily close to its most radical demand simply by withdrawing from the streets at the policy adjacent to that demand.

search for the efficient abbreviated version by the technique just described. Naturally, it makes no sense to call a strategy efficient without specifying some initial schedule of demands as a frame of reference.

Abbreviating a strategy is one form of compromise that allows a movement to obtain a final, though incomplete, concession in return for restoring tranquility to the streets. The technique is essentially an end game gambit in the nature of closing a deal. The movement agrees to suspend its activities if the regime agrees to a somewhat bigger concession than the prevailing equilibrium. This is the usual method for reaching negotiated settlements in labor disputes, for example. The maneuver has a curious and slightly paradoxical air about it. In a system of conflict where power depends solely on numbers, it allows the movement to win extra concessions by reducing the level of disruption in the streets.

An interesting example of this kind of end game bargaining arises in the history of the American civil-rights movement. During the voter registration campaign waged by the Southern Christian Leadership Conference in Selma, Alabama, broad support developed for what later became the Voting Rights Act of 1965. Eventually, President Johnson summoned Dr. Martin Luther King, Jr. to the White House for discussions about the wording of the new legislation. Before King arrived, however, the President's counsel, Lee White, drafted a memorandum warning LBJ about a rumor that thousands of King's followers might descend on Congress to launch a sit-in protest. "You may wish to stress the need for some restraint on the part of the civil rights group," he cautioned. "There is considerable national interest in voting legislation . . . but it can be drained off by mistakes."[5]

This memorandum suggests how regimes may react by withdrawing concessions if they are greeted by further disruption. The movement's enemies inside the regime inevitably argue that making concessions will only provoke more radical demands (i.e. more disruption). If the movement is too weak to achieve everything it wants, it can be disastrous to supply ammunition for these arguments. In this case, the proper strategy was not to punish the President and the Congress *after* a coalition had formed to enact the reforms, but rather to reward their concessions with tranquility. This, in fact, is just what the SCLC did. Thus, the fact that there is power in numbers does not always imply

[5] See David J. Garrow, *Protest at Selma* (New Haven: Yale University Press, 1978), pp. 68-69.

that more mobilization is better than less. Mobilizing against too broad a spectrum of policies sometimes backfires.

The Logic of Compromising Demands

THE TECHNIQUE of withdrawing from the streets is theoretically interesting because it illustrates how to milk the maximum potential from a particular schedule of demands. By no means, however, is it the only political alternative when a strategy results in an unhappy outcome. Another possibility is to compromise demands in an effort to create more pressure for a bigger concession.

Explaining how this approach works and the political dilemmas it entails are the central problems in a theory of peaceful protest. The political dynamics of defining and adjusting demands depend on the interplay of three elements in the system of conflict described by our model. The first might be called the fundamental fact of political life—namely, that power resides in numbers. When movements find themselves struggling to win their demands, attracting more support becomes the paramount concern. How much additional support they need depends on the responsiveness of the regime. Responsiveness, our measure of the power of numbers, therefore decides the political necessity for, and the effectiveness of, programmatic adjustments.

The second element of the problem is the connection between demands and popular support established by the recruiting process. Simple ideological recruiting locks the two together like a political vice, punishing extreme demands and rewarding moderation. Other systems of recruiting make compromise gratuitous by severing the connection between political substance and popular support. And there are many alternatives in between.

The dissident leaders' own aspirations form the third link in the chain. How much they value partial concessions and how committed they are to maintaining principles also affect the choice among alternative demands. Some movements eagerly pursue any political concession, however slight, while others spurn compromise like a political virus. To understand why, we must understand the differences separating the Bolsheviks and Mensheviks, the Mountain and the Gironde, and other "purists" and "pragmatists" whose debates animate the literature of radical thought. Devising a story that draws these threads together into a coherent political tapestry is a real challenge. It shall occupy us for the remainder of this chapter and several to follow.

Steadfast and Evolutionary Strategies

RADICAL politics attracts people with markedly different strategic predispositions. Among the fault lines dividing dissident movements, few
are more important than the cleavage between pragmatists and purists. Before we investigate these political types in the chapters to follow, it is important first to understand the properties of the strategies
they characteristically pursue.

Purists are intensely committed to ultimate goals and abstract principles. They take their principles seriously and prefer not to compromise them. Nor do they trust the "waverers" and opportunists who
somehow manage to see two sides in every issue. The ideological rigi-
dity of the purist favors a politically rigid strategy. The purist feels
most comfortable with steadfastness and sincerity, while compromise
and flexibility evoke the deepest suspicion, if not dismay.

Where steadfastness and uncompromising adherence to principle are
the hallmarks of the purist mentality, the pragmatist wants results. If
tangible concessions can be won by compromising demands, then the
pragmatist is all for flexibility. A consistent proponent of the pragmatic
philosophy is the American organizer Saul Alinsky, who captures its
tenets especially well in his discourse on the word *compromise*:

> Compromise is a word that carries shades of weakness, vacillation, be-
> trayal of ideals, and surrender of moral principles. . . . When virginity was
> a virtue, one referred to a woman's being "compromised." The word is
> generally regarded as ethically unsavory and ugly.
>   But to the organizer, compromise is a key and beautiful word. It is
> always present in the pragmatics of operation. It is making the deal,
> getting that vital breather, usually the victory. If you start with nothing,
> demand 100 per cent, then compromise for 30 per cent, you're 30 per cent
> ahead.[6]

The short-term expedient of compromising demands to win partial
concessions generalizes naturally to a broader conception of strategy
based on evolutionary change. The idea is to force the regime to move
incrementally toward the movement's goal rather than to strive to
achieve it in one fell swoop. At each step in the process, the movement
tries to mobilize the broadest possible opposition against the regime's
prevailing course. With every new concession, the movement regroups

---

[6] Saul Alinsky, *Rules for Radicals: A Pragmatic Primer for Realistic Radicals* (New
York: Vintage Books, 1972), p. 59.

its forces, adopts a somewhat more radical demand, and then renews the struggle. As Alinsky says,

> A free and open society is an on-going conflict, interrupted periodically by compromises—which then become the start for the continuation of conflict, compromise, and on *ad infinitum*.[7]

The Political Logic of the Steadfast Strategy

IN VIEW of the powerful impulses that propel radical politicians toward the steadfast and evolutionary strategies, let us spend some time to consider their political characteristics. First, the steadfast strategy:

RULE 4: Moderate demands mobilize more support than radical demands when recruiting is ideological. Note: The terms *moderate* and *radical* refer to relative distances from the regime's ideal point.

This rule places a fundamental political constraint on strategy making in our hypothetical society. It follows straightforwardly from our assumptions about the continuity of popular opinion and the nonextremeness of both sides' political platforms. Examine Figure 3.2 and consider the effectiveness of the two demands, P_X and P_Y. The level of support mobilized by these demands against the government's ideal policy, P_G, is given by the value of the cumulative distribution at the halfway mark associated with each one. Of course, the halfway point determined by a radical demand always lies farther to the left than the halfway point of a moderate demand. Since the cumulative distribution is strictly increasing from left to right in the range of the political spectrum occupied by the two sides (remember, their positions are not extreme), it follows that radical demands mobilize smaller demonstrations than moderate demands.

RULE 5: Among steadfast strategies, the moderate outmobilize the radical when recruiting is ideological.

This rule is a straightforward generalization of rule 4, derived by applying it serially inside an interval where the target intervals of two steadfast strategies overlap. Figure 3.3 shows how the mobilization curves of radical steadfast strategies always lie below those of their

---

[7] Ibid.

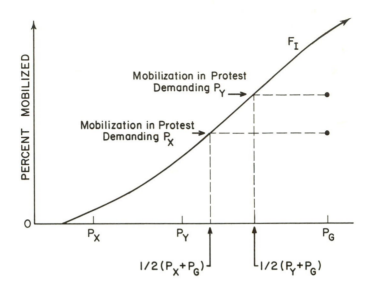

FIG. 3.2
Radical Demands Never Outmobilize
Moderate Demands

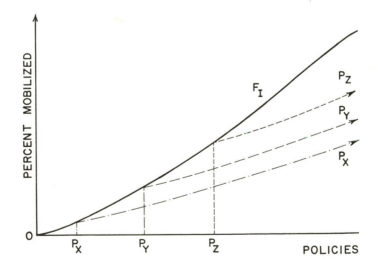

FIG. 3.3
A Family of Mobilization Curves

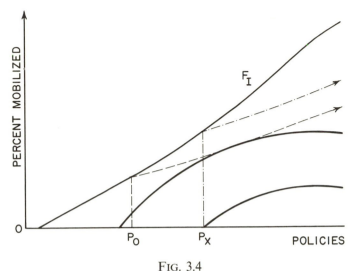

FIG. 3.4
When a Strategy Succeeds, So Do More
Moderate Strategies

moderate cousins. In fact, these mobilization curves are simply lateral translations of each other.

RULE 6: When a steadfast strategy is successful, so too are the steadfast strategies with more moderate demands. Note: The rule naturally refers only to the stubborn versions of each strategy, recalling rule 2.

Figure 3.4 illustrates the reasoning behind the rule. Let P_O be the successful demand of a steadfast strategy, and P_X be any demand lying closer to the regime's ideal point. When faced with the original strategy, the regime finds it more advantageous to accept the demand P_O than to adopt any of the compromise policies closer to its ideal point. The more moderate strategy creates even greater disruption against these intermediate policies (by rule 5) but demands less. The new demand therefore becomes an equilibrium policy.

RULE 7: The demands of successful and unsuccessful steadfast strategies span two continuous intervals along the ideological spectrum.

Canvass the sequence of successful demands on the left of the regime's ideal point, and proceed to the leftward limit of the sequence.

All the strategies with more radical demands are necessarily unsuccessful; otherwise the leftward limit has not been reached. All the less radical demands are successful (by rule 6). Hence the rule.

RULE 8: The Moderation Rule for Steadfast Strategies
If a steadfast strategy is unsuccessful, then some more moderate strategy neccessarily wins a bigger concession.

This rule is a fundamental political consequence of the ideological system of recruiting. It means that dissident groups sacrifice concessions whenever they cling to a sincere strategy (or any other steadfast schedule) without mobilizing enough support to win their demand.

To verify the rule, we must consider two situations. The most interesting case arises when the stubborn version of a steadfast strategy turns out to be unsuccessful. The second case is largely a curiosity. It involves instances where the stubborn version would be successful if the dissidents used it, but instead they withdraw from the streets prematurely. The abbreviated versions of successful strategies are unsuccessful because of human error rather than political necessity. Curiously enough, they still can be improved by moderating demands, though doing so would only compound the first blunder with a second. We leave it to the reader to verify the rule for these cases.

Far more important are those steadfast demands that cannot be won by pursuing them stubbornly. To verify the moderation rule in these instances, it is necessary to show that by demanding less, it is always possible to outperform *the efficient version* of such a strategy. Figure 3.5 illustrates the reasoning that sustains this conclusion.

Here the stubborn strategy demanding P_X forces the government initially to the policy P_E. If the dissidents are clever enough, they can use the disturbances against P_E to bargain for a somewhat bigger concession. The indifference curve defining the original equilibrium also determines the appropriate amount of abbreviation. In this case, the biggest concession attainable with the demand P_X lies adjacent to the policy P_{X*}. By agreeing to suspend their demonstrations if the government adopts this policy, the dissidents exploit the demand P_X to its fullest potential. According to the moderation rule, it should be possible to design a strategy that demands less than P_X but wins more than P_{X*}. Of course, if we succeed, we shall have found a better strategy than every conceivable strategy demanding P_X.

Certainly, any demand that might be an improvement must lie between P_X and P_{X*}. We shall never win a bigger concession than

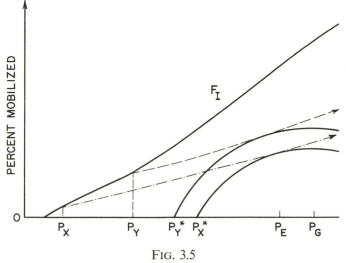

FIG. 3.5
The Moderation Rule

P_{X*} by demanding less, after all. As a matter of fact, any of these demands can be used to win a bigger concession. To see why, let us pick one at random and use it in a stubborn strategy. If the new strategy happens to be successful, it wins a bigger concession than P_{X*} straightforwardly. The new strategy might not be successful, however. In Figure 3.5, the strategy demanding P_Y illustrates this possibility. Although it fails to win its demand, the new strategy does mobilize more people against the policies to its right (by rule 5) than the original strategy did. Its mobilization curve therefore rests on a higher indifference curve than the one defining the equilibrium at P_{X*}. Since higher indifference curves intersect the policy axis farther from the regime's ideal point than lower curves, the efficient version of the new strategy wins a bigger concession that P_{X*}. Hence, the rule.

RULE 9: The Optimal Steadfast Strategy
None of the steadfast strategies wins a bigger concession than the most radical one that succeeds.

What is the most effective way to exploit the political situation while holding fast to a single demand? The answer is simple—choose the most radical demand that succeeds. In other words, never demand more than you can get.

To understand why (save for a slight technical wrinkle), let's begin at the regime's ideal point and canvass the class of (stubborn) steadfast strategies as their demands become more radical. Moving to the left, we enter the span of successful demands and continue until we reach the most radical of the lot.[8]

Among the successful demands, the most radical wins the biggest concession. The only conceivable rivals to our candidate for the optimum therefore lie in the span of unsuccessful demands farther to the left. But rule 8 assures us that none of these demands can be optimal, since we can always moderate an unsuccessful demand to secure a bigger concession. This process inexorably draws us back to the right until we arrive again at the most radical of the successful demands.

Figure 3.6 illustrates this reasoning and alerts us to a curious strategy that defies our descriptive taxonomy. In the upper panel, the stubborn demand P_X proves to be unsuccessful. We know that any demand between P_X and P_{X*} (the equilibrium policy attained by abbreviating the target interval efficiently) has greater political potential, so we pick one at random (here P_Y). The second panel shows that the new demand, P_Y, is unsuccessful too. However, the span of more effective demands shrinks to the interval between P_Y and P_{Y*}. Continuing this iterative process of informed trial and error reduces our options even further in the lower panel. In this fashion, we can locate the optimal demand within an arbitrarily narrow interval.

Note, however, that when the dissidents choose a demand a bit more moderate than P_Z, the new equilibrium-defining indifference curve intersects the policy axis precisely at the new demand. This maverick strategy poses something of a semantic problem, defining, as it does, at least two equilibrium outcomes—one inside the target interval and a second at the demand itself. Is it successful or unsuccessful or just plain ambiguous? To avoid endless qualifications, let's give it a special name—the boundary strategy[9]—since it lies on the boundary of the

---

[8] Note that the set of successful steadfast strategies cannot be empty when the government's policy is not extreme.

[9] The existence of the boundary strategy creates a number of complications in our system of definitions and rules, and not a few headaches if we choose to treat it as more than an infinitesimal tempest in a teapot. We would prefer not to, but those who like to worry about such things should be alert to the difficulties it causes.

Consider first the problems that arise if we decide to call the boundary strategy successful. (It does fit the definition of successful strategies set forth earlier, after all.) This approach has the virtue of ensuring that the set of successful demands contains its boundary on the left. We can then talk about the *most radical* of the successful demands without ambiguity. Rule 9 is no longer true, however, because the government may not adopt the demand of the boundary strategy as its concession. (It could equally well move to the equilibrium inside the target interval.) This is unfortunate because rule 9 is a convenient and natural way to describe an important feature of steadfast strategies.

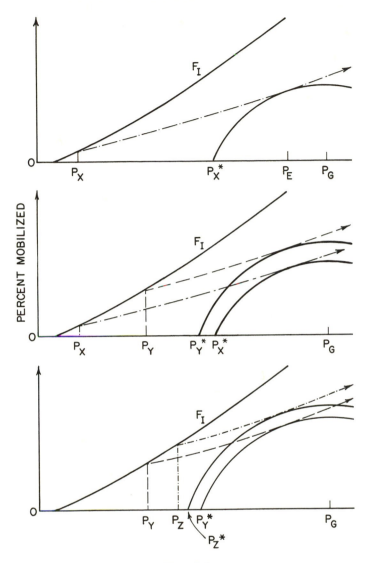

FIG. 3.6
Locating the Optimal Demand

successful and unsuccessful spans. Figure 3.7 shows what the boundary strategy looks like.

RULE 10: A Law of Diminishing Returns
As the demands of steadfast strategies diverge in either direction from the optimum, they win continuously smaller concessions. Note: with the exception of the boundary demand.

This assertion is trivially true for less radical demands than the optimum because they are all successful. As they demand less, they achieve less—it is as simple as that.

For the unsuccessful demands to the left, we rely again on the reasoning of the moderation rule. If the stubborn version of a steadfast strategy fails to win its demand, we know the demand immediately to its right has greater political potential. Since the unsuccessful demands lie in a continuous span, applying this reasoning serially, from left to right, yields the conclusion we want.

One of the interesting features of steadfast strategies is the way the message to compromise demands emanates quite directly from the sit-

---

Suppose, then, that we call the boundary strategy unsuccessful, on the grounds that a successful strategy should establish equilibrium *uniquely* at its demand. The problem now is that neither rule 8 nor 9 is true if the government does accede to the boundary demand. It seems that we have taken one step forward, but two steps back.

These difficulties reflect an inherent uncertainty about the government's response to the boundary strategy. Rather than arbitrarily calling it successful or unsuccessful, it seems wisest to regard it as an essentially different kind of strategy, which deserves its own name. We can then partition the ideological spectrum into three sets of demands. The open interval bounded by the boundary demand on the left and the government's ideal point on the right contains the demands that are successful in an unambiguous sense (each becomes a unique equilibrium when used in a steadfast strategy). The half-open interval between the ideological fringe of the population on the left and the boundary demand on the right contains demands that are assuredly unsuccessful. And finally, the boundary demand itself lies on the boundary of the two intervals.

unsuccessful		successful	
demands		demands	

P_L P_B P_G
Leftward limit of   Boundary   Government's
political preference   demand   ideal point
in population

The great virtue of this taxonomy is that we can use the words successful and unsuccessful in a politically meaningful way. Care must be exercised, however, in using expressions like "the most radical successful demand" or "the most moderate unsuccessful demand." Properly speaking, no such demands exist when the sets of successful and unsuccessful demands are open. We shall use these expressions informally to denote arbitrarily small neighborhoods on either side of the boundary demand.

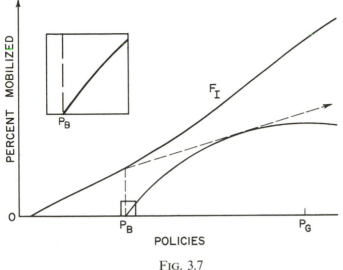

FIG. 3.7
The Boundary Strategy

uation itself, rather than from an extended analysis of the situation. If the dissidents' sincere strategy is unsuccessful, more moderate demands achieve continuously bigger concessions until the optimum is reached. To locate the best strategy, the dissidents do not need a picture of the regime's responsiveness map or a detailed reading of popular opinion. Nor do they have to understand the logic of bargaining underlying the abbreviated strategies. They only need to know whether their strategy is successful or not—an immediately obvious fact—and then moderate their demand if it isn't. Unlike many game theoretical analyses of political life, we need not assume mathematical sophistication on the part of radical strategists to imagine that our theory might tell us something about their behavior. This is not to say, however, that the world of radical politics is necessarily populated by mathematical dunces. Leon Trotsky, for example, showed promise as a mathematician before he launched his career as a revolutionary.[10]

Evolutionary Strategies of Confrontation

WHEN RADICAL groups abandon the constraint of steadfastness and begin tailoring their demands to fit the political situation, it is hardly

[10] See Leon Trotsky, *My Life* (New York: Pathfinder Press, 1970).

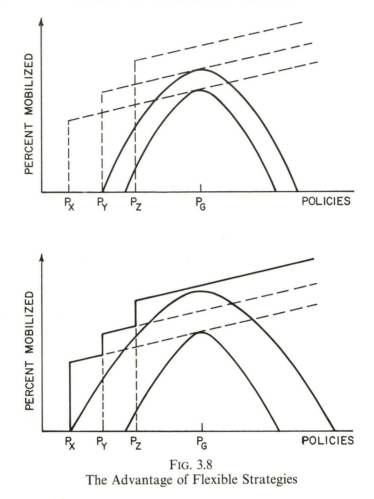

FIG. 3.8
The Advantage of Flexible Strategies

surprising that their strategies should become more effective. The moderating bias of ideological recruiting favors the flexible strategy over its steadfast cousin by making it a more potent mobilizer.

Figure 3.8 illustrates how the advantage arises. The upper panel shows the mobilization curves of three steadfast strategies; the middle one, demanding P_Y, is the optimal member of its class. Now let's adopt the perspective of a group whose goal is P_X and consider the options when our sincere strategy fails. If we feel bound to a steadfast approach, a real dilemma arises because our sincere demand is less effective than P_Y. Either we compromise our principles, or we sacrifice tangible concessions.

The dilemma becomes less acute, however, if we adopt a flexible strategy. The lower panel of Figure 3.8 shows how we can reach our goal by lodging incrementally more radical demands as the regime moves its policy from right to left. By first demanding P_Z (until the government adopts that policy), and then demanding P_Y, and finally P_X, our sincere demand ultimately becomes the regime's most attractive alternative. The flexible strategy succeeds where its steadfast cousin fails because it mobilizes bigger demonstrations in the crucial middle range between P_Y and P_G. This capacity to stir up greater opposition to the regime's partial concessions makes the flexible strategy an inviting alternative when a steadfast strategy fails to win its demand.

RULE 11: Minimal demands create maximal disruption when recruiting is ideological.

Pushing rule 4 to its logical limit leads, as a natural corollary, to rule 11. If moderate demands outmobilize radical demands, it follows that disruption increases continuously as the dissidents' demand converges toward the government's policy—reaching a maximum at the minimal demand adjacent to it. The rule captures the essential advantage of flexibility in our theoretical system of conflict. By adjusting their demand when the government changes its policy, the dissidents can sustain the maximal level of disruption at all times.

DEFINITION: Minimalist Strategy
A minimalist strategy lodges the minimal demand against every policy inside its target interval.

RULE 12: The mobilization curve generated by a minimalist strategy is identical to the cumulative distribution.

A minimalist strategy mobilizes all the people on the left of the government's policy, whatever it may be. Thus, $M(P_X) = F_I(P_X)$ for all P_X inside the target interval.

RULE 13: The Optimal Peaceful Strategy (Analogue of Rule 9)
No peaceful strategy wins a bigger concession than the most radical of the successful, minimalist strategies. Note: We decide whether one flexible strategy is more radical than another by comparing the most extreme demands inside their target intervals.

Figure 3.9 illustrates the rule graphically. The mobilization curves of all the minimalist strategies are defined by the cumulative distribution. The trick to choosing the best one, then, is knowing when to withdraw from the streets. Here we can rely on familiar techniques.

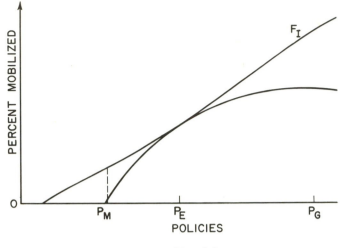

FIG. 3.9
The Optimal Peaceful Strategy

The political potential of the minimalist approach is ultimately determined by the lowest indifference curve grazing the cumulative distribution. To secure the biggest concession, the dissidents must suspend
their demonstrations infinitesimally to the right of the point where this
indifference curve intersects the policy axis.

In Figure 3.9, this reasoning leads the dissidents to withdraw from
the streets when the government adopts the policy, P_M. Under a minimalist strategy, the demand P_M is lodged against the policy immediately to its right. The optimal strategy therefore establishes equilibrium
at its most radical demand—i.e. it is successful. Any strategy lodging a
more radical demand than P_M is necessarily unsuccessful, while the
less radical, minimalist strategies all succeed. Thus, when the minimalist strategies are indexed by their most radical demand, they define a
partition of the ideological spectrum into continuous spans containing
achievable and unachievable demands (plus one boundary demand
separating the spans). We have then an analogue for rule 7.

Unlike the steadfast approach, however, the flexible approach does
not define an essentially unique optimal strategy. Clearly, no other
program of demands wins a bigger concession than the strategy described by our rule. Doing so would require a larger protest against the
policy P_E (where the indifference curve grazes the cumulative distribution), but a minimalist demand already creates maximal disruption at

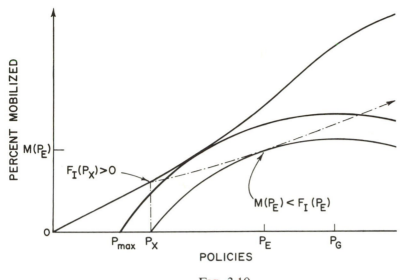

FIG. 3.10
Flexible Strategies Outperform Steadfast Strategies

this point.[11] The minimalist strategy creates more disruption against the other policies, however, than the minimum required to reach P_M. Other demands could therefore be substituted in these cases, without changing the end result.

RULE 14: The best steadfast strategy is less effective than the best flexible strategy, unless every steadfast strategy succeeds.

Flexible strategies are clearly better adapted to the moderating bias of ideological recruiting than steadfast strategies. Still, it is interesting to ask whether a steadfast approach might be just as effective in certain situations. While the answer, in fact, is yes, the circumstances are so bizarre that it might just as well be no.

Figure 3.10 shows why the best of the minimalist strategies generally outperforms the optimal steadfast strategy. Here the demand P_X is the optimal choice in a steadfast strategy. Two features of the situation guarantee that a better flexible strategy exists. First, the stubborn demand for P_X generates less than maximal disruption inside its target interval. Second, the cumulative distribution remains positive for policies on the left of P_X (meaning that people with more radical views are

---

[11] The same argument holds when there are multiple tangencies.

available to be mobilized against it). As a result, it is possible to design a flexible strategy whose mobilization curve rests higher on the regime's indifference map. In this case, the best minimalist strategy achieves the concession P_{max}.

The only circumstance in which a steadfast strategy cannot be improved upon occurs when the optimal steadfast demand happens to coincide with the leftward boundary of popular opinion. Then no one can be mobilized to push the government further to the left. In this unlikely situation, every steadfast strategy succeeds.

THE THEORY of peaceful protest is schematic and stark, but its virtues more than compensate for the inevitable lack of literalism in any highly idealized representation of a complex reality. We build abstract models to acquire a sense of underlying structure, not to understand minute details (though such details often remain incomprehensible without a sense of structure). In this case, the model rewards us by rendering in bold relief the most basic of all the strategic dilemmas in radical politics—whether to hold fast to principles or to compromise them for political concessions. In the circumstances described by the present theory, the dilemma is inescapable whenever sincere strategies fail. The dilemma tends to become less acute, however, as the assumptions underlying the theory are relaxed.

The Distribution of Preferences

WHEN the population is arrayed ideologically in discrete groups or factions, rather than continuously across the political spectrum, several modifications must be introduced into the rules of strategy described in this chapter. Although the underlying logic of peaceful protest remains the same, the impulse to moderate unsuccessful demands may be attenuated or even disappear entirely. The basic complication arises in rules 4 and 5, since it can no longer be assumed that moderate demands result in strictly greater mobilization than radical demands. When the cumulative distribution has "flats," corresponding to unpopulated stretches of the ideological spectrum, moderate demands produce mobilization greater than, *or equal to*, that produced by radical demands. The reason is simple. If the crucial middle ground between the radicals' position and the regime's is not continuously populated, compromising demands does not necessarily bring new people into the movement's span of support.

This possibility requires in turn that rule 8 (the moderation rule) be weakened. In the circumstances of a factionally divided society, it is no longer true that an unsuccessful strategy can necessarily be improved by compromising its demand. Rule 9 remains in force, but without the presumption that the optimal demand is (essentially) unique. Thus, rule 10, the law of diminishing returns, must be amended as follows:

> Within the set of unsuccessful, steadfast strategies, the more radical win concessions smaller than, *or equal to*, those won by the less radical.

A compact summary of these amendments can be accomplished with diagrams that plot the demand of each (efficient) steadfast strategy against the concession it secures. The general shape of the heavily shaded strategy-potential curve in the upper panel of Figure 3.11 conforms to the rules of strategy when preferences are distributed continuously. P_L denotes the leftward limit of popular opinion, P_G denotes the ideal point of the government, and P_{max} denotes the most radical of the successful demands. In accord with rule 10, the unsuccessful demands between P_L and P_{max} achieve continuously smaller concessions as they become more radical.

When the assumption of continuity is relaxed, the political potential of the unsuccessful demands need not be *strictly* decreasing. Instead, their potential may diminish in fits and starts as shown in the middle panel of Figure 3.11. Depending on the location of the movement's ideal point and the particular shape of such a curve, there may be no incentive to moderate a sincere strategy that fails to win its demand. In general, it is fair to say that a continuously distributed population is friendlier to a compromising strategy than is a factionally divided population, but such a global generalization must be handled gingerly. In particular ideological neighborhoods, the incentive to compromise unsuccessful demands may be pronounced even when the population is partitioned in discrete political blocs. And conversely, the potential of progressively more moderate demands may increase only marginally in a continuously distributed population.

Organizational Recruiting

WHEN movements adopt a system of recruiting that does not rely on ideological incentives, the linkage between programmatic strategy and mobilization is severed completely. The only strategic problem facing the radical leaders is when to withdraw from the streets. If they have enough support to win their demand, they should of course adopt a stubborn strategy. Otherwise, the lowest indifference curve grazing

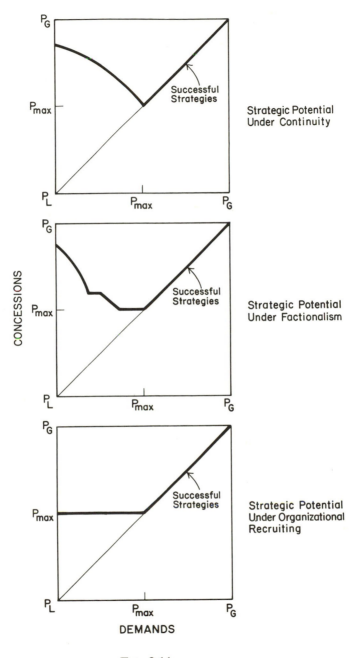

FIG. 3.11
Strategy-Potential Curves

their (level) mobilization curve defines the optimal boundary for the target set (in the fashion of Figure 3.1). Since the height of the mobilization curve no longer depends on the choice of demands or the government's policy, it follows that every unsuccessful demand has equal capacity to win concessions. The strategy potential curves associated with the organizational approach to recruiting therefore have the shape shown in the lower panel of Figure 3.11. Clearly, no movement that relies on organizational recruiting ever has any incentive to compromise its sincere demand. Such a system of mobilization provides one avenue of escape from the dilemmas imposed by an "immature" political situation. It allows the radical leaders to pursue grandiose goals in an unfriendly political environment without sacrificing support.

The strategy-potential curves arising from organizational and ideological recruiting represent boundary conditions, in a sense, between which similar curves from hybrid systems of recruiting must fall.

CHAPTER FOUR

Pragmatists and Purists

IN THE LAST chapter, we developed a bare-bones model of protest and used it to explore the potential for winning concessions with several kinds of strategy. Having acquired the necessary means for assessing the effectiveness of alternative strategies, we must now ask how this latent potential for change is translated into political action. The most straightforward (and naive) solution to the problem is simply to assume that dissident leaders choose the strategy that brings them closest to realizing their ideal policy. This method of deriving predictions about actions from a description of the movement's political environment is simple and plausible. Nonetheless, the history of radical politics evokes grave doubts about the utility of such a theoretical stratagem. The purpose of this chapter is to develop a richer and more fruitful approach to understanding how radical movements develop a strategy. Although our focus shall remain on the problem of choosing demands in strategies of peaceful protest, the implications of this approach extend far beyond the narrow confines of our current theory.

The difficulties arising in a naive, concession-maximizing model of strategic choice become evident when we consider movements that lack enough support to achieve their goals with a sincere strategy. If a radical group has the wherewithal to get what it wants just by demanding it, there is little occasion for controversy in predicting that it will do so. The more challenging problem is to foresee what road a movement will travel after its sincere strategy fails. In the idealized setting described by our theory of peaceful protest, the straightforward, rational-choice perspective suggests that movements will compromise their demands whenever they find themselves in this predicament. The distaste for turbulent crowds among those in authority and the system of ideological recruiting both favor moderation as the politically pragmatic course to follow.

Historical accounts of radical politics, on the other hand, show that compromise rarely occurs without political friction. When dissidents are forced to choose between tangible concessions and doctrinal purity, intense factional strife often results. Nor do the proponents of compromise always prevail in these disputes. Innumerable movements have shunned compromise altogether, despite the manifest political costs of doing so.

Explanations for this apparent shortcoming of the theory can be sought in three places. Some cases can be disposed of within the existing framework, simply by revising the description of the situation. For example, we know that compromising may not be useful in populations that are distributed in discrete groups rather than continuously across the political spectrum. Nor does every radical group rely on ideological recruiting. Other instances can be explained only by extending the menu of strategic choice within the theory. For example, resorting to violent tactics is sometimes politically more effective than compromising demands. A simple model of peaceful protest then becomes too narrow to yield useful predictions about the political alternatives to a faltering sincere strategy. Finally, it may be that radical leaders evaluate strategies by criteria other than their capacity to secure concessions. This possibility is the focus of the present chapter, while the others await future consideration.

Radical circles are notoriously contentious, and the process of fashioning political demands occasions some of the bitterest factional infighting. This fact alone suggests that considerations other than political effectiveness may influence the design of strategy. One enlightening way to investigate this possibility is by building theoretical models of how factional disputes arise and testing the models' ability to capture the main contours of real factional debates in the literature of radical thought. Among the numerous cases one might select for this purpose, none is more fascinating, better documented, or historically more consequential than the debates within the European revolutionary socialist movement about the "revisionist" theories of Eduard Bernstein.

The prosperous decades before World War I created widespread doubts about the Marxian theory of capitalism's demise. In an atmosphere of disquieting theoretical uncertainty, the Social Democratic parties faced the difficult choice of whether to follow the revolutionary road laid out by Marx and Engels in *The Communist Manifesto* or the "practical" program of incremental reformism advocated by Bernstein.[1]

In the classical Marxian theory, the transformation to socialism follows a general and catastrophic commercial crisis resulting from the contradictions inherent in the capitalist system of production. According to Marx, the irreconcilable economic interests of the bourgeoisie and the proletariat fuel a bitter class struggle that resolves itself only in the revolutionary overthrow of the bourgeois order. Bernstein argued, on the other hand, that capitalist development produces mechanisms of adaptation or adjustment, which attenuate the contradictions identified by Marx and reduce the likelihood of a catastrophic collapse. From this vantage point, he concluded that Social Democrats ought not to strive, in their day-to-day activities, for the abolition of private property, the conquest of state power, and a dictatorship of the proletariat. Instead he campaigned for a strategy of reform-minded trade-union and parliamentary work, directed toward the gradual betterment of the workers' lot. The piecemeal extension of the proletariat's political and economic rights, Bernstein insisted, would produce an evolutionary transformation of the bourgeois order into a higher socialist form.

Bernstein's revisionist ideas sent shock waves through the Social Democratic movement, provoking a rancorous dispute among Europe's leading socialist theorists about political strategy. In the remainder of this chapter and in the following two chapters, we shall

[1] Our account of the revisionist debates considers the writings of those participants who best exemplify various strategic mentalities. The following works are the focus of the discussion to follow: Edward Bernstein, *Evolutionary Socialism*, trans. Edith C. Harvey (New York: Schocken Books, 1961); Karl Marx, "Wage Labour and Capital," and Karl Marx and Friedrich Engels, "Manifesto of the Communist Party" in *The Marx-Engels Reader*, ed. Robert C. Tucker (New York: W. W. Norton, 1972); Rosa Luxemburg, *Selected Political Writings*, ed. Robert Looker (New York: Grove Press, 1974); Rosa Luxemburg, *Rosa Luxemburg Speaks*, ed. Mary-Alice Waters (New York: Pathfinder Press, 1970); V. I. Lenin, *Selected Works* (New York: International Publishers, 1967).

Information about the historical setting of the debate can be found in Peter Gay, *The Dilemma of Democratic Socialism* (New York: Collier Books, 1962); Fritz Stern, *Gold and Iron* (New York: Alfred A. Knopf, 1977); Karl Kautsky, *The Class Struggle* (*Erfurt Program*), trans. W. E. Bohn (New York: W. W. Norton, 1971); Massimo Salvadori, *Karl Kautsky and the Socialist Revolution 1880-1938*, trans. Jon Rothschild (London: NLB, 1979); Gary P. Steenson, *Karl Kautsky, 1854-1938* (Pittsburgh: Pittsburgh University Press, 1978); Robert Michels, *Political Parties*, trans. Eden and Cedar Paul (New York: Free Press, 1962); Theodore S. Hamerow, *Restoration, Revolution, Reaction* (Princeton: Princeton University Press, 1958); Robert C. Tucker, *The Marxian Revolutionary Idea* (New York: W. W. Norton, 1970); Carl Schorske, *German Social Democracy, 1905-1917* (New York: Russell & Russell, 1970); and Georg Lukács, *History and Class Consciousness*, trans. Rodney Livingstone (Cambridge: MIT Press, 1971).

consider several mechanisms that might explain how the dispute arose and the shape it took. Surprisingly, the highly schematic model of peaceful protest requires only slight modifications to accomplish these tasks. Despite its silence about many important questions, it proves to be well suited for analyzing the processes at work in this complicated controversy.

Purists versus Pragmatists: The Intensity Model

LET US EXPLORE first, and try to make more precise, the vague intuitive idea that the revisionist controversy was a dispute between "pragmatists" and "purists." The immediately evident requirement for such an argument to make sense is that radical leaders seek, in formulating their strategy, to maintain the integrity of their political principles as well as to gain concessions from the regime. Unhappily, these objectives are not always compatible, as the theory of peaceful protest vividly shows. The political situation sometimes forces the dissidents to choose between tangible concessions and doctrinal purity. Factional tensions may then develop if the movement's strategy makers disagree about how the two objectives should be reconciled.

But by what mechanism would such disagreements arise? The most obvious answer is that the two political types attach different weights to the competing objectives, purists giving higher priority to maintaining principles and pragmatists giving higher priority to securing concessions. The trouble with this account is that it simply redescribes the phenomenon we are trying to understand, leaving unexplained why different individuals would attach unequal weights to the two concerns in the first place.

Let us consider another approach, then, which might provide a deeper understanding. Suppose that radical leaders differ with respect to the intensity of their preferences for policies across the ideological spectrum. We shall not assume, at least for the time being, that any disagreement exists about ultimate political objectives. The differences of opinion turn instead upon the relative attractiveness of intermediate positions along the way to the final destination. The question is whether a model based solely upon differences in intensity can explain the salient features of strategic debates between pragmatists and purists (that is to say, a model that makes no prior assumption that radical

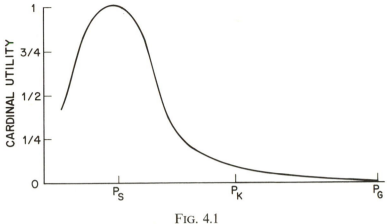

FIG. 4.1
The Purist Pattern of Preference

leaders assign different priorities to achieving concessions and preserving principles).

First consider the ideological purist who is typically described as doctrinaire, dogmatic, narrow-minded, and politically intense. If we were to describe the purist pattern of preference by a cardinal utility function defined over the ideological spectrum[2] (where the utility of the regime's ideal policy, P_G, is assigned a value of zero and the individual's ideal policy, P_S, takes on a value of one), a reasonable interpretation of the anecdotal descriptions would resemble the function in Figure 4.1. In accord with the assumptions of the theory, the utility of alternative policies diminishes continuously as they recede from the purist's preferred policy. The distinctive feature of the purist outlook, of course, is the intense disliking for policies only slightly removed from the ideal point. Thus the level of utility decays rapidly as we depart from the immediate neighborhood of P_S, leaving the purist hostile toward, and essentially indifferent between, a broad span of policies ranging far across the political spectrum.

Pragmatists, on the other hand, are less doctrinaire about the policies in the middle ground between their ideal point and the regime's

---

[2] A function that gives rise to an interval scale of measurement, so that differences in the utility numbers can be meaningfully compared. See Fred S. Roberts, "Measurement and Utility," *Discrete Mathematical Models* (Englewood Cliffs, N.J.: Prentice-Hall, 1976). For a fuller description of cardinal utility functions and how they may be constructed, see Chapter 8 of the present book.

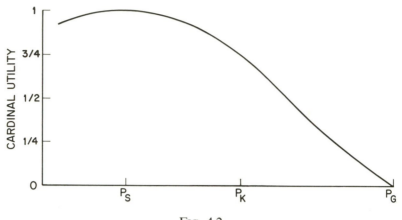

FIG. 4.2
The Pragmatist Pattern of Preference

position. The pragmatist differs from the purist in attaching relatively more value to policies outside the immediate vicinity of his ideal point. The pragmatist's open-mindedness can be represented by a function like the one in Figure 4.2, which is literally broader and more open than the purist's. The question, then, is how these differences might influence attitudes about strategy.

Suppose the dissidents of both types consider doctrinal purity and tangible concessions to be equally important objectives in designing a campaign of disruption. If their (steadfast)[3] demand is denoted by P_D and the concession it produces by P_C, we can define the

$$\text{Net Value of a Strategy} = \text{Loss from Compromise} + \text{Gain from Concession}$$

$$= [U(P_D) - U(P_S)] + [U(P_C) - U(P_G)]$$

The loss from compromise is the difference in utility between a sincere demand (P_S) and the actual demand (P_D). The gain from concession is the difference in utility between the regime's ideal point P_G (status quo ante) and the new policy it adopts (P_C).

Consider the utility functions in Figures 4.1 and 4.2, and suppose the steadfast strategy demanding P_K turns out to be successful. Then the demand is identical to the concession, and the net value of the

---

[3] The discussion that follows assumes the dissidents follow a steadfast strategy. An essentially similar, though less tidy, story can be told for flexible strategies.

strategy can be calculated as follows:

	Loss from Compromise	Gain from Concession	Net Value
	$L = U(P_K) - U(P_s)$	$G = U(P_K) - U(P_G)$	$L + G$
Pragmatist	$-\frac{1}{4} = \frac{3}{4} - 1$	$\frac{3}{4} = \frac{3}{4} - 0$	$+\frac{1}{2}$
Purist*	$-1 = 0 - 1$	$0 = 0 - 0$	-1

* Values for the purist are approximate

The same procedure yields net values for every conceivable strategy, varying between $+1$ for a successful sincere strategy (P_S, P_S) and -1 for acquiescing to the status quo (P_G, P_G). The strategic predispositions of each strategist can then be summarized in diagrams like the ones in Figure 4.3.

Each point in the two squares corresponds to an ordered pair of the form (P_D, P_C), describing the demand lodged by the movement and the concession it secures. Strategies along the 45° bisector are successful $(P_D = P_C)$, while those above it are not $(P_D > P_C)$. We can ignore the points below the bisector since they violate our theory's assumptions about responsiveness (regimes never grant bigger concessions than dissidents demand). The upper half of each square is overlaid with indifference curves connecting points with equal net value. The point (P_S, P_S) corresponds to a successful sincere strategy and has the highest possible score $(+1)$. As the indifference curves diverge from this point, they take on lower net values. Of course, the relative steepness of these curves distinguishes the purist from the pragmatist. From the purist's point of view, only substantial new concessions justify compromises in questions of principle. His indifference curves are accordingly far steeper than those of the pragmatist, who willingly moderates demands for even slight new concessions.

The point (P_S, P_G), representing an absolutely ineffective sincere strategy, establishes a floor on the movement's fortunes. The dissidents can always guarantee themselves the net value of this outcome (0), just by lodging a sincere demand. The strategies yielding negative net values are thus unattractive in principle. These points lie beyond the indifference curve labeled $V = 0$, which therefore defines (at its intersection with the 45° bisector) the largest doctrinal compromise either kind of strategist could ever accept. Strategies with more moderate demands

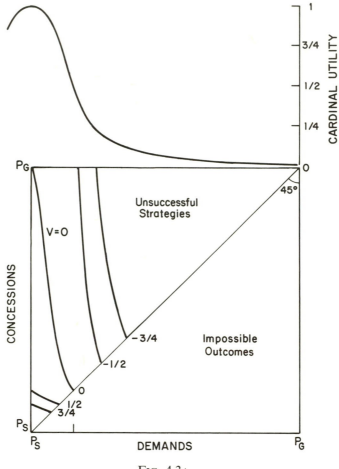

FIG. 4.3A
The Purist's Evaluation of Strategies

necessarily yield negative net values, even when they succeed. Naturally, the purist reaches his limit far sooner than does the pragmatist.

If we superimpose the two diagrams in the fashion of Figure 4.4, the potential for factional discord between the two political types becomes obvious. Their respective break-even indifference curves (V = 0) partition the space into three subsets; one containing mutually attractive outcomes, a second containing mutually unattractive outcomes, and a third containing outcomes that are potentially acceptable to the pragmatist but unattractive in principle to the purist. The more these strate-

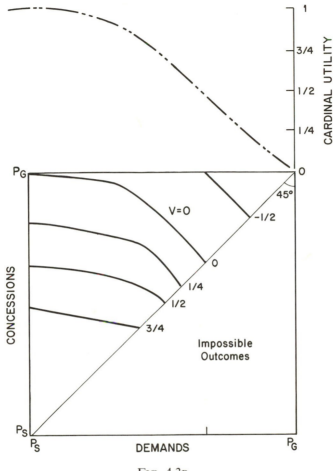

FIG. 4.3B
The Pragmatist's Evaluation of Strategies

gists differ with regard to the intensity of their preferences, the larger the disputed territory becomes.

This potential for factional strife remains unrealized, of course, until unfriendly political circumstances conspire against the movement's internal harmony. The gross outlines of this process are shown in Figure 4.5. We know already how to represent a radical group's political environment with a responsiveness map and the cumulative distribution of preferences. A more compact and useful summary of the same information is accomplished by plotting the demand of each steadfast

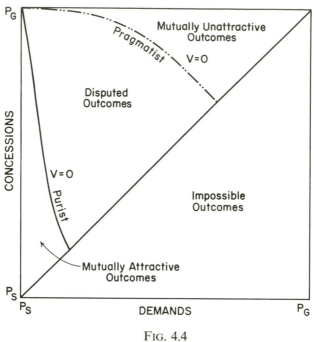

FIG. 4.4
Strategic Disputes between Pragmatists
and Purists

strategy against the concession it secures. The three heavily shaded strategy-potential curves (SPC's) in Figure 4.5 share the general shape dictated by the rules of Chapter 3. P_{max} denotes the most radical of the successful demands and thus the biggest concession the movement can attain (rule 9). The demands lying between P_{max} and P_G are successful too (rule 6), while the more radical strategies win continuously smaller concessions (rule 10).

Despite their similarity in these respects, the three curves have very different factional implications. In the upper panel, the forces of the left are so weak generally that even the optimal strategy (P_{max}) accomplishes very little. Neither the purist nor the pragmatist finds compromise attractive in this climate because a sincere strategy is nearly as effective as any other. The sincere strategy yields the highest net value from both perspectives, and there is no controversy about pursuing it.

The politically more favorable circumstances in the middle panel are far more likely to aggravate the underlying differences in outlook. Here

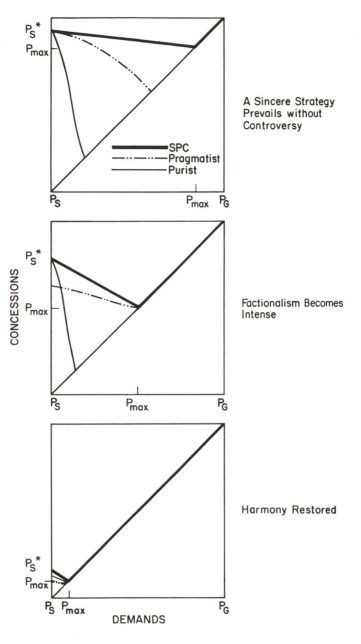

FIG. 4.5
Dynamics of Factional Discord

a sincere strategy achieves relatively little, while the moderate demand P_{max} forces the regime substantially closer to the movement's goal. Thus, the most effective strategy makes a tangible difference but requires a large measure of ideological flexibility. The pragmatist and the purist now part company as their preferred strategies diverge sharply. The purist still rejects compromise altogether, insisting, no doubt, that the movement's principles ought not to be sacrificed for such trifling handouts. The pragmatist, on the other hand, regards P_{max} as a real political advance and despairs at the thought of letting it go for the sake of ideological abstractions. Nothing seems more doctrinaire or more hopelessly impractical than clutching to an ineffective strategy when real gains can be made by responding flexibly to the political alignment of forces. The purists and pragmatists are now hopelessly divided, each finding the other's strategy fatally flawed. Charges of political deviation soon fill the air, the purists denouncing the pragmatists as opportunists and ideological running dogs of the regime while the pragmatists deplore the utopianism and sectarian disregard for reality among the purists. At this point, the movement faces a grave internal crisis that threatens to wrench it apart.

The lower panel in Figure 4.5 shows how the strategic inclinations of the two factions converge again as the political outlook continues to brighten. Now a sincere demand is nearly successful, and the optimal demand is nearly sincere. Maintaining principles no longer exacts a heavy toll in lost concessions, while the most pragmatic compromise requires only minimal doctrinal distortions. The tensions arising in the second panel therefore evaporate as the situation improves.

This simple model of factionalism provides a far richer and politically more interesting account of strategy making than an approach that mechanically identifies the most effective demand as the one most likely to be heard in the streets. Such an approach renders the salient differences among the situations in Figure 4.5 politically irrelevant, since each conforms to rule 10 of the theory. If we regard concessions as the dissidents' only objective, rule 10 implies that P_{max} will be the favored demand in all three settings. We are left, alas, with dubious predictions and not the slightest clue about how a movement's external environment affects its internal cohesion.

By slightly complicating our conception of the dissidents' objectives, the political tensions in Figure 4.5 come to life, and we see how the political harmony of radical groups can be disrupted from within or without. In some cases, the political cohesion of a single-minded leadership core may disappear when new leaders emerge from the rank and file to join the old guard, bringing with them disparate strategic predispositions. In other instances, the prevailing facade of harmony may crumble when shifting political circumstances aggravate the underlying, but previously unnoticed, differences between pragmatists and purists. People who have struggled together for years may suddenly find themselves unable to agree about anything. Ironically, up-and-coming movements are most likely to suffer this unhappy fate. The transition from the upper to the middle panel in Figure 4.5 describes a change from unambiguous political weakness to middling political strength. This could happen if the regime became more responsive or the climate of opinion shifted toward the movement's position. In either event, the disparity increases between the effectiveness of the sincere and the optimal strategies, exciting tensions between purists and pragmatists who had earlier agreed that compromise was useless.

Our model of factional discord introduces a new constellation of forces into explanations of how radical movements behave, taking us well beyond the rigid situational determinism of a theory based on maximizing concessions. If the revisionist controversy was essentially a dispute between pragmatists and purists, several patterns ought to emerge in the historical evidence about the substance and the timing of the debates. The basic premise of the model is that dissidents seek not only to win concessions but to preserve the integrity of their principles. When political conditions make these goals incompatible, tensions may develop between radical leaders who share the same ideal policy but who differ about the attractiveness of transitional policies. Those with intense or narrow preferences are reluctant to bend demands to secure partial concessions, which seem to them trivial and unsatisfying. Individuals with broader preferences are more inclined to the opposite viewpoint. The main bone of contention, then, is the relative worth of tangible concessions and doctrinal purity. With regard to the occasion for such debates, the model suggests two mechanism that might explain how a relatively harmonious atmosphere can suddenly be poisoned by controversy. On one hand, pragmatists and purists of the same political stripe might cooperate together for years, remaining unaware of their differences until shifting political tides outside the movement bring them to the surface. Alternatively, the movement's internal cohesion may suffer when a homogeneous leadership for one reason or another accepts new members of the other strategic persuasion.

Notes on the Revisionist Struggle

BY THE END of the nineteenth century, a plausible case could be made in most of industrialized Europe that a strategy based strictly on Marxist aspirations was materially less effective than moderate strategies seeking broader electoral rights, better working conditions, higher wages, shorter hours, and other piecemeal reforms. "Sincere" demands for the abolition of private property and a dictatorship of the proletariat were simply too extreme to mobilize significant pressure on the ruling coalitions of aristocrats and industrialists. A central problem raised by Bernstein's theory, therefore, was how to balance the competing objectives of preserving Marxian principles and enhancing the material well-being of the proletariat. As Rosa Luxemburg put it:

> The basic question of the socialist movement is how to bring its immediate practical activity into agreement with its ultimate goal. The various schools and trends of socialism are differentiated according to their . . . solutions to this problem.[4]

The flexible and gradualist strategy advocated by Bernstein reflected the value he attached to social and material progress for working people. Although he surely accepted the goals elaborated by Marx in a general sense, Bernstein was never prepared to let "preconceived theories" impede the political and economic advance of the proletariat, however halting or slow.

> Preconceived theories which go beyond a generally expressed aim, which try to determine the direction of the movement without an ever-vigilant eye upon facts and experience, must necessarily pass into utopianism, and at some time or other hinder the practical progress of the movement.[5]

The problem was that a radical revolutionary line alienated Social Democracy from its natural base of support in the trade unions and among the liberal bourgeoisie. "The desire of the industrial working class for socialistic production is for the most part a matter of assumption than of certainty," he pointed out,[6] while the bourgeoisie

[4] Luxemburg, "Opportunism and the Art of the Possible," *Selected Political Writings*, p.73.
[5] Bernstein, *Evolutionary Socialism*, p. 205.
[6] Ibid., p. 107.

is a highly complex class which is composed of a large number of strata with very divergent interests. These groups stick together only if they feel menaced.[7]

Thus, Bernstein rejected Marx's rigidly bifurcated model of capitalist society, replacing it with a model whose elements were arrayed far more continuously across the political spectrum. As we know from our theory, such a model is much friendlier to a strategy of compromise and moderation. Social Democracy's political influence would be greatly enhanced, Bernstein concluded, if it

> could find the courage to emancipate itself from a phraseology which is actually outworn and if it would make up its mind to appear what it is in reality today: a democratic, socialist party of reform.[8]

Nothing captures Bernstein's pragmatic resolution of the Social Democrats' strategic dilemma with more economy or clarity than his own famous proposition: "The ultimate aim of socialism is nothing but the movement is everything.[9]

This phrase became notorious among the more orthodox and doctrinaire Marxists who were genuinely appalled by the idea of compromising Marx's revolutionary theory to court the support of bourgeois liberals for reformist legislation. Among Bernstein's critics, Karl Kautsky was the most visible and influential at the time.[10] Rosa Luxemburg and V. I. Lenin developed, however, the most consistently "purist" attack, while Kautsky's in many ways vacillated between the polar extremes.

Lenin's first sustained assault on the "opportunist" trend appeared in his book *What Is To Be Done?*[11] His irreconcilable hostility to the Bernsteinian program animates every page. From the standpoint of our theory, the interesting feature of Lenin's argument is its open admission that reforms could be won by compromising strategies. What Lenin vehemently denied was the revisionist assertion that such reforms were worth the ideological cost. Why shouldn't a socialist "charm the bourgeois world with orations on class collaboration," or join the bourgeois cabinet, or "personally take part in greeting the

---

[7] Quoted in Gay, *Dilemma of Democratic Socialism*, p. 225.

[8] Bernstein, *Evolutionary Socialism*, p. 197.

[9] Ibid., p. 202.

[10] For Kautsky's role in the controversy, see Salvadori, *Karl Kautsky 1880-1938*, and Steenson, *Karl Kautsky, 1854-1938*. Kautsky was a central figure in the debates, but his viewpoint is a curiously inconsistent amalgamation of purism in thought and pragmatism in deed.

[11] V. I. Lenin, *Selected Works*, Vol. 1: *What Is To Be Done?*, pp. 97-256.

Tsar," Lenin asks sarcastically, if Social Democracy is simply a party of reform?

> The reward for this utter humiliation and self-degradation of socialism in the face of the whole world, for the corruption of the Socialist consciousness of the working classes ... the reward for this is pompous projects for miserable reforms, so miserable in fact that much more has been obtained from bourgeois governments![12]

In much the same way, Rosa Luxemburg deplored

> the playful ease, the imperturbable calmness, indeed, even the serene grace with which principles are undermined, principles which must have entered the flesh and blood of every comrade who does not interpret the party's good in a wholly superficial manner.[13]

The fundamental characteristic of the "opportunists," she explains, is that they consistently "sacrifice the movement's ultimate goal, namely the liberation of the working class, to its most immediate interests."[14]

> In all opportunistic political speculation, we see the great aims of socialist class emancipation sacrificed to petty practical interests of the moment, interests, moreover, which ... prove to be essentially illusory.[15]

Thus, where Bernstein saw "practical progress," Lenin, Luxemburg, and the other purists saw "petty" and "miserable" reforms. The Marxist principles Bernstein dismissed as "preconceived theories" and "vague speculation about the future," they defended as the lifeblood of the movement and "the only basis that can guarantee our victory."[16] Where Bernstein proclaimed "the ultimate aim is nothing, the movement everything," Lenin insisted " without revolutionary theory there can be no revolutionary movement."[17]

These brief though telling glimpses of the dialogue between Bernstein and his critics make it abundantly clear that the tensions arising in the mathematical structure of the theory were very much a living force in European Social Democracy before World War I. The polemics of the two trends are closely in accord with the factional positions derived from the intensity model. The timing of the debates also supports the idea that variability in the intensity of preferences was

---

[12] Ibid., p. 104.
[13] Luxemburg, "The Militia and Militarism," *Selected Political Writings*, p. 89.
[14] Ibid., p. 81.   [15] Ibid., p. 82.
[16] V. I. Lenin, *What Is To Be Done?*, p. 104.
[17] Ibid., p. 117.

a catalyst in the volatile political reactions that divided the Social Democratic movement.

One compelling piece of evidence for this view is the history of Bernstein's own career. While the composition of the Socialist parties changed dramatically in the later years of the nineteenth century, Bernstein was anything but an upstart newcomer importing alien ideas into the ranks. When he began publishing his revisionist papers in 1896, Bernstein had already served the SPD for nearly twenty-five years, including seven as the editor of the party newspaper *Sozialdemokrat*. By all accounts, he was highly esteemed by the leading figures of German Social Democracy, including the great Engels himself, who named Bernstein to be the executor of his literary estate. The interesting feature of this historical record is the total absence of evidence to suggest that Bernstein had anything like a reputation as an ideological renegade or free thinker before the appearance of his controversial essays. On the contrary, the founding fathers entrusted him with the great responsibility of editing the party's newspaper—surely no place for a person of dubious political outlook.

It is difficult, then, to ascribe Bernstein's split with the orthodox wing of the party to disagreements about ultimate purposes, differences that would have been obvious in the years when the movement was struggling.[18] Our simple model of factionalism offers a more plausible interpretation based upon the steadily improving political prospects of the workers' movement in the years before *Evolutionary Socialism* appeared. Following the depression of 1873 and the passage of the Anti-Socialist Bill outlawing their party in 1878, the German Social Democrats enjoyed remarkably good fortune for the next twenty years. Bismarck introduced progressive social insurance programs for working people, an economic boom began in 1879 that lasted nearly without interruption until 1914, the anti-Socialist legislation was repealed in 1890, and the Social Democratic vote increased nearly four-fold between 1874 and 1890, when the party won nearly 20 percent of the votes cast and thirty-five seats in the Reichstag.

These events suggested a very different appraisal of the German regime's responsiveness and the potential for proletarian political initiatives than the view developed in the days of *The Communist*

---

[18] Admittedly, Bernstein's political aspirations may have changed, though I have yet to see compelling evidence for this view.

Manifesto forty years earlier. At that time, the predominant impression of the political situation was akin to the upper panel in Figure 4.5. The workers were weak and divided, and it appeared that the bourgeoisie would never make concessions to their demands. Indeed, Marx's theory was designed to explain why the bourgeoisie would blindly pauperize the proletariat until a revolutionary explosion destroyed its exploitative regime. There was, in short, little occasion for controversy about the value of partial concessions in an atmosphere where the most moderate demands were treated as subversion.

By the 1890s, the Socialists controlled pivotal swing votes in the Reichstag, membership in the unions and the party had grown geometrically, and Bernstein was describing the franchise for the Reichstag as Social Democracy's "most effective means for asserting its demands."[19] Although the party was far from achieving its objectives, the situation was manifestly more favorable than it had been during the dark days of reaction following the abortive Revolution of 1848. The German party had thus reached a stage of middling political strength of the very kind likely to excite hostilities between purists and pragmatists. Little wonder, then, that even Bernstein's closest comrades like Karl Kautsky and Victor Adler were overcome with surprise and anguish when his heretical arguments appeared in print, and were thrown into confusion about how to respond to them. "I do not know what I should think of Ede," Kautsky wrote in a letter to his wife. "What does Adler say about it?"[20] Later he wrote to Adler directly, describing Bernstein's "unbelievable theoretical retrogression" but expressing great reluctance to attack his friend in print.[21] Their differences had remained hidden behind commonly shared goals and years of friendship, only to surface with a vengeance after their arduous struggle began to bear fruit.

Summing Up

THE MOST interesting feature of the intensity model of factionalism is its ability to explain rancorous disputes among people who share a common goal. The apparent ideological consensus in radical groups and their relative isolation from the political mainstream often conceal

[19] Bernstein, *Evolutionary Socialism*, p. 194.
[20] Quoted in Steenson, *Karl Kautsky, 1854-1938*, p. 122.
[21] Ibid.

more subtle discontinuities in outlook. Factional debates seem like pre-posterous exercises in ideological hairsplitting, only to be dismissed as window dressing for clashes of personality, struggles for power, or some other essentially personal or accidental process. Even Engels attributed his good friend Bernstein's fascination with reformism to "a nervous illness."[22] A noteworthy virtue of our model is its ability to dispel the aura of paradox surrounding factional disputes without disregarding their systematic political underpinnings.

Despite its good agreement with the facts, as well as the insights it supplies about the political origins of cohesion and discord in radi-cal groups and the nature of strategic decision making, the intensity model still provides a very limited understanding of the revisionist debates. The model appears to be at its best in identifying the poli-tical dynamite that made the debates so explosive, but it tells us very little about the content of Bernstein's revisionist theory and his funda-mental disagreements with Marx. To understand these problems, we must adopt new perspectives.

[22] Gay, *Dilemma of Democratic Socialism*, p. 68.

CHAPTER FIVE

Reformers and Revolutionaries

IF THE "revolutionary idea" was the keystone of Marx's theoretical structure,[1] the reformist idea was surely the keystone of Bernstein's. The divergent perceptions of reformers and revolutionaries were very much at the core of the revisionist controversy, igniting the passions of its participants and shaping their arguments. In the pages that follow, we shall explore our own theoretical system for insights about the political foundations of these perspectives, their strategic implications, and their factional meaning. This task may seem a bit ambitious, if not altogether wrongheaded, given the currently modest dimensions of the theory. It certainly is not obvious on the face of things that a schematic model of peaceful protests should have anything to say about the political inclinations of revolutionaries. For the purposes we have in mind, however, the crucial limitations reside mainly in the present interpretation of the theory rather than in its structure per se. The politically essential feature of our story about protests is that power resides in numbers, and this is certainly no less true in revolutionary conflicts than in struggles for reforms. Ultimately, the success of most revolutionary movements depends on bringing the masses into the streets, and our model already captures important elements of this process. With a slight modification, it becomes a powerful tool for exploring the political character of reformist and revolutionary thinking and the tensions in the contrasting points of view.

The Revolutionary Threshold

THE MODEL of protest is limited as a description of revolutionary situations mainly by its rendering of the regime's responsiveness to disruption. The theory is framed within a two-dimensional space whose axes

---

[1] The phrase is Robert C. Tucker's. See *The Marxian Revolutionary Idea* (New York: W. W. Norton, 1970), p. 3.

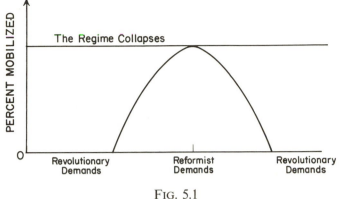

FIG. 5.1
The Revolutionary Threshold

measure the location of the regime's policy along the political spectrum and the percentage of the population mobilized against it. Indifference curves filling the space represent the regime's willingness to trade concessions for tranquility.[2] Unfortunately, this schema breaks down in the extreme circumstances of a revolutionary high tide. After all, no regime can survive when an entire population is mobilized against it, and most can be toppled by substantially smaller disturbances. When demonstrations become large enough to drive a regime from power, there is little sense in describing its "responsiveness" to them.

This difficulty can be remedied by adding a threshold to each responsiveness map, indicating how much disruption the regime can tolerate before it collapses. The existence of a revolutionary threshold like the one in Figure 5.1 immediately implies that some demands are so repugnant to the regime, or so far beyond its physical capacity to meet, that a successful insurrection becomes necessary to achieve them. The indifference curve resting against the revolutionary threshold therefore partitions the demands along the ideological spectrum into two sets—those on the interior of the curve can be won without overthrowing the incumbent regime and those on the exterior cannot. The first set of demands we call reformist, the second revolutionary. Clearly, the less responsive the regime (i.e. the steeper the indifference curves), the broader the spectrum of revolutionary demands becomes. This is surely what the Russian terrorists of the *Narodnaya Volya* ("People's Will")

---

[2] This discussion carries over straightforwardly to the full indifference surfaces described in Chapter 2.

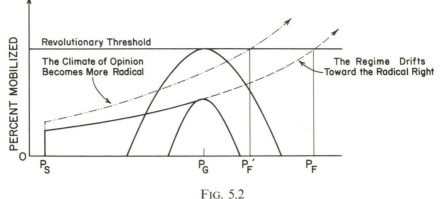

FIG. 5.2
The Revolutionary Outlook

meant when they wrote:

> Social reform in Russia is the revolution. With our existing regime of
> despotism and complete rejection of all the people's rights and wishes,
> reform can only assume the form of revolution.[3]

A vital issue facing every radical movement is whether its own
strivings are reformist or revolutionary. In fact, this became a burning
question among the European socialists before World War I. To understand better the significant strategic consequences resting upon such
an assessment, let us examine first the outlook of the revolutionary.
Figure 5.2 illustrates the situation of a fairly isolated movement with
a clearly revolutionary goal (P_S). The sincere demand P_S attracts only
limited support when the regime's policy lies near its ideal point (P_G),
as shown by the heavy mobilization curve, and the sincere strategy
quickly proves itself to be ineffective. The dissidents then face the difficult question, "What is to be done?"

One option is to compromise demands. If the movement's leaders
have any regard for principles, however, they may well decide that all
the concessions in the reformist interval are unattractive in principle
(by the reasoning of the intensity model). Naturally, the more extreme
the movement and the more unresponsive the regime, the more likely
this assessment becomes. The model does suggest, however, two dynamics that might allow the movement to maintain an uncompromising political posture and still achieve its goals. If, for some reason,

---

[3] Quoted in Franco Venturi, *Roots of Revolution*, trans. Francis Haskell (London:
Weidenfeld and Nicolson, 1960), p. 672.

the regime drifted into extremism and its policy began migrating to the right, the movement's sincere demand, P_S, would become steadily more attractive to the masses until eventually it mobilized enough support to cross the revolutionary threshold. In Figure 5.2, the culmination of this process is a successful insurrection against the policy P_F. From the perspective of a revolutionary movement, then, better is worse and worse is better.

A second favorable dynamic that obviously enhances the movement's prospects is the radicalization of popular opinion. If the distribution of preferences shifts uniformly to the left, the demand P_S generates more disruption against the entire spectrum of policies available to the regime. Local shifts of sentiment enhance the mobilization against some policies but not all. The tendency in either event is to accelerate the revolutionary process by hastening the approach toward the threshold of insurrection. In Figure 5.2, the mobilization curve generated by a sincere strategy is displaced upward as the population becomes more radical. The regime's day of reckoning then shifts from P_F to $P_{F'}$, that is, closer to its present position and backward in time.

The Logical Structure of Marx's Revolutionary Theory

As THE LOCOMOTIVE forces driving the bourgeois order to its inevitable demise, these two dynamics were pivotal elements in Marx's model of the proletarian revolution against capitalism. The theory Marx built around them implied that workers could realize their ultimate class interests without abandoning a strategy built upon sincere demands. It is not surprising, then, that the theory became a focal point of intense controversy between the revisionists and their detractors. Marx's revolutionary reasoning justified an intransigent political line during the struggle against the bourgeoisie and thus became an impediment to the aspirations of the reformers. One of Bernstein's central objectives therefore was to refute Marx's reasoning about revolutionary dynamics under capitalism. To understand the character of his attack, we must first explore the structure of Marx's revolutionary vision more carefully.[4]

---

[4] Our account follows the earlier, though extremely influential, writings of Marx and Engels in "Manifesto of the Communist Party," and "Wage Labour and Capital." Both essays appear in *The Marx-Engels Reader*, ed. Robert C. Tucker (New York: W. W. Norton, 1972).

According to Marx and Engels, the fundamental conflict in capitalist society is the class struggle between the proletariat and the bourgeoisie. The goals of the two classes are assumed to be strictly incompatible, since the proletariat's interest in higher wages conflicts with the bourgeoisie's interest in higher profits. There develops a class struggle characterized by ruthless exploitation and bitter hatred. For a time, the bourgeoisie prevails, but the contradictions residing in the system of industrial competition propel the bourgeois order toward a revolutionary cataclysm. "Modern bourgeois society . . . is like the sorcerer who is no longer able to control the powers of the nether world he has called by his spells," Marx warns ominously.[5]

We can give Marx's argument a spatial interpretation by identifying the political spectrum in our model with some quantitative measure of the material well-being of the two classes.[6] Let the scale represent the share of the national wealth held by the bourgeoisie, for example. Moving to the right on the scale (toward 100 percent) corresponds to enriching the bourgeoisie at the expense of the proletariat. Moving to the left has the opposite interpretation. The zero point on the scale represents the expropriation of the means of production by the proletariat and the destruction of the bourgeois class. The proletariat is pauperized as we approach the other extreme. Note that since the interests of the two classes are assumed to be strictly incompatible, one scale is sufficient to describe the welfare of both. One class's gain is the other's loss.

Given this interpretation of the stakes of the game, we can then array the population across the spectrum according to its class sympathies and identify the regime's "policy" with the prevailing distribution of wealth. This is not to suggest, by the way, that governmental decree determines economic outcomes in Marx's theory. Instead, the state plays a subordinate (or rather superstructural) role, being simply a "committee for managing the common affairs of the whole bourgeoisie."[7] We shall therefore use the term *regime* broadly to mean the entire system of class rule, including the mode of industrial production as well as the political organization of the state.

Under this interpretation, the intractable contradictions discerned by Marx and Engels can be said to have revolutionary consequences

[5] "Communist Manifesto," p. 340.
[6] Ambiguities in Marx's argument make this more difficult than one might think.
[7] Ibid., p. 337.

of two kinds. Either they drive the regime to the right by concentrating more of the national wealth in the hands of the bourgeoisie (pauperizing the proletariat), or they drive the population to the left by multiplying the ranks of the proletariat (and shrinking the bourgeoisie).

The root of these evils (or blessings, depending on one's viewpoint) lies in the system of cutthroat competition that engages each and every capitalist in an endless struggle for economic survival. The bourgeois producer attempts to drive his rivals from the marketplace by producing cheaper goods than they can. Gaining a competitive advantage requires the capitalist to increase the productive power of labor, which he accomplishes "above all by a continual improvement of machinery and a greater division of labor."[8] To the extent that these efforts succeed, the capitalist gains a temporary advantage—but not without a rub. "The more powerful and costly means of production . . . enable him, indeed, to sell his commodities more cheaply, they compel him, however, at the same time to sell more commodities."[9] Nor is the new-found advantage secure for long. Other producers introduce similar technical and organizational innovations and soon "the game begins again."

The system of competition therefore produces a relentless downward pressure on prices and a simultaneous expansion of productive capacity. The harried capitalist find himself caught on a nightmarish treadmill, having always to produce more goods at lower prices, just to hold his own. Alas, "every weapon he forges against his rivals recoils against himself."[10] As prices fall toward the cost of production, the producer must sell enormous quantities of goods to maintain a constant amount of profit. Eventually, there are no longer enough consumers to absorb the colossal output of bourgeois enterprise. The system falls victim to an "epidemic of over-production," throwing the capitalist economy into commercial crises "that by their periodical return put on trial, each time more threateningly, the existence of the entire bourgeois society."[11]

One revolutionary consequence of this system of production is the constant enlargement of the proletariat. The marginal elements of the bourgeoisie find the struggle for survival ever more harrowing as

[8] "Wage Labour," p. 185.   [9] Ibid.   [10] Ibid., p.187.
[11] "Communist Manifesto," p. 340.

competition from giant industrial enterprises develops. The small capitalists who succumb to the competitive pressures are left without any means of support save for the sale of their own labor:

> The lower strata of the middle class—the small tradespeople, shopkeepers, . . . the handicraftsmen, and peasants—all these sink gradually into the proletariat partly because their diminutive capital does not suffice . . . partly because their specialized skill is rendered worthless by new methods of production.[12]

In this way, the distribution of preferences tilts continually to the left as capitalism matures. The ranks of the proletariat swell while the bourgeoisie shrinks to a tiny circle of capitalist barons.

At the same time, the owners of the surviving enterprises control a growing proportion of the national wealth, which increasingly takes the form of heavy industrial capital equipment. And as the producers invest more of their profits in fixed (machine) capital, the wages of the workers collapse to subsistence levels:

> The greater division of labor enables one worker to do the work of five, ten, or twenty; it therefore multiplies competition among the workers fivefold, tenfold and twentyfold.[13]

The demand for skilled labor thus evaporates while the number of workers competing for unskilled factory positions mushrooms. The development of an "industrial reserve army" allows the capitalists to cut costs by reducing wages to the minimum required for "maintenance and the propagation of the race."[14] Thus, as their numbers multiply, the economic lot of the proletariat deteriorates precipitously. "The forest of uplifted arms demanding work becomes thicker, while the arms themselves become ever thinner."[15]

The inevitable consequence of these dynamics, say Marx and Engels, is the revolutionary destruction of the bourgeois order by the proletariat. As capitalism matures, its contradictions become so severe and uncontrollable that the proletariat seizes the means of production, abolishes the anarchical system of private property, and develops a socialist society.

> The modern laborer . . . instead of rising with the progress of industry . . . becomes a pauper, and pauperism develops more rapidly than population

---

[12] Ibid., pp. 441–42.   [13] "Wage Labour," p. 187.
[14] "Communist Manifesto," p. 341.   [15] "Wage Labour," p. 190.

and wealth. And here it becomes evident that the bourgeoisie is unfit any longer to be the ruling class in society . . . because it is incompetent to assure an existence to its slave within his slavery.[16]

The revolutionary's belief that his movement's ultimate goals are impossible to achieve while the incumbent regime holds power elevates the problem of how to reach the threshold of insurrection to the highest priority. Herein lies the central paradox of revolutionary theories like Marx's. When it appears that the fastest approach to the threshold lies in retrograde political developments, better becomes worse and worse becomes better. According to Marx, then, the ruination of the proletariat is the pathway to its salvation. We shall see in a moment how profoundly alien this view of politics is to the reformist mentality.

The Reformist Perspective

THE ESSENTIAL differences between reformers and revolutionaries rest upon their perception of the regime's responsiveness, not upon the relative extremeness of their aspirations per se. The reformer believes his movement's goals can be attained without overturning the regime, while the revolutionary does not. Naturally, this perception supports a markedly different pattern of strategic thinking. Before we consider Bernstein's revisionist criticism of Marx, let us return once again to the model to consider how the reformer is likely to react when a sincere strategy fails to return substantial concessions.

The reformer's fundamental optimism about the political situation leads him to part company with the revolutionary on several basic points of strategy. Most importantly, the reformer accepts the possibility that ultimate goals can be reached by forcing the regime to *converge* toward his movement's position, while the revolutionary believes the incumbent regime will not or cannot bend its policy that far. These divergent appraisals spawn radically different attitudes about the desirability of retrogressions in public policy. The revolutionary, in his anxiety to reach the insurrectionary threshold, welcomes reversals in the regime's political course as a positive spur to mobilization. To the reformer, however, waiting for the regime to drift into a catastrophically unpopular position seems neither necessary nor desirable, even if he accepts the possibility that it might happen. After all, why

[16] "Communist Manifesto," p. 345.

suffer the calamity of a progressively worsening situation if one's goal can be reached by a path of steady advances?

These reflections lead in turn to a parting of the ways over the political costs of maintaining an unsuccessful sincere strategy and the value of compromising demands. From the revolutionary's vantage point, compromise leads, at best, to partial concessions and never to a final victory. When a sincere strategy falters, the revolutionary is therefore more likely to seek refuge in dynamics that transform the situation than to pin his hopes on moderate strategies adapted to it. Moreover, as soon as it appears that revolutionary dynamics are in motion, the sincere strategy works as well as any other.

The key political problem from the reformer's viewpoint is how to get the regime moving in the right direction. If there is a bloc of unmobilized support located between the movement's position and the government's, the natural response to an ineffective sincere strategy is to compromise demands. This approach not only compels the regime to adopt more favorable policies, but sets it on a course that may lead to the movement's ultimate victory. For as soon as the dissidents accept the idea that their objectives are reformist, there is no logical contradiction in assuming that an evolutionary strategy can succeed where the sincere strategy failed (Chapter 3, rule 13). In light of this potential, the sincere strategy appears to be a real political albatross, weighing down the movement's progress and prolonging the struggle unnecessarily.

Bernstein's Attack on Marx

WHEN DISAGREEMENTS develop within a radical movement about whether its goals are revolutionary or not, political fireworks are the inevitable consequence. Such disagreements were another element of the factional strife surrounding Bernstein's heretical doctrines. Because Marx's theory of the revolutionary transition to socialism had become a formidable obstacle to his reformist initiatives, Bernstein launched a two-pronged attack against its very foundations.

The first line of assault was directed against the dynamic reasoning in Marx's model, which propels bourgeois society toward economic catastrophe and revolutionary collapse. Surveying the progress of economic development in the capitalist countries, Bernstein argued vigorously against the Marxian hypotheses that wealth becomes more concentrated as capitalism matures, while the proletariat swells and the bourgeoisie shrinks. The increase in the national wealth, he insisted,

> is not accompanied by a diminishing number of capitalist magnates but by an increasing number of capitalists of all degrees. . . . Far from society being simplified as to its divisions in earlier times, it has been graduated and differentiated both in respect to incomes and business activities.[17]

Moreover, the vast wealth generated by capitalist enterprise is simply too much for a tiny circle of industrial barons to consume.

> If the capitalist magnates had ten times as large stomachs as the popular satire attributes to them, and kept ten times as many servants, their consumption would only be a feather in the scale of yearly national product.[18]

The question, then, is what happens to the rest of the colossal cornucopia of goods and services. For Bernstein, the answer was both simple and devastating to Marx's theory. Either the proletariat grows richer or the bourgeoisie grows larger; "these are the only alternatives which the increase in production allows.[19]

Nor did Marx's theory of commercial crises escape Bernstein's critical scrutiny. Crashes and depressions resulting from the anarchy of cutthroat competition play a two-sided role as precipitants in Marx's analysis of the revolutionary process. On one hand, their continual return deepens the alienation and insecurity of the workers, spurring the mobilization of a revolutionary opposition to the bourgeois order. On the other hand, the mechanisms seized upon by the capitalists to overcome the crises only aggravate the underlying contradictions that produce them, and hasten their return on a larger scale.

Against these views, Bernstein assembled evidence to show how the bourgeoisie developed adaptive mechanisms like the credit system and cartels to regulate output and avoid the disastrous consequences of overproduction. Without asserting categorically that general commercial crises were remnants of the past, Bernstein concluded all the same that at least "for some time, they must be regarded as improbable."[20]

The underlying intention of Bernstein's economic critique was to undermine the political standing of the orthodox Marxists in his party who appealed to the theory of revolution laid out in *The Communist*

---

[17] Eduard Bernstein, *Evolutionary Socialism*, trans. Edith C. Harvey (New York: Schocken Books, 1961), pp. 49–51.
[18] Ibid., p. 52.   [19] Ibid., p. 50.   [20] Ibid., p. 80.

Manifesto to defend a steadfast and uncompromising strategy. Deploring "the doctrine which assumes that progress depends on the deterioration of social conditions,"[21] Bernstein tried to convince his party that the dynamic reasoning in Marx's theory was fundamentally unsound as a description of capitalist development and therefore as the basis of Social Democracy's political strategy.

> I set myself against the notion that we have to expect shortly a collapse of the bourgeois economy, and that social democracy should be induced by the prospect of such an imminent . . . social catastrophe to adapt its tactics to that assumption.[22]

After dismissing the dynamic arguments used by his opponents to defend a sincere strategy, Bernstein set out next to build a positive defense for an evolutionary approach. The cornerstone of the defense was a drastic reworking of the orthodox interpretation of the liberal bourgeois state. Here, then, was the second frontal assault against Marx. The contrast between Bernstein's description of liberal democracy and Marx's could not be more stark. Where Marx argued that the bourgeois state was so blindly unresponsive to proletarian needs that it could not even "assure an existence to its slave within his slavery," Bernstein described liberal democracy as the "absence of class government where political privilege belongs to no one class."[23] The electoral representatives of the working classes check the bourgeoisie's blind exploitation and criminal neglect of the people's basic needs:

> The parties and the classes standing behind them soon learn to know the limits of their power. . . . Democracy is the high school of compromise. . . . The right to vote in a democracy makes its members virtually partners in the community.[24]

All of which was only to say that bourgeois democracy was vastly more responsive to the political and economic demands of the proletariat than Marx had assumed. Bernstein even went so far as to claim that a democratic political system could alter the laws of economic development and, with a judicious legislative program, avoid the calamities Marx had prophesied.

> It is clear that where legislation . . . interferes in an appropriate way, the working of the tendencies of economic development is thwarted, and under some circumstances can even be annihilated.[25]

21 Ibid., p. 213.   22 Ibid., p. xxiv.   23 Ibid., p. 143.
24 Ibid., p. 144.   25 Ibid., p. 208.

In keeping with the logic of our theory, Bernstein's optimistic appraisal of the state's responsiveness led him to fundamentally different conclusions about strategy than the ones reached by the revolutionary elements in Social Democracy. Above all, he rejected the idea that the transition to socialism was a revolutionary aspiration requiring the destruction of the bourgeois political order. Bernstein foresaw "a transition, free from convulsive outbursts, of the modern social order into a higher one,"[26] and described Social Democracy as "a party that strives after the socialist transformation of society by means of democratic and economic reform."[27] He also denied the political utility of waiting for catastrophic developments (or worse still encouraging them), even if they were possible. Was a "sudden catastrophe" in Social Democracy's interests?

> I have denied it ... because in my judgment a greater security for lasting success lies in a steady advance than in the possibilities offered by a catastrophic crash.[28]

And, finally, Bernstein argued that an evolutionary strategy based on a step-wise progression of ever more radical demands could realize for the working classes all their fundamental objectives. Pointing to the experience of the British working class struggle, he expressed the conviction that

> The working classes would certainly increase their demands, but would desire nothing that could not be shown each time to be necessary and attainable beyond all doubt.[29]

The Revolutionary Counterattack

> What is now happening to Marx's theory has, in the course of history, happened repeatedly to theories of revolutionary thinkers and leaders. ... After their death, attempts are made to convert them to harmless icons. ... The bourgeoisie and the opportunists within the labor movement ... omit, obscure, or distort the revolutionary side of this theory, its revolutionary soul. Our prime task is to reestablish what Marx really taught.[30]

So writes Lenin in the opening lines of *The State and Revolution*, describing the political challenge facing orthodox Marxists after the

---

[26] Ibid., p. 146.   [27] Ibid., p. 197.   [28] Ibid., p. xxviii.   [29] Ibid., p. 203.
[30] V. I. Lenin, *Selected Works*, Vol. 2: *The State and Revolution* (New York: International Publishers, 1967), p. 269.

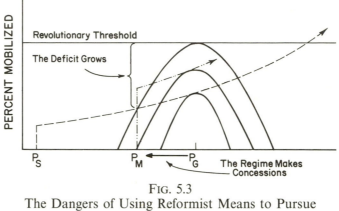

FIG. 5.3
The Dangers of Using Reformist Means to Pursue
Revolutionary Ends

appearance of Bernstein's revisionist theory. Figure 5.3 suggests one explanation for the distress created among revolutionary Social Democrats by the revisionist doctrines. The picture describes the political situation facing a movement whose goal, P_S, is in fact revolutionary. The lower mobilization curve in the diagram arises from a sincere strategy, the higher one belongs to the more moderate demand P_M. Now suppose the movement's leaders disagree about the regime's responsiveness and therefore about whether their goal is revolutionary or not. If the reformist faction carries the day and implements an evolutionary strategy originating with the demand P_M, a triple onus is then placed on the revolutionaries' sincere strategy of insurrection.

First, the moderate demonstrations arrest any rightward momentum in the regime's policy, thwarting a potentially powerful revolutionary dynamic. As the government's policy moves instead to the left, support for the revolutionary demand P_S diminishes and the distance to the revolutionary threshold increases. Any remaining hope for reaching the threshold then depends on radicalizing the population, a task that becomes more formidable as the regime expropriates the middle ground of the political spectrum, and the discrepancy between existing mobilization and the number required for revolution grows larger. The reformist strategy therefore has a distinctly counterrevolutionary effect, undermining the two vital dynamics that might eventually produce a successful insurrection under the movement's political banner.

REFORMERS AND REVOLUTIONARIES

It comes as little surprise, then, that the revolutionary socialists blasted Bernstein's theories with fiery polemics. Their counterattack came, in fact, in two thrusts. The first barrage of arguments sought to refute the assumptions underlying Bernstein's approach, while the second explained how its implementation would be politically disastrous. Among the arguments of the first type, some merely reasserted the positions developed by Marx and Engels. Karl Kautsky, for example, asked the delegates at the famous SPD Party Congress in 1898 (the first of the so-called Bernstein debates), "Does anyone believe that this victory is possible without catastrophe? I desire it, but I don't believe it."[31] Others developed new lines of reasoning to refute revisionist speculation about the future of the capitalist economy. Rosa Luxemburg devoted much of her pamphlet *Reform or Revolution*[32] to a detailed rebuttal of Bernstein's economic reasoning. Since the contours of Bernstein's theory have already been discussed fairly carefully, there is no need to elaborate the refutation of each point. It suffices to note that not a line of what Bernstein wrote about the dynamics of capitalist development went unchallenged. To take one example, consider how Luxemburg's interpretation of the credit system differs from Bernstein's:

> Credit reproduces all the fundamental antagonisms of the capitalist world. It accentuates them. It precipitates their development and pushes the capitalist world forward to its own destruction.[33]

More interesting were the arguments about the political implications of an evolutionary strategy, for these revealed some of the deep-seated stresses residing in the revolutionary point of view. On the face of things, the dynamic Marxian model of revolution implied that Bernstein's approach was doomed to failure. It could neither arrest the self-destructive evolution of the capitalist system in the long run, nor secure "meaningful" concessions from an unresponsive bourgeois regime in the short run. By these lights, Bernstein's program ought not to have aroused hostility among the orthodox Marxian revolutionaries, but merely amusement at its futility. Indeed, this was a recurrent theme

---

[31] Quoted in Peter Gay, *The Dilemma of Democratic Socialism* (New York: Collier Books, 1962), p. 77.

[32] Rosa Luxemburg, "Reform or Revolution," *Rosa Luxemburg Speaks* (New York: Pathfinder Press, 1970), pp. 33–91.

[33] Ibid., p. 43.

in the anti-Bernstein polemics. Luxemburg, for instance, returns again and again to the idea that a revisionist strategy must flounder. "Trade unions cannot suppress the law of wages," she writes, nor can "the fundamental relations of the domination of the capitalist class . . . be transformed by means of legislative reforms."[34] On the contrary, "The phenomenon of capitalist exploitation does not rest on a legal disposition, but on purely economic [facts]."[35] Luxemburg even tries to make a virtue of the reformers' futility by arguing that the proletariat's inability to secure meaningful reforms will only radicalize its members' perceptions (i.e. create an awareness that their goals are revolutionary).

> As a result of its trade-union and parliamentary struggles, the proletariat becomes convinced of the impossibility of accomplishing a fundamental social change through such activity and arrives at the understanding that the conquest of power is unavoidable.[36]

Despite the implications of a Marxian position, one needs only to skim the anti-Bernstein polemics to sense the deep anxiety his evolutionary approach created. No sooner does Luxemburg finish arguing that a reformist strategy may, by its ineffectiveness, advance the revolutionary cause than she attacks the Bernsteinians for pursuing just such a strategy. The problem, she explains somewhat inconsistently, lies not in what they do but rather in how they think about what they are doing.

> As soon as immediate results become the principal aim of our activity, the clear-cut, irreconcilable point of view, which has meaning only insofar as it proposes to win power, will be found more and more inconvenient. . . . [Trade union and parliamentary activity] lose not only their usual effectiveness, but cease being means of preparing the working class for the conquest of power.[37]

Thus, reformism that aims to fail is revolutionary, but reformism that aims to succeed is not. The difference, evidently, lies in the implicit message conveyed to the workers by the reformers' demands. Adopting an attitude that reforms are important for their own sake and attainable by evolutionary methods can only create an impression among the proletariat that its interests are compatible with the regime's. Pursuing reforms seriously therefore blunts the development of a revolutionary consciousness within the movement's base.

---

[34] Ibid., p. 79.   [35] Ibid.   [36] Ibid., p. 58.   [37] Ibid., pp. 58–59.

This acute two-mindedness about reformism suggests a certain incompatibility between the strategic mentality of the purist and the historical reasoning in Marx's model of revolution. On one hand, the purist's preference for maintaining principles creates a definite sympathy for any doctrine that justifies the sincere strategy. The same historical reasoning does not, however, justify the purist's reluctance to compromise principles. The driving forces in Marx's theory lie beyond the influence of the workers' movement. The same transforming dynamics that allow the purists to defend an ineffective sincere strategy presumably mitigate the political shortcomings of a compromising strategy as well. At least, so one might suppose. Much, then, as the purist would like to embrace a model that makes the revolution historically inevitable, the relative indifference of such a theory to the movement's choice of strategy is just too hard to swallow. Consequently, the purist is forced to tinker with the theory in order to repair its unfortunate tolerance for the reformer's folly. The political emphasis inevitably shifts away from the large-scale historical dynamics that negate the importance of strategy toward more proximate factors, like revolutionary consciousness, that restore the movement's political activity to a meaningful role.

This pattern of thinking is especially pronounced in Lenin's *What Is To be Done?* Lenin's perception of the threats posed by an evolutionary approach rests on assumptions that depart markedly from Marx's, and his indictment of the "opportunists" stretches the Marxian vision of revolution dramatically. Like Luxemburg, Lenin argues that a reformist strategy dulls the revolutionary consciousness of the workers. The Bernsteinian trend, he says,

> demoralized the socialist consciousness by vulgarizing Marxism, by advocating a theory of the blunting of social contradictions, by declaring the idea of the social revolution ... to be absurd.[38]

He then goes on to argue that a revolutionary consciousness can *only* be brought to the workers from outside their class by the conscious efforts of a revolutionary vanguard party:

> The history of all countries shows that the working class, exclusively by its own effort, is able to develop only a trade union consciousness. ... A Social-Democratic consciousness ... would have to be brought to them from without.[39]

---

[38] V. I. Lenin, *Selected Works*, Vol. 1: *What Is To Be Done?*, p. 111.
[39] Ibid., p. 122.

The strategy chosen by the Social Democrats is therefore anything but a matter of indifference. The fate of the revolution depends critically upon it because the historical patterns of development under capitalism do not create spontaneously a revolutionary consciousness among the proletariat.

A second threat posed by a reformist strategy is the possibility that it might actually win some concessions. In keeping with the reasoning of Figure 5.3 (and contrary to the dynamic reasoning of Marx), Lenin warns that

> economic concessions (or pseudo-concessions) are, of course, the cheapest and most advantageous from the government's point of view, because by these means it hopes to win the confidence of the working masses. Social Democrats must not under any circumstances . . . create grounds for the belief that we regard [economic reforms] as being particularly important.[40]

Here, again, Lenin recoils from the idea that reformism is politically innocuous. And, in defense of his view, he is forced once again to reformulate basic propositions in Marx's theory about the historical direction of the bourgeoisie's economic policy. Hence we can speculate that the flight from Marx's dynamic reasoning among Bernstein's revolutionary critics was a consequence of strategic constraints imposed by their purist mentality.

Summing Up

OUR SECOND model of factional tension enriches our understanding of the schism in Social Democracy by supplementing rather than replacing the intensity model. At first glance, the two mechanisms seem not to have much in common; the intensity model turns on variations in structures of preference, while the rift between reformers and revolutionaries rests on empirical disagreements about the regime's responsiveness and the operation of revolutionary dynamics. Certainly, these differences in perspective account for the ability of the new model to illuminate many facets of the debate about which the original model is silent.

Still, there is a noticeable political resonance between the two systems of cleavage and considerable mutual reinforcement when they op-

[40] Ibid., p. 150.

erate together. For example, the reformist perspective is surely more congenial to the pragmatist than it is to the purist (when the status of the movement's goals is open to question and a sincere strategy is ineffective) because both outlooks favor a compromising strategy. Similarly, a revolutionary perspective reinforces the purist's disinclination to moderate a faltering sincere strategy. A revolutionary estimate of the regime's responsiveness implies that compromising strategies can never attain more than partial concessions, though partial concessions may delay the approach to the revolutionary threshold. It is also interesting to note that both lines of cleavage are likely to be aggravated by the same kinds of political developments. When the political situation is bleak and the regime appears stubbornly unresponsive, a consensus is more likely to form around the revolutionary perspective. As the situation brightens, however, the revolutionary view is harder to defend and the reformers (especially pragmatic reformers) are likely to assert themselves. Thus, in periods of middling strength, the factional stresses are most intense because empirical uncertainty about the movement's prospects reaches a peak. These stresses are likely to ease up again as the movement's fortunes improve and a new unity develops around the reformist perspective. In short, the occasions for cohesion and controversy are the same for reformers and revolutionaries as they are for pragmatists and purists.

Nonetheless, it is a mistake to assume that the two systems of factional cleavage are equivalent. The intensity model, for instance, is fully capable of generating factional strife in strictly reformist movements, while disputes about the movement's political status can easily arise among radical leaders of equal intensity. We have also discovered interesting signs of stress between the strategic reasoning of the intensity model and the dynamic historical reasoning associated with Marx's revolutionary perspective. Thus, both models contribute independently to our understanding of factionalism, but in ways that are richly interactive.

CHAPTER SIX

Moderates and Radicals

The Diversity Model of Factionalism

ONE OF THE bitterest ironies of prewar Social Democracy was the stormy relationship that developed between trade unionists and the movement's Marxist theoreticians. Marx, it is true, embraced the trade unions as "schools of socialism," but this seemingly natural alliance disintegrated as the nineteenth century wore on. By the turn of the century, Lenin was describing trade unionism as "the ideological enslavement of the workers by the bourgeoisie," and emploring his party "to divert the working-class movement from this spontaneous, trade-unionist striving to come under [the bourgeoisie's] wing."[1]

In Germany, the conservative stance of the unions created enormous difficulties for the SPD's orthodox purists who already faced determined opposition from the revisionist camp. As the unions built up an extensive mass following during the 1890s, they developed powerful organizations of their own and gradually intensified their efforts to subvert the revolutionary wing of the party. The unions' decisive victory in the fierce struggle that followed produced fundamental changes in the SPD's political strategy and led ultimately to the party's official (and to many, unthinkable) endorsement of German militarism in August 1914. If we hope to explain the process of deradicalization that sapped the SPD's revolutionary zeal, it is therefore imperative that we understand the political relationship between the party and the unions.[2]

The breach between the trade unionists and the more radical Marxian socialists suggests another source of factional tension in radical politics. What happens if a movement's leaders do not share a common

[1] V. I. Lenin, *Selected Works*, Vol. 1: *What Is To Be Done?* (New York: International Publishers, 1967), p. 130.

[2] Our account of this struggle relies mainly on evidence provided by Carl Schorske, *German Social Democracy, 1905–1917* (New York: Russell & Russell, 1970) and Peter Gay, *The Dilemma of Democratic Socialism* (New York: Collier Books, 1962).

goal but, rather, hold diverse opinions about the ideal outcome of their struggle against the regime? Certainly, very few movements draw their support from a point source along the ideological spectrum, and the same can be said about the people who filter up to positions of leadership. Under what circumstances, then, and on what terms can a consensus develop about strategy among leaders who maintain different ideal policies? And what kinds of factional coalitions are likely to crystallize when unity breaks down?

To answer these questions, we can rely upon the kind of reasoning developed earlier in the intensity model of factionalism. The keystone of that model was a simple rule that established the net value of all possible strategies, given a cardinal utility function to describe the dissident leader's relative liking for policies across the ideological spectrum. The net value of a strategy is defined as the loss from compromise plus the gain from concession. The loss from compromise equals the difference in utility between the dissident leader's ideal point and the policy actually demanded. The gain from concession equals the difference in utility between the regime's ideal point (assumed without loss of generality to be the status quo ante) and the concession won by the strategy. Thus,

$$\text{Net Value} = (U(P_D) - U(P_I)) + (U(P_C) - U(P_G))$$

where P_D is the policy demanded, P_I is the dissident leader's ideal point, P_C is the policy conceded, and P_G is the regime's ideal point. We may, for convenience, assign a utility value of one to the dissident's ideal policy, and a utility value of zero to the policy P_G. The net values of strategies will then vary between plus and minus one. The highest possible net value is achieved when a sincere strategy succeeds. Then the loss from compromise is zero (when $P_D = P_I$, $U(P_D) - U(P_I) = 0$), and the gain from concession is one (when $P_C = P_I$, $U(P_C) - U(P_G) = 1$). A sincere strategy that produces no concession has a net value of zero (the loss from compromise and the gain from concession both equal zero). It follows that dissident leaders who share a common ideal policy always can *guarantee* themselves a net value of zero, simply by adhering to a sincere demand. Strategies that produce negative net values are therefore unattractive in principle.

To describe a dissident leader's strategic preferences in general, we must evaluate the net values of all possible strategies from his point of view. This information can be summarized by a net value indifference

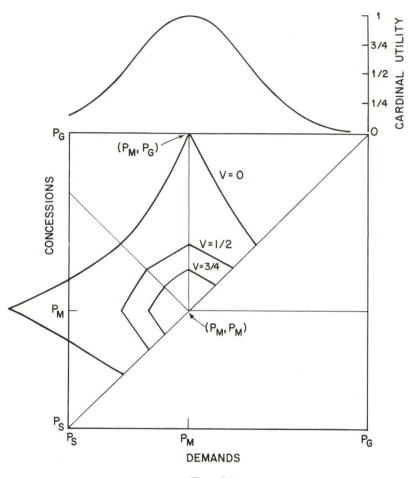

FIG. 6.1
The Moderate's Evaluation of Strategies

map like the one in Figure 6.1. This picture describes the strategic preferences of a dissident leader whose ideal policy is P_M. The cardinal utility function resting above the horizontal axis defines this individual's relative liking for every policy between P_S and P_G. Notice that the utility value assigned to P_M is one while the utility of P_G equals zero, in accord with our usual convention. P_S represents the ideal point of the politically most extreme elements in the movement's leadership circle. Relative to the extremists at P_S, then, our friend at P_M is a "moderate." From his point of view, the policy P_S is only slightly more attractive than the regime's position at P_G.

The square below the utility function describes the entire universe of strategic situations that the leaders of this movement might encounter. The square is defined by two axes, one describing demands along the political spectrum and the other describing concessions. The movement's potential demands range between P_S (the sincere demand for those leaders on the extreme left) and P_G. Likewise, the government's concessions may range, in principle anyway, between P_S and P_G. Each point in the square corresponds to an ordered pair of the form (P_D, P_C), the first coordinate describing the demand of a potential strategy and the second describing the concession it produces. As we move from left to right in the square, the movement's demands become less extreme relative to the government's position. The government's concessions increase as we move from top to bottom. The points in the square and on its boundaries exhaust every conceivable combination of demand and concession over the interval between P_S and P_G. Of course, we can disregard those points lying below the 45° bisector. They represent strategies that produce larger concessions than the movement demands. Such outcomes are incompatible with the political reasoning of Chapter 3. The points lying along the bisector itself denote successful strategies (demand equals concession), and the points above the bisector denote unsuccessful strategies (demand exceeds concession).

The net value indifference curves, which are superimposed on the square, summarize the strategic preferences of the particular moderate leader whose utility function rests above. Each curve joins combinations of demands and concessions that yield a constant net value, V. The curve labeled $V = 0$ describes strategies for which the gain from concession exactly equals the loss from compromising principles. Notice how this curve passes through the point (P_M, P_G). From the perspective of our moderate leader, this point represents a sincere strategy that fails to produce any concession.

The reader might wish to verify that the other points along this curve also yield net values of zero. For any point on the curve, one must first determine the utility of the policy demanded and the utility of the policy conceded, and then apply the rule for calculating net value. The utility of the policy demanded can be ascertained directly by proceeding vertically from the point in question to the graph of the utility function

above. Finding the utility of the policy conceded is slightly more complicated, because the utility function is graphed over the horizontal,
rather than over the vertical, policy axis. A simple geometric trick
solves the problem. The utility of the concession is found by moving
horizontally from the point in question to the 45° bisector and then
proceeding vertically to the graph above. Consider the point (P_M, P_G).
The utility of the demand P_M is given by the level of the utility function
directly over this point. In this case, the utility of the policy demanded
is one, and the loss from compromise is therefore zero. The utility of the
concession P_G is found by moving horizontally to the bisector (which
we reach in this case at the upper right corner of the square) and then
checking the level of the utility function above. Here, the utility of the
concession equals zero, and so does the gain from concession. Thus,

$$\text{Net Value } (P_M, P_G) = (U(P_M) - U(P_M)) + (U(P_G) - U(P_G)) = 0$$

where we have simply substituted P_M for P_D, P_M for P_I, and P_G for
P_C in the general expression for net value.

The curve labeled $V = 0$ identifies those strategies that break even
exactly with regard to concessions gained and principles lost. The
nested indifference contours that lie inside the break-even curve represent increasingly attractive strategies. As the level of net value
approaches one, these curves converge on the point (P_M, P_M), which
denotes a sincere demand successfully pursued. This outcome is clearly
ideal from our moderate leader's point of view. As demands or concessions or both diverge from the point (P_M, P_M), net value diminishes.
Those outcomes outside the break-even indifference curve yield negative net values, making them unattractive in principle.

The derivation and interpretation of this indifference map are identical to those in Figure 4.3. The more elaborate appearance of the picture here results simply from mapping outcomes on *both* sides of the
leader's ideal point. When we studied the intensity problem, we assumed tacitly that the movement's leaders shared a common goal. In
that case, it was sufficient to consider only those demands and concessions that lay between the leaders' shared ideal point and the government's preferred position at P_G. Notice that the northeast quadrant
of the present indifference map is identical in form to the ones constructed earlier. This quadrant contains demands and concessions that
lie between our moderate leader's ideal policy, P_M, and P_G. Now, how-

ever, we want to understand the factional implications of political diversity within the movement's leadership. We must therefore consider the moderate leader's attitude toward those demands between P_M and P_S, which may be advocated by the radicals on the left. The northwest and southwest quadrants of the indifference map in Figure 6.1 describe the moderate's evaluation of strategies with more radical demands than P_M.

Cohesion and Factionalism among Moderates and Radicals

To IDENTIFY the occasions when moderates and radicals are likely to disagree about which demand their movement should pursue, we must be able to derive each group's preferred demand in particular situations. Once again, the steps required to solve this problem are familiar from Chapters 3 and 4. The first step is to describe the empirical relationship between demands and concessions in whatever political environment the movement happens to find itself. In Chapter 3, we learned how to deduce the effectiveness of every potential demand (steadfast strategy) from the cumulative distribution of political opinion and curves describing the government's responsiveness to disruption. This information can be summarized in a strategy-potential curve (SPC) that describes how much concession each demand secures from the government (see Chapter 3, Appendix B, for a review).

Next we superimpose the strategy-potential curve (describing the movement's menu of choices) on the net value indifference maps of the various dissident leaders (describing their strategic predispositions). In each case, the individual's preferred strategy is found by locating the point on the SPC that yields the highest net value. Of course, the indifference maps will vary in shape according to the ideal points and intensity of preferences of the movement's leaders. Different individuals will not necessarily agree about which strategy is best, even when they agree about how much each strategy will accomplish. The final step in the analysis is to vary the shape of the strategy-potential curve to reflect a variety of political climates. The natural way to proceed is from the bleakest circumstances, in which no strategy accomplishes much, to more favorable situations, in which the movement can largely secure what it wants. In this way, we shall acquire a broad understanding of the political occasions for cooperation and factionalism among moderates and radicals.

The Political Intransigence of Moderates

THE CURVES in Figure 6.1, taken together with the rules of Chapter 3, imply interesting and rather surprising conclusions about the factional tendencies of moderate elements in dissident groups. Our reasoning leads us to the following rule:

> The dissident strategist in a leftist movement may sometimes prefer demands on the right of his ideal point, but under no circumstances does he prefer the more radical demands on his left.

This rule implies that in factional disputes the moderate wing of a dissident movement should be more united and unyielding in resisting demands to its left than the radical wing is in resisting demands to its right. In ordinary discourse, we tend to associate "moderateness" with political softness, while the term "radical" connotes both extremeness and inflexibility. The rule may therefore seem rather counterintuitive to those who aren't accustomed to drawing a careful distinction between the intensity of preferences and their ideological location.

To verify the rule, we must consider two situations. Suppose first that the strategist's movement is sufficiently strong to force the regime beyond his preferred outcome (taking Figure 6.1 as a general prototype, let's call the individual's ideal point P_M). It follows that the most radical of the successful demands (P_{max}) lies to the left of P_M, and that P_M will also be successful if it becomes the movement's demand (Chapter 3, rule 6). Since a successful, sincere strategy yields the highest net value, and uniquely so, P_M is unambiguously the preferred demand of our dissident leader. More radical strategies require compromising principles (to the left) and necessarily achieve net values less than one (even if they produce the concession P_M, which they generally will not).

Let us suppose, then, that P_{max} falls to the right of P_M (and therefore that a sincere strategy demanding P_M is unsuccessful). Might our strategist prefer demands to the left of his ideal point in this case? Certainly not. According to the law of diminishing returns (Chapter 3, rule 10), the unsuccessful strategies using more radical demands than P_M deliver either smaller concessions that P_M or at best the same concession (if the population is factionally divided). In either event, these strategies provide no compensation to the strategist for compromising his principles to the left. Thus, more radical strategies always seem less attractive than a sincere strategy. Of course, less radical strategies may become attractive when a sincere strategy is unsuccessful, because they typically offer some compensation for compromising principles (i.e. bigger concessions). This possibility is already familiar from the intensity model.

The political imperatives embodied in our rules obviously contain the seeds of factional disagreements between moderates and radicals. It remains to study their timing, which forms a mirror image of the disputes between purists and pragmatists. This interesting inversion is illustrated by Figure 6.2, which contains six panels arranged in two columns and three rows. The panels in the left column depict the strategic calculations of a moderate leader (ideal point at P_M) in three different political situations. The panels on the right, reproduced from Figure 4.5, illustrate the calculations of two radical leaders, one purist and one pragmatist (both with ideal points at P_S), in the same three situations. In each square, a heavy strategy-potential curve represents the dissidents' political options. This curve describes the amount of concession (vertical axis) that can be won by each potential demand (horizontal axis), given the balance of forces in the movement's political environment. Notice that the SPC remains constant in each row, but changes as we move down the two columns. The lighter curves in each square are the particular net value indifference contours that define the strategist's preferred demand.

Let P_S and P_M represent the ideological boundaries of the movement's leadership. We can then trace how the strategic preferences of leaders on each pole evolve as the political situation improves from the gloomy circumstances in the upper row to the favorable circumstances below.

The upper row of our illustration models those trying political conditions in which the movement has limited support and minimal impact. The most effective demand, P_{max}, not only delivers a very small concession but requires that leaders of every stripe abandon their principles. Under these conditions, purists and pragmatists who share common goals unite around their sincere strategy. Moderates and radicals disagree about which demand is best.

Consider first the moderate leader's assessment of the situation in the upper left panel. From his point of view, the sincere strategy demanding P_M is clearly the most attractive. This demand defines an outcome on the strategy-potential curve that also rests on the single indifference contour shown in the illustration. In order to appear more

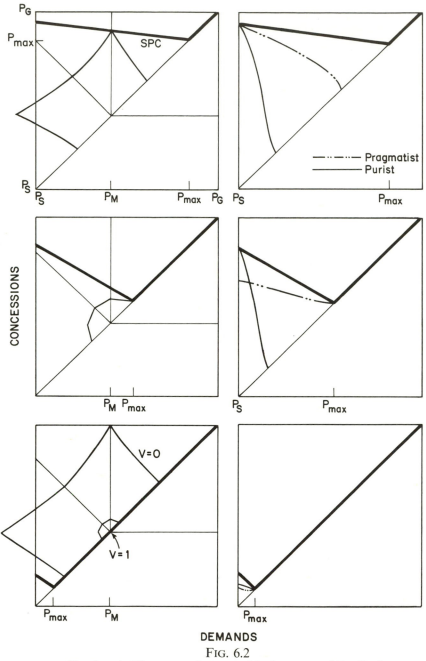

FIG. 6.2
Factional Alignments between Moderates and Radicals

attractive, other demands would have to produce outcomes on the SPC that would lie inside this indifference curve (i.e. that deliver higher net value). In this case, no such demand exists and P_M is the strategy of choice.

The radical leaders in the movement (upper right panel) similarly prefer their sincere demand, P_S. The two indifference curves in this square (one for the purist, the other for the pragmatist) show that from the radicals' point of view, every other demand produces a less attractive outcome than P_S. (Recall from Chapter 4 that net value diminishes in this diagram as we move from the southwest corner of the square, where $V = 1$, toward the northeast corner, where $V = -1$.)

The same reasoning applies to other members of the dissident leadership whose ideal policies lie between P_S and P_M. Compromise returns so little in the way of extra concessions that everyone takes refuge in a sincere strategy. Political adversity therefore conceals differences between pragmatists and purists but aggravates cleavages between moderates and radicals. Even though our model implies that a strategic conflict of interest will exist in this movement, notice that we cannot readily predict how the conflict will be resolved.

The middle panels describe a significantly more favorable political climate. Here the dissidents can force the government substantially to the left if they are willing to compromise their demands toward P_{max}. As a result, the previous pattern of cleavage reverses. Now the original radical coalition is split; the purists hold fast to their sincere demand P_S while the pragmatists defect to the moderate camp in support of the demand P_{max}. Meanwhile, the moderates remain united. We have, then, a powerful coalition favoring political moderation arrayed against the isolated purists on the left.

If it happens that the left wing holds sway in the adverse circumstances of the upper row, a significant deradicalization of strategy is likely to occur when the balance of forces becomes more auspicious. Not only will the left purists face the combined opposition of moderates and pragmatists (which may alone spell their defeat), but the political dynamics of recruiting will compound their difficulties. A salient feature of political situations like the one in the middle row is that moderate demands (like P_{max}) will usually mobilize substantially greater support than radical demands (like P_S). Even if the advocates of moderation have only limited success in the initial phases of their struggle with the purist radicals, the movement's mass following will now increase as its

strategy becomes less extreme, and new growth will draw dispropor-
tionately on previously unmobilized moderate elements in the underlying population. As this happens, the internal composition of the
movement will usually change, sometimes dramatically, in the moderates' favor. The rightest coalition will only grow larger and more
powerful as it prevails on the left to compromise the party line. Every
victory it achieves therefore makes the next victory more likely.

These factional alignments are upset in the lower panel as the movement grows even stronger. Now P_{max} passes the moderate position and
approaches the radical demand P_S. The moderates and radical pragmatists part company, while the radical coalition regroups. Having
achieved their goals, the moderates try to arrest the government's rush
past their position by preventing any further radicalization of the
movement's demands. The radical pragmatists, on the other hand,
retreat toward their sincere demand as the incentive to compromise
evaporates. Thus, as the movement's political potential increases, the
radical pragmatists and purists are reunited, while the moderates and
radicals are split.

Moderate versus Radical Social Democrats

A CONSIDERABLE body of evidence about German Social Democratic
politics can be informed by the diversity model of factionalism. Most
importantly, it helps explain the political relationship between the
radical, theoretical wing of the socialist movement and the moderate
leaders of the trade unions.[3] If we investigate the patterns of alliance
and cleavage that crystallized during the politically optimistic period
around the turn of the century, for example, we find them very much
in accord with the model's predictions.

On one hand, the German trade-union leaders became hostile and
openly defiant toward the purist wing of the SPD's radical leadership.
The first signs of trouble appeared after the repeal of the Anti-Socialist
Bill in 1890, and things only got worse after the onset of an economic
boom in 1895, when the trade-union movement entered a period of

---

[3] On the relative conservatism of the trade unions' national leadership, see Gay,
Dilemma of Democratic Socialism, Chapters 5 and 8; Schorske, *German Social Democracy*,
Chapters 1, 2, and 4; and Rosa Luxemburg, "The Mass Strike, the Political Party and
the Trade Unions," in *Rosa Luxemburg Speaks* (New York: Pathfinder Press, 1970).

explosive growth. At the trade-union congress of 1892, the leader of the Free (i.e. socialist) Trade Unions, Carl Legien, asserted the "neutrality" of the unions for the first time. This was a polite though ominous way of saying that the trade-union movement no longer regarded itself as a subordinate arm of the SPD but rather as a separate and equal political entity, free to pursue its own strategy.[4]

The unionists, in fact, were far less interested in making a revolution than they were in achieving immediate and tangible improvements in wages, hours, and working conditions. According to Carl Schorske, the trade unionists found the "revolutionary character of the party a handicap in recruiting" and preferred instead "to emphasize only the pursuit of the workers' material interest."[5] They called their strategy *Gegenwartsarbeit*, meaning "work for the present time." We should notice here that the union leaders made no attempt to portray their program as the first step in either an evolutionary or revolutionary march toward socialism. As Schorske puts it, they regarded their "positive work" and "practical little tasks" as "triumphs in and for themselves, to be further expanded within the framework of the capitalist order."[6] It is in this sense that the trade-union leadership can be distinguished as "moderate" from the radical Marxists of the SPD (that is, from both the revisionist and revolutionary wings of the party who wanted to transform capitalist society).

The uneasy relationship between the party and the unions deteriorated rapidly during the next several years. The popularity of their program and its relatively greater capacity to mobilize support made the unions formidable opponents of the radical, revolutionary line. As the ratio of party voters to union members shrank from eight to one in 1893 to only three to one in 1903, the unions acquired power in numbers of their own. Gradually, they abandoned the pretense of "neutrality" and fought aggressively to keep the party on a moderate course.

During the late 1890s, for example, the unions' general commission openly defied the party's long tradition of "pure opposition" by officially recognizing various institutions of the German state (particularly the state labor exchanges and the social insurance system). Shortly thereafter, the unionists fought a pitched battle with the party's left

[4] See Gay, p. 134, and Schorske, pp. 11–15.
[5] Schorske, *German Social Democracy*, p. 12.
[6] Ibid., p. 15.

wing to forestall a political mass strike on the model of the Russian Revolution of 1905.

At the Fifth Trade Union Congress held at Cologne in May of 1905, the union leaders voted by an "overwhelming majority" to denounce the idea of a mass strike as "indiscussible," and warned their followers not to be "distracted by the reception and propaganda of such ideas from the small day-to-day tasks of building up the organization of labor."[7] Only one leader of a major union rose to disagree with Auer's famous quip that "the general strike is general nonsense."[8] Thus, on the mass strike issue (and all others) the unions' national leadership remained united and intransigent in resisting efforts to pursue a more radical strategy than their own *Gegenwartsarbeit*.

While the leaders of the unions refused to compromise their program to the left, the radicals were divided about whether to compromise their program to the right. The Marxist purists like Lenin and Luxemburg were dismayed by the conservatism of the unions and vehemently resisted their program as a dangerous threat to the revolution. In Lenin's view, the unionists' arguments that "a kopek added to a ruble is worth more than any socialism" and that workers should fight "not for the sake of some future generation but for themselves" were nothing more than "a favorite weapon of the West-European bourgeoisie" to divert the proletariat from a revolutionary course.[9] To accept a purely trade-union struggle was "bowing to spontaneity" and "allowing the subordination of the working class movement to bourgeois ideology."[10] The task of Social Democracy, he concluded, was not to bow to the immediate material desires of the workers, but rather to create among them an awareness of "the irreconcilable antagonism of their interests to the whole of the modern political and social system."[11]

In Germany, Luxemburg was similarly distressed by the separation and independence of the two wings in the labor movement. "The illusion of equality" between the party and the unions, she observed, created "the monstrous spectacle that ... on the same questions ... diametrically opposite decisions are taken."[12] In her opinion, the theory of "equal authority" and "neutrality" was nothing but another manifestation of the "opportunist tendency to reduce the political struggle of the working class to a parliamentary contest ... and to

---

[7] Ibid., p. 40.   [8] Gay, *Dilemma of Democratic Socialism*, p. 243.
[9] V. I. Lemin, *What Is To Be Done?*, p. 127.
[10] Ibid., p. 130   [11] Ibid., p. 209   [12] Luxemburg, "The Mass Strike," p. 217.

change social democracy from a revolutionary proletarian party into a petty bourgeois reform one."[13] Luxemburg's answer to the dilemma was similar to Lenin's. The worst possible approach, she insisted, was seeking a negotiated truce between the two camps. "Nothing could be more perverse or hopeless than a desire to attain . . . unity by means of sporadic negotiations . . . between the Social Democratic Party leadership and the trade union central committees."[14] Instead, the party had to bypass the "bureaucratic minority" of trade-union officials and go directly to the masses. Only in the "consciousness of the mass of proletarians who have been won for the class struggle can the unity of social democracy and the trade unions be restored."[15] Thus, purists like Luxemburg and Lenin sought to repair the schism between moderates and radicals, not by compromising principles, but through a program of political agitation among the masses that would deprive the moderates of their base.

The evolutionary strategy devised by Bernstein, on the other hand, was essentially equivalent, at least in the near term, to the trade unionists' preferred course. Along with the moderates, radical pragmatists like Bernstein expressed greater interest in the possibilities of the moment than in ideal models of the future. His concern, he wrote, was not "with what will happen in the more distant future, but with what can and ought to happen in the present,"[16] The moderation of his program, its gradual pace, and its emphasis on forward movement rather than political regression were far more congruent with the unionists' political sensibilities than the harsh (and ineffective) revolutionary dogma of the purists. Naturally enough, Bernstein expressed much warmer sentiments about the unions than did the purists. Replying to critics like Rosa Luxemburg "in whose eyes the union is only an object lesson to prove the uselessness of any other than political revolutionary action,"[17] Bernstein described the unions as "indispensable organs of democracy," and attached "the greatest value" to their work.[18]

Despite these affinities in outlook, it is important to emphasize once again that revisionism and trade unionism were not simply different guises for a single political mentality. Scholars of this period are quite

---

[13] Ibid., p. 209   [14] Ibid., pp. 217–18,   [15] Ibid., p. 218.

[16] Eduard Bernstein, *Evolutionary Socialism*, trans. Edith C. Harvey (New York: Schocken Books, 1961), p. 163.

[17] Ibid., p. 140.   [18] Ibid.

explicit in drawing a careful distinction between the two tendencies, and there is good evidence to show that their basic consensus about strategy was not at all unshakable, but highly contingent upon the contours of the political situation.

Gay, for example, describes the relationship between the revisionists and trade unionists as a "marriage de convenance."[19] The unionists, he argues, were not only uncommitted to the grand designs of Marxian theorists but completely uninterested in them. The arcane doctrinal controversies within the radical left were, in the unionists' view, mere "intellectual pastimes of no value for practical affairs."[20] Even Bernstein's reformulation of Marxist theory "left the unions completely cold."[21] Thus, the trade unions were ready allies of the revisionists "insofar as revisionism was a practical reform movement,"[22] but they did not in any way share the revisionists' aspiration to achieve a socialist transformation.

As a result, the revisionists and the trade unions tended to part company (as our model predicts they should) during those periods of political regression that occasionally interrupted the general advance of labor in the years between 1890 and World War I. The contingent nature of their alliance became evident during the dark days of 1905, in particular, when the German employers' associations made a concerted effort to bust the unions by coordinating mass lockouts on a national scale. While the unions' leadership steadfastly opposed the mass political strike, the revisionists withdrew to the "left," partially anyway, by defending its use under carefully circumscribed conditions. Bernstein argued that the mass strike could legitimately be mobilized as a last resort to defend universal suffrage. Although this tame suggestion was a far cry from the revolutionary mass strike advocated by Luxemburg, it nevertheless outraged the unions.[23] Thus, the unions and the revisionists represented distinct political viewpoints whose strategic inclinations generally, but not always, coincided.

The Consolidation of the Antirevolutionary Coalition

THE STRUCTURAL alignment of the German left at the turn of the century placed the revolutionary wing of the SPD in mortal peril. In a

---

[19] Gay, *Dilemma of Democratic Socialism*, p. 140.
[20] Ibid., p. 138.   [21] Ibid.   [22] Ibid.
[23] Ibid. and Schorske, *German Social Democracy*, Chapter 2.

political situation that resembled the middle panel of Figure 6.2, the
forces of deradicalization enjoyed a decided advantage in the struggle
to determine the strategy of the labor movement. The fundamental
basis of their political strength was the fact that a moderate program
of demands mobilized broad support, while the radical platform remained isolated. According to Schorske, the trade unions simply "out-
ran the party in securing the active allegiance of the working class"
in the years between 1895 and 1906.[24] The unions' strategy of *Gegenwartsarbeit* succeeded where a sincerely Marxist strategy failed by
affording to workers "what the party could not directly give: a measure
of economic security in the here and now. Tangible benefits exerted
a more immediate attraction on the working man than the more rarefied ideas of socialism."[25]

In a situation that rewarded compromise with substantial material
concessions, the orthodox purists then encountered three enormous
difficulties in trying to retain supremacy in the party. First, the Marxist
left was hopelessly split into revisionist and revolutionary factions.
Even though they shared the common goal of achieving socialism, the
purists and pragmatists of the radical camp were bitterly divided about
the utility of sincere and evolutionary strategies. Second, the moderates
of the trade unions remained steadfast and united in their commitment
to a strictly reformist course. They did not experience the self-consuming factional strife that sapped the strength of the left. And third,
the moderates enjoyed mass support that conferred on them power
in numbers. The fear that the unions might desert the SPD, taking with
them a membership that outnumbered the party's by four to one in
1906, made the party executive increasingly sensitive to the unionists'
demands.[26] The potential had therefore developed for a powerful coalition of radical pragmatists (revisionists) and moderate trade unionists
to seize control of the party and, by doing so, to strike a heavy blow
against the revolutionary impulse in German socialism.

In these unfriendly political circumstances, the radical purists sought
refuge in antidemocratic rules of party organization. In order to secure
their own position and to thwart their determined and numerous
opponents, the orthodox left became in Schorske's words, "firmly
wedded to the idea of party discipline and strong central authority."[27]

---

[24] Schorske, *German Social Democracy*, p. 13.
[25] Ibid.   [26] Ibid., p. 110.   [27] Ibid., p. 24.

By retaining control over the party's central institutions, and by denying to local party organizations the autonomy to fashion a moderate political strategy that reflected the relative conservatism of German labor, the purists hoped to subvert the forces of deradicalization from above.

These efforts encountered fierce resistance from revisionists and trade unionists alike. The revisionists, naturally enough, became the defenders of intraparty democracy and looser, federalist forms of organization. They argued that broad popular support was incompatible with strict party discipline, and that "the unhealthy omnipotence of the executive committee is not consonant with the democratic sentiment of the party comrades."[28] Particularly in the south, where their forces were strongest, the revisionists attempted to secure their position by establishing financially autonomous umbrella organizations at the state level, which could serve as buffers between the national executive and the locals. Although weak initially, these regional institutions gradually spread throughout the country and eventually became powerful bastions of entrenched conservatism in the party.[29]

The unions resisted the authority of the purist left, initially anyway, by declaring their independence ("neutrality") and withdrawing from the party's control. The orthodox Marxists simply had no leverage to prevent the unions from exploiting their mass support to develop large and financially self-sufficient organizations of their own. Having done so, the unions were able to pursue whatever strategy they pleased.

By the turn of the century, then, the champions of Marxist orthodoxy were steadily losing their grip on the day-to-day activities of the labor movement. They nevertheless managed to retain control over the party congress and its executive committee. In 1899, for example, the party congress reaffirmed the idea of class struggle and rejected "any attempt to alter or obscure the party's antagonistic attitude toward the existing state and social order."[30] Four years later, the purist left repulsed the rising tide of deradicalization again, this time at the party congress at Dresden. The famous Dresden resolution, which carried only after bitter debate, denounced "revisionist efforts to supplant the policy of a conquest of power by overcoming our enemies with a policy of accommodation to the existing order."[31] The congress insisted that class

---

[28] Ibid., p. 26.
[29] See Schorske, *German Social Democracy*, especially Chapter 8, sections 4–5.
[30] Ibid., p. 23,   [31] Ibid., p. 24.

antagonisms were increasing, and rejected in principle any proposal that Social Democracy participate in bourgeois government.

But here, too, the left purists were fighting a losing battle. Their protracted struggle with the forces of moderation finally ended in a rout at the Mannheim party congress of September 1906 when the explosive issue of the unions' relationship to the party came to a head.

The paramount question before the Mannheim congress was how to define, once and for all, the lines of authority between the party and the unions. The decisive blow to the purist cause was the defection of the party executive to the moderate camp. The executive's spokesman, August Bebel, proposed a resolution that recognized the absolute parity of the unions with the party. Even worse, the resolution gave the parity principle political teeth by declaring that "the central leadership of both organizations should seek a mutual understanding in order to achieve a unified procedure" in all actions that affected their mutual interests.[32] This resolution was tantamount to giving the unions veto power over the party's strategy, insofar as it implied that the party executive could do nothing without the trade unions' approval.

The orthodox wing of the party denounced the parity principle, maintaining that the activities of the unions should be subordinated absolutely to the will and direction of the party. The trade unions were transient creatures of the capitalist era, the purists argued, while the party represented "the total struggle for the liberation of the proletariat" and by its nature was "the higher authority."[33] The radical left was at a loss, however, to devise an institutional mechanism by which to enforce discipline on the unions. Their resolution, formulated by Karl Kautsky, simply proclaimed the "duty" of each party comrade "to feel bound by the decisions of the party congresses in his trade-union activity," and declared the "absolute necessity" that the trade unions be "ruled by the spirit of Social Democracy."[34]

When it appeared that Kautsky's resolution might pass by a close vote, the party executive engineered a parliamentary ruse. First they amended some of Kautsky's language (the vague admonition to infuse the unions with a Social Democratic spirit) to their own resolution supporting the parity principle. Then Bebel closed off debate and forced the issue to a vote.

When the amended resolution carried, the unions passed, in Schorske's words, "from a position of independence of the party to one

---

[32] Ibid., p. 49.   [33] Ibid., p. 50.   [34] Ibid.

of effective control over it."[35] While the Mannheim resolution molli-
fied the purist left with lofty and empty statements about the spirit of
Social Democracy, it canonized in the party rules the power of the
unions' general commission to veto all of the executive committee's
political decisions. In one bold stroke, the antirevolutionary coalition
had finally consolidated its power in the party's ruling apparatus and
effectively routed the forces of the radical left.

Even though Kautsky tried to defend the Mannheim resolution as
a "decided shift to the left" in trade-union policy,[36] it was clear to
partisans on both sides that the moderates had achieved a momentous
victory. In language that belied Kautsky's wishful appraisal, the general
commission celebrated the agreement as the beginning of a new era in
the labor movement.

> It is to be hoped that the frequent ructions between the party and the
> trade unions . . . will have a lasting good effect in that the complete co-
> operation that now exists will never again be endangered by theorists and
> writers who attach greater value to mere revolutionary slogans than to
> practical work inside the labor movement.[37]

Meanwhile, Rosa Luxemburg ruefully, and accurately, compared the
relationship between the unions and the party to the "parity" arrangement between a domineering peasant woman and her husband: "On
matters of question between us, when we agree, you will decide; when
we disagree, I shall decide."[38]

The political dynamics that carried the advocates of moderation to
their victory in 1906 are fully consistent with the predictions of our
theory. Taken together, the diversity and intensity models imply that
periods of rising political optimism will align radical pragmatists and
moderates against purist radicals, providing the former with a decided
advantage in numbers. In Carl Schorske's post-mortem on the events
at Mannheim, we see that our formal reasoning captures perfectly the
basic pattern of deradicalization in German Social Democracy:

> The line of division in the labor movement which, in the radical years,
> had run between the party and the trade unions was now shifted back
> into the party itself. The real locus of power, on the other hand,
> shifted . . . to the unions which in turn strengthened the reformist wing
> within the party, and laid the groundwork for the ultimate break-off of
> the isolated radicals.[39]

[35] Ibid., p. 52   [36] Ibid.
[37] Gay, *Dilemma of Democratic Socialism*, p. 134.
[38] Quoted in Schorske, *German Social Democracy*, p. 52,   [39] Ibid., p. 53.

In the years between 1906 and World War I, the revisionists' control over the party's regional bureaucracy and the unions' domination of the executive allowed the antirevolutionary coalition to marshal the organizational apparatus of the SPD against the radical left. The moderates implemented a virtual tyranny of the majority—relying upon censorship of the party press, manipulation of funds, rule by administrative fiat, malapportionment in the party congress, and, in the end, termination of membership—to suppress their opponents. And while the new leadership waged its repressive campaign inside the party, it pursued electoral alliances with the liberals and voted consistently to support the regime's militaristic foreign policy. The political alignment that crystallized in 1906 propelled the SPD toward its ultimate accommodation with the German state in August 1914, when the Social Democratic delegation to the Reichstag voted overwhelmingly to support the regime's war credits bill, and then to the fateful rupture in 1917 when the revolutionary Spartacist left finally abandoned the party of Marx and Engels.

CHAPTER SEVEN

Organization and Strategy

IF WE PROCEED on the assumption that political effectiveness alone governs the dissidents' choice of strategy, their strategy-making organization fades into a neverland of theoretical irrelevancy. The game boils down to surveying the political situation and identifying the strategy that accomplishes the most. As soon as we move beyond naive models of rational choice, however, the problem of organization assumes a central theoretical role. The evidence about the revisionist controversy makes the following points clear:

1. Tangible concessions are not the only criterion governing decisions about strategy. Principles matter too.

2. Radical movements sometimes harbor people with markedly dissimilar strategic inclinations. Disparities in political aspirations and the intensity of political preferences can easily fuel violent disagreements about strategy, even when everyone agrees about the alignment of political forces (i.e. about which strategy is most effective).

3. Real-life factional disputes reflect multiple systems of political cleavage, operating simultaneously in highly interactive ways.

All of these considerations suggest that good explanations of strategy must do more than elaborate the opportunities and constraints in a movement's external environment. They must also consider its internal political climate, that is, the composition of the strategy-making core and the process by which factional disagreements are resolved. Far from being a theoretical irrelevancy, then, problems of organization are intimately bound up with problems of strategy. Nothing like a full treatment of their reciprocal influences is possible here. Instead, we shall simply attempt to outline how the two questions are related by reviewing a famous debate about political organization among the Russian Social Democrats.

Organizational Form and Strategic Choice

AS THE REVISIONIST controversy simmered to a boil, it became increasingly apparent that the organizational form of the Socialist parties exerted a decided influence on their strategic course. Political strategy was neither conceived nor implemented in an organizational vacuum, making it impossible to ignore the strategic consequences of decisions about organizational design. An excellent way to appreciate the intimate connection between strategy and organization is to recall the story of the famous Second Party Congress held by the Russian Social Democratic Labor Party in 1903.[1] At this historic meeting, the Russian Social Democrats split into Bolshevik and Menshevik factions. The congress was really a constituent assembly, convened by the editors of the émigré newspaper *Iskra*[2] to organize a political party that could lead the workers' revolutionary movement in Russia. The debates among the delegates about the design of their party illustrate vividly how the strategic tendencies described in earlier chapters give life to, and draw sustenance from, various organizational structures.

The agenda of the congress included a bewildering menu of topics, but two central problems of organizational design emerged as the focus of controversy. The first had to do with the location of the party's boundaries. Given the full breadth of the movement's political base, where were the lines to be drawn that separated the strategy-making core from the larger following? The debate about who should be admitted to the party was a matter not so much of evaluating particular individuals and groups but rather of defining how much ideological

---

[1] Our description of the congress relies mainly on the following historical accounts: V. I. Lenin, *Selected Works*, Vol. 1: *One Step Forward, Two Steps Back* (New York: International Publishers, 1967); Leon Trotsky, *My Life* (New York: Pathfinder Press, 1970); Adam Ulam, *The Bolsheviks* (New York: Collier Books, 1965); Donald Treadgold, *Lenin and His Rivals* (New York: Frederick A. Praeger, 1955); Isaac Deutscher, *The Prophet Armed: Trotsky 1879–1921* (New York: Vintage Books, 1965); Georg Lukács, *Lenin*, trans. Nicholas Jacobs (Cambridge: MIT Press, 1971); Rosa Luxemburg, "The Organizational Question of Social Democracy," in *Rosa Luxemburg Speaks* (New York: Pathfinder Press, 1970).

[2] *Iskra*, "The Spark," was the illegal newspaper edited by Lenin between 1900 and 1903.

breadth the party would span and the degree of political commitment required from its members. The second problem concerned the structure of authority within the party. Should the pattern of decision making be centralized and hierarchical or broadly democratic? Would lower party officials be allowed any discretion in tailoring a strategy to fit local circumstances? Or would binding decisions about strategy emanate from the party's center?

These questions provoked such intense controversy that the party split, quite to everyone's surprise, in the midst of its own creation. The interesting feature of this dramatic and fateful rupture was its striking parallelism with the factional cleavages that had crystallized during the revisionist debates. As the Marxist theorist Georg Lukács put it nearly sixty years ago:

> On the level of pure theory the most disparate views and tendencies are able to co-exist peacefully. . . . But no sooner are these same questions given organizational form than they turn out to be sharply opposed and even incompatible.[3]

Lenin's Organizational Plan

THE PARTY congress convened during a period of intense factional turmoil within the larger Social Democratic movement. While the revisionist debates were raging in the German party, the editors of the *Iskra*, especially Lenin and Plekhanov, became active participants in the theoretical war against the Bernsteinians. Among the Russians, and perhaps in all of Social Democracy, no one exemplified the unalloyed purist mentality more completely than Lenin. Even in the rarefied atmosphere of underground émigré politics, the intensity of his ideological passion was startling. According to Trotsky,[4] Lenin's favorite words were "irreconcilable" and "relentless," and they aptly describe his behavior at the congress.

Lenin probably appreciated the strategic implications of organizational design more deeply than anyone in his party, and he struggled with ferocious zeal to create a party organization that would remain immune to the moderating, revisionist tendencies in the Russian move-

---

[3] Georg Lukács, "Towards a Methodology of the Problem of Organization," in *History and Class Consciousness*, trans. Rodney Livingston (Cambridge: MIT Press, 1971), p. 299.

[4] Leon Trotsky, *My Life*, p. 161.

ment. As the congress began, Lenin perceived a dual threat to the steadfast, revolutionary course he championed. On one hand, the vast majority of the party's base was politically moderate (at least by Lenin's standards). The Russian proletariat seemed to him ideologically immature and incapable of forging a truly revolutionary perspective on its own. At the same time, his own comrades at the movement's center no longer seemed especially reliable either. Judging by the recollections of Trotsky, it appears that tensions of the kind we expect between pragmatists and purists had been brewing on *Iskra*'s editorial board for several months before the congress.

Lenin's closest collaborator on the paper was Julius Martov. The two revolutionaries had been companions in arms for nearly a decade, first as leading members in the St. Petersburg Union of Struggle for the Liberation of the Working Class and later as exiles. Their falling out bore the same marks as Bernstein's split with the orthodox wing of the German party. Evidently, Martov's ideological position on the eve of the congress was indistinguishable from Lenin's. Nonetheless, a subtle and only vaguely perceived discontinuity in outlook was already straining their relationship. "Lenin was 'hard' and Martov was 'soft.' And they both knew it," Trotsky recalls.

> Although no marked divisions really existed, there was a difference in point of view, in resoluteness and readiness to go on to the end.... Martov lived much more in the present; Lenin, on the other hand ... was always trying to pierce the veil of the future.... A certain coldness was beginning to creep into their mutual relations.... When Lenin spoke to me of Martov, there was a peculiar intonation in his voice: "Who said that? Julius?"—and the name Julius was pronounced in a special way, with a slight emphasis, as if to give warning: "A good man, no question about it, even a remarkable one, but much too soft." [5]

Lenin entered the congress with a single purpose in mind. Whatever the cost, he was determined to combat "opportunism in matters of organization." [6] Like the Alaskan Inuits who can distinguish 100 types of snow, Lenin perceived opportunists in finely graduated shades from "minor" to "middling" to "major." [7] He fought tenaciously for a system of party rules that would neutralize the moderating influence of both moderates and pragmatists on the party's strategy. Lenin wanted,

---

[5] Ibid., p. 151.
[6] V. I. Lenin, *One Step Forward, Two Steps Back*, p. 260   [7] Ibid., p. 374.

above all, to create a resolutely revolutionary organization that would never compromise its ultimate objectives for the "petty reforms" his rivals valued so highly.

The Membership Question

No SOONER did the congress begin than Lenin engaged Martov in a violent dispute about how to define membership in the party. Martov's inclination was to extend the boundaries of the party as broadly as possible across the working-class movement. "The more widespread the title of party member the better," he declared. "We could only rejoice if every striker, every demonstrator . . . could proclaim himself a party member."[8] From Lenin's exquisitely hardened perspective, this proposal was little short of heresy. He found preposterous the idea of extending membership in the revolutionary vanguard party to politically immature elements of the working class. Such a plan was nothing but "tailism," an open door to "vagueness and vacillation," and a blueprint for letting "the most backward elements in the party gain the upper hand."[9]

Many historians of the Russian Revolution call special attention to the apparent similarity of Martov's draft of the party rules about membership to Lenin's.[10] Where Martov defined a party member as someone who "rendered the party regular personal assistance under the direction of one of its organizations," Lenin insisted that a member of the party "personally participate in one of the party organizations."[11] The intentions underlying the definitions were entirely distinct, however. Martov wanted to create a truly mass party by opening its doors to anyone who wanted to join. Lenin, on the other hand, envisioned a vanguard party composed only of the ideologically most mature and intensely committed people. By adopting a narrow definition, Lenin hoped to exclude from the party those elements in its base who threatened to challenge an uncompromising revolutionary strategy.

> The stronger our party organization consisting of *real* Social Democrats, the less wavering and instability there is within the party. . . . Why Comrade Martov's suggestion is no good is that it allows any opportunist, any windbag, any professor, to proclaim himself a party member. . . .

---

[8] Ibid., p. 307.   [9] Ibid., p. 315.
[10] See, for example, Ulam, *The Bolsheviks.*
[11] V. I. Lenin, *One Step Forward, Two Steps Back,* p. 294.

The idea of Paragraph I as formulated by me ... consists in *guaranteeing* actual control and direction.[12]

Authority Patterns in the Party

THE SAME pattern of cleavage divided the congress on the question of how decision-making authority should be constituted within the party. The purist wing headed by Lenin advocated a rigorous centralism designed to guarantee strict control by the party's core over the broader periphery. Lenin insisted that the party be built "from the top downward ... upholding the rights and powers of the center in relation to the parts."[13] To realize such control in practice, he elaborated a circular system of formal authority intended to insulate the strategy-making center from the "opportunist" influences originating in the party's lower levels.

In Lenin's scheme, the "supreme organ of the party," at least formally, was the party congress. The delegates to this body represented "all the active organizations" in the party.[14] These delegates appointed in turn the members of the "central institutions," who then directed the party's affairs until the next congress convened. The practical (rather than formal) supremacy of the Central Committee was guaranteed, in "Catch 22" fashion, by its right to appoint all of the party's local committees and thus to determine the composition of the party congress. The success of such a closed-loop arrangement depended, of course, on putting the right people inside the loop initially. Thus, the definition of membership in the party was an integral part of a larger design to combat the "opportunist" trend. As Lenin declared in his attacks on Martov's arguments:

> The party, as the vanguard of the class, should be as organized as possible ... [and] should admit to its ranks only such elements as allow of at least a minimum of organization. My opponent, on the contrary, lumps together in the party ... those who lend themselves to direction and those who do not, the advanced and the incorrigibly backward.[15]

Lenin's approach to constituting the party was intended, of course, to exclude the "incorrigibly backward" elements by raising the price of admission beyond the means of less than fully committed adherents of revolutionary socialism. As he openly admitted, the whole rationale for

---

[12] Ibid., p. 306.   [13] Ibid., p. 424.   [14] Ibid.   [15] Ibid., p. 304.

giving the Central Committee absolute control over the delegations to
the party congress was to provide the strategy-making institutions

> with a membership which satisfies the advanced elements of the party
> more than the backward and is more to the taste of its revolutionary than
> its opportunist wing.[16]

The Menshevik Counterattack

THE "SOFTER" .delegates at the congress, echoing the German revisionists, attacked Lenin's organizational scheme with genuine passion,
denouncing it as a "system of autocratic and bureaucratic government
of the party."[17] The so-called Menshevik faction lamented "the systematic suppression of individual initiative," and deplored the "monstrous centralism" that allowed lower echelons in the party "only one
right—to submit without a murmur to orders from above."[18] In addition to a broader conception of membership, they defended democratic
forms of authority within the party and substantial autonomy for its
local committees. Their purpose was to create a mass proletarian party
that would remain responsive to the aspirations of its base.

What the Mensheviks feared most about Lenin's plan was the possibility that a vanguard party would become divorced from the working
masses. The idea that the party might be overwhelmed and transformed by "immature" elements, as the German party later was, hardly
concerned them. After all, the party's purpose was to advance the interests of the proletariat. "We must take care not to leave outside the
party ranks people who consciously, though perhaps not very actively,
associate themselves with that party," argued Pavel Axelrod, one of
Lenin's coeditors on the *Iskra* and a collaborator with the Mensheviks
at the congress.[19] In much the same spirit, Martov insisted that

> The Central Committee in order not to leave a multitude of organizations
> outside the party will have to legitimize them despite their not quite
> reliable character.[20]

In the Menshevik's view, the mass base was anything but a threat to
the party—it was its lifeblood. The real danger was "a doctrinaire
policy which loses contact with life."[21]

---

[16] Ibid., p. 424.   [17] Ibid., p. 394.   [18] Ibid., p. 300
[19] Ibid., p. 306.   [20] Ibid., p. 315.   [21] Ibid., p. 426.

The Organizational Dilemma

STRATEGIES prevail not simply by a process of superior adaptation to a political environment but also because the organizational forms assumed by radical movements have definite strategic biases. Effecting a political strategy requires thinking about organization, and explaining a strategy does too.

The principal objective of the political purist is to preserve the integrity of his movement's principles. When the movement's base is ideologically immature, this means isolating the strategy-making process from the corrupting influences of those who would bow to the base's "spontaneous" aspirations. Lenin devised a dual system of checks on the forces of moderation in his party. By enforcing a rigorous centralism and erecting narrow organizational boundaries, he hoped to institutionalize an uncompromising strategy. "Our Party Rules, and the whole system of centralism," he wrote, "are nothing but a 'state of seige' in respect to the numerous sources of political vagueness."[22]

Pragmatists and moderates, on the other hand, strive for tangible concessions, even at the expense of the purist's doctrinal sensibilities. The political tendency most inimical to their program is the sterile and ineffectual extremism of the radical purist. To secure the mass support needed to win concessions, and to maintain the responsiveness of the party to its following, the compromisers must neutralize the influence of the movement's political hard core. This can be accomplished organizationally by extending membership in the party broadly across its mass base and designing democratic decision-making procedures that provide the lowest echelons of the party with political leverage over the center.

Each organizational schema therefore reflects an underlying strategic imperative, and the dilemmas of organizational design then assume the character of the underlying strategic dilemmas. The Leninist approach defies, at least on its face, the basic political canon that power resides in numbers. When a movement's support depends on the content of its political program, placing organizational constraints on demands threatens its political survival. The party that opens its doors to all and sundry, on the other hand, imperils its ideological identity. This was the fate of Marx's own party, the SPD. The German Social

---

[22] Ibid., p. 361.

Democrats organized a "democratic mass party,"[23] which conveyed membership on all comers and subjected its leaders to numerous democratic controls. When the SPD's membership exploded during the 1890s, the Marxist intellectuals who had organized and designed the party lost control over its political direction. By 1914, the party was openly endorsing German militarism, and its place in the vanguard of revolutionary socialism became a bitter memory for those who remained captivated by Marx's vision. In the words of the Bolshevik Nikolai Bukharin, the "betrayal" of the German Social Democrats was "the greatest tragedy of our lives."[24]

The minutes of the Second Party Congress record a metamorphosis of the fundamental tensions arising in our theory of strategic choice into political conflicts about the organizational form of Russian socialism. The strategic dilemma of whether to pursue tangible concessions by compromising principles became an organizational dilemma of whether to build a hierarchical vanguard party or an open and democratic mass party. In the perceptive words of Rosa Luxemburg, the socialist movement had to tack precariously

> betwixt and between the two dangers by which it is constantly being threatened. One is the loss of its mass character, the other the abandonment of its goal. One is the danger of sinking back to the condition of a sect, the other the danger of becoming a movement of bourgeois social reform.[25]

As the subsequent history of the German and Russian socialists shows, the political implications of these organizational decisions sometimes extend far beyond the movement's immediate fortunes. In the rules of its political organizations, the radical movement creates a system of political authority that often defines its vision of the state when it comes to power. Certainly, Lenin's conception of the revolutionary vanguard party bore the essential marks of the Soviet state he created in 1917, including:

1. Rigid centralism, demanding absolute subordination of the constituent parts to the center.

---

[23] See Peter Gay, *The Dilemma of Democratic Socialism* (New York: Collier Books, 1962), pp. 110–20.

[24] Cited in Stephen F. Cohen, *Bukharin and the Bolshevik Revolution* (New York: Oxford University Press, 1980), p. 22.

[25] Luxemburg, "The Organizational Question of Social Democracy," p. 129.

2. Hostility to spontaneous, autonomous, democratic institutions (including bodies like the soviets, which were quickly emasculated by the "Soviet" regime).

3. A vision of the state/party as a transforming apparatus rather than the purely superstructural phenomenon described by Marx.[26]

As Stephen Cohen argues persuasively in his political biography of Bukharin, the Bolsheviks had nothing like a systematic plan of political and economic development in hand when they seized power in 1917.[27] Their reactions to the bewildering and chaotic circumstances surrounding them were conditioned largely by the years of political struggle that preceded their fortuitous coup. But these struggles were focused not so much against the old regime as against factional rivals within the socialist camp. Our model of strategy therefore becomes a powerful lens for perceiving the origins of the revolutionary Soviet state in the factional strife of the revisionist period. For Lenin and his opponents, centralism and democracy were not abstract philosophical problems in a theory of the just state. They were pressing problems of strategy. As Lenin explained long before he dreamed about organizing a revolutionary socialist government:

> Bureaucracy versus democracy is in fact centralism versus autonomism: it is the organizational principle of revolutionary Social Democracy as opposed to the organizational principle of opportunist Social Democracy.[28]

---

[26] For further discussion of this important discontinuity between Marx's and the Bolsheviks' political thought, see Cohen, *Bukharin*, Chapter 3, "The Politics of Civil War."

[27] Ibid.

[28] V. I. Lenin, *One Step Forward, Two Steps Back*, p. 424.

CHAPTER EIGHT

Repression

Repression and Mobilization

IN THIS chapter, we shall consider the impact of repression on recruiting and strategy in dissident movements. Understanding the strategic implications of repression requires first that we explain why people make personal sacrifices for dissident causes. In other words, we need an explicit model of the cost-benefit calculations that motivate individuals to join demonstrations when it appears that participating in them will be dangerous and unpleasant. Thus far, we have assumed that individuals simply compare the movement's demand to the government's policy in deciding whether or not to take to the streets. Let us continue to assume that this comparison defines the potential benefit of participation for prospective recruits. It then remains to specify the calculation of costs associated with repression.

Although our empirical knowledge of these matters is scanty and inconclusive, it appears that repression can be a double-edged sword, sometimes deterring and intimidating and sometimes producing a political backlash that enhances the movement's support. It should be clear that bringing such a double-edged mechanism into our theory will enormously complicate matters and will cloud our conclusions with a large measure of indeterminacy. Rather than tackling these difficulties at the outset, however, it is advantageous to set them aside for a time. Above all, we want at this stage to develop a systematic, step-by-step understanding of the logical connection between the micro-level effects of repression on individual behavior and the ultimate macro-level impact on the movement's choice of strategy. It is much easier to appreciate the big picture here if we refrain from introducing all sorts of complications into the cost-benefit model of individual recruiting. Let us therefore begin by considering only the net impact of repression (deterrent effect net backlash effect), and by assuming that impact to be negative (or costly to the individual). Later (in the next chapter) we shall explicitly disaggregate the net impact of repression into separate components representing the deterrent and backlash effects. The important point to notice is that the methods of reasoning developed in this chapter will not change when we adopt a more elaborate recruiting model. We shall simply tally up the net impact of repression component by component and then proceed as we do here.

To sum up briefly, then, our plan of attack in this chapter will be to keep the number of variables in the recruiting model to a minimum by subsuming all of the separate effects of repression into a single measure that describes their net impact. We shall, for the time being, rely on a highly schematic cost-benefit model that includes only two considerations for the potential recruit: the benefit derived from moving the government's existing policy to the movement's demand and the net costs of repression.

Even in this simple model, an important problem remains to be solved. How shall we calculate the relative value to the individual of changes in policy and avoiding repression? When can it be said that the costs outweigh the benefits, if such different experiences are being compared? Without a common currency in which to express the values of policies along the political spectrum and the unpleasantness of repression, our cost-benefit model won't be very helpful.

This problem is not as intractable as it might appear, but it does require that we reformulate the purely ordinal model of political preferences presented in Chapter 2. Heretofore, we have considered only demonstrations in which participation is costless, and it has been sufficient to assume that potential recruits simply *rank* alternative policies in order of preference. A simple ordinal ranking based on distance from the individual's ideal point told us in every case whether or not the radicals' demand was preferred to the government's policy and provided all the information the ideological model of recruiting required. Now, however, we need a more detailed description of political preferences that tells us *by how much* one policy is preferred to another.

Let us suppose that each person's political preferences can be represented by a cardinal utility function that enables us to compare meaningfully differences in the magnitude of the utility numbers assigned to policies. More specifically, let the utility scale be of the interval type— which is to say, unique up to a positive linear transformation. Thus, if $U(P)$ is an admissible utility function defined over the ideological spectrum, so too is $(a \cdot U(P) + b)$ where $a > 0$. Like the familiar temperature scales such a utility function admits two degrees of freedom. Once utility values are assigned (arbitrarily) to two benchmark policies, the utilities for all the other positions along the ideological spectrum are determined. With such scales, it makes no sense to say that one outcome is X times more favorable than another because there is no fixed zero point under all the admissible transformations of the utility numbers. Differences in the utility numbers can be compared, however, just as differences in temperature can. (With an interval scale, ratios of differences are preserved under admissible transformations.)[1]

Figure 8.1 shows the graphs of two such utility functions, each conforming to the assumption of single-peakedness and obeying the additional constraint of symmetry as well.[2] Thus, policies continue to be ranked in order of preference according to their distance from the ideal point. Note that a utility value of one is assigned to each person's ideal point, while the utilities of less favorable policies go to zero as they approach some benchmark located far away from the most preferred position. The two functions have similar shapes but differ in spread. In each case the utility function is fairly flat in the immediate neighborhood of the ideal point, indicating that the individual is relatively insensitive to small departures from the ideal state of affairs. Leaving this neighborhood produces a more rapid decline in satisfaction, at least for a time. We can imagine a liberal who does not discriminate too finely among various liberal shadings, but who immediately experiences distress when the government adopts policies on the radical left or the conservative right. Eventually, however, the rate of decay abates again as the individual becomes relatively indiscriminate among policies in the (psychologically) remote reaches of the ideological spectrum. The liberal, for example, might not find much to choose between ultraconservative and ultra-ultraconservative policies, but presumably would express a preference for the ultraconservative if pressed to make a choice.

---

[1] For a discussion of meaningful statements under various types of scale, see Fred Roberts, *Discrete Mathematical Models* (Englewood Cliffs, N.J.: Prentice-Hall, 1976).

[2] The restriction that utility functions be symmetrical is largely adopted for convenience. In any large population, surely some people's preferences are skewed to the left and some to the right. Unless skewness is systematically related to ideological position, however, there is little harm in ignoring it.

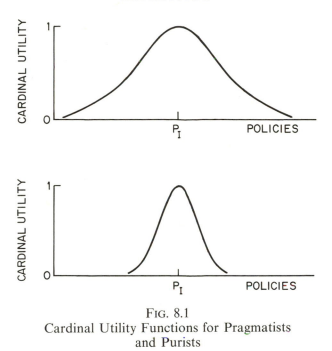

FIG. 8.1
Cardinal Utility Functions for Pragmatists
and Purists

While the utility functions in Figure 8.1 share the same general form and a common location over the ideological spectrum, they are notably different in spread. This feature captures the now familiar distinction between the broad-minded pragmatist and the doctrinaire purist. As we shall see, this distinction becomes important as soon as political activism becomes a dangerous undertaking.

Von Neumann and Morgenstern have developed one procedure by which such a utility function might be constructed. We begin by selecting two positions along the political spectrum as benchmarks and assigning to them utility values of one and zero respectively. Here we will assign a utility value of one to the individual's ideal point. For the other benchmark, we can select a policy in the far reaches of the political spectrum, well beyond the interval being contested by the movement and the government.[3] The utility values of other policies can now be determined by a simple lottery procedure.

---

[3] Recall that in Chapters 4 and 6, we had occasion to use the government's ideal point as a benchmark when we analyzed the preferences of the dissident leaders. The choice of benchmark is not of great moment, though some benchmarks can be more useful than others in particular problems.

Let's call the individual's ideal point P_I, the second benchmark P_B, and the intermediate policy whose utility we want to determine P_X. We ask the individual to choose between the certainty of the policy P_X, or a lottery with P_I and P_B as possible outcomes. Let the probability of winning P_I be p and the probability of the dreadful policy P_B be $(1 - p)$. When the probability p approaches one, the individual will presumably prefer the lottery option to the certainty of having P_X, since the likelihood is great that he will achieve his ideal policy. As p approaches zero, however, the lottery option will become the less attractive alternative. If we allow the probability mixture in the lottery to vary continuously between these extremes, there will be some particular value of p at which the individual becomes indifferent between the two options. Suppose this transitional value is $\frac{1}{4}$. Then $\frac{1}{4}$ becomes the utility of P_X.

The same procedure can be used to measure the individual's relative liking for all the policies that are less extreme than P_B. For those policies more attractive than P_X that lie closer to P_I, indifference between the two options will occur at higher values of p. The utilities of policies very close to P_I will approach one, for example, because the individual will prefer the certainty of an already attractive policy to the lottery option unless the probability of winning P_I is very high indeed. Conversely, the utilities of less attractive policies will approach zero as they diverge from P_I.

We can also use this procedure to measure the disutility of various forms of repression. We simply ask the individual to choose between a lottery whose possible outcomes are again P_I and P_B, and the certainty of experiencing some kind of repression, say six months in jail. Now, however, we shall let the probability of the dreadful policy P_B be p, and the probability of winning the ideal policy be $(1 - p)$. Here again, the probability mixture that produces indifference between the lottery and certainty options will define the disutility of the particular form of repression.

Suppose we want to evaluate the disutility of a minimal amount of repression, say a week in jail. If the probability of winding up with the dreadful policy P_B is at all substantial, the individual will clearly prefer the certainty of spending a short time behind bars. He will be indifferent between the two options only when p is very low, and the disutility of this form of repression will therefore be close to zero. What happens, however, when the repression option is ten years in jail? The individual will then prefer the lottery until the value of p gets quite large, and the disutility of repression will be much higher than before.[4]

The Von Neumann-Morgenstern approach allows us to measure the relative unpleasantness of each form of repression on the same (dis)utility scale we use for describing political preferences. Let us assume finally that the total utility derived from displacing the government's policy and experiencing repression can be partitioned into additively separable components. This is an abstract way of saying that the satisfactions and miseries derived from joining protests are in a certain sense independent. On one hand, the painfulness of a particular form of repression should not vary with the demands and policies being contested in the streets. And, since the policies of the government are essentially public goods, bearing the private costs of repression does not, in many cases, prevent the individual protester from enjoying the fruits of his efforts. Of course, people die for political causes, and we do not want to insist too adamantly that successful protests can be enjoyed from beyond the grave. Instead, we endorse the assumption of independence as a useful point of departure—not as the final word.

The Recruiting Function under Repression

A PIVOTAL element in our theory of strategy is the recruiting function. This function describes formally the process by which a movement recruits people into its demonstrations and establishes the crucial connection between the radicals' choice of demands and the level of disruption in the streets. In order to analyze the strategic implications of repression, we must now generalize the simple model of ideological recruiting to account for the hazards of protesting as well as its rewards.

We can describe the ideological recruiting process in a repressive society by a real valued function of four variables—the prevailing policy of the regime, P_R; the demand lodged against P_R by the dissidents' strategy, P_D; the level of repression inflicted upon the protesters, R; and the ideal policy of the potential recruit, P_I. The recruiting function assigns to individuals at every location across the political

---

[4] For a more complete discussion of this procedure see R. D. Luce and H. Raiffa, "Utility Theory," *Games and Decisions* (New York: John Wiley, 1957).

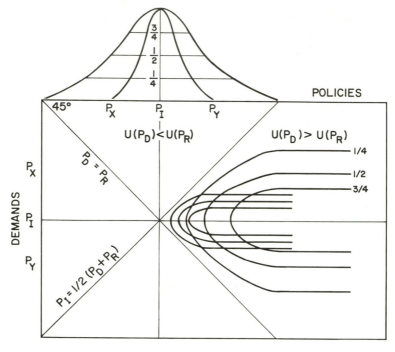

FIG. 8.2
Attractive Sets

spectrum the conditional probability of participation given the demand lodged, the policy being protested against, and the level of repression. Presumably, each person must feel that the political stakes are sufficiently important in order to accept the risks in the streets. Accordingly, we define the probability function as follows:

$$\Pr(\text{Participation}\,|\,P_D, P_R, R, P_I)$$

$$= \begin{cases} 1 & \text{if } [U(P_D) - U(P_R)] - C(R) > 0 \\ 0 & \text{otherwise} \end{cases}$$

In other words, the difference in utility between the radicals' demand and the government's policy (the potential political gain) must exceed the net costs of repression, $C(R)$, if protesting is to seem worthwhile. This apparently simple model provides the tools we need to ascertain the main effects of repression on individual behavior.

Figure 8.2 illustrates these effects geometrically. It takes the original utility functions in Figure 8.1 and translates them into a form that defines explicitly the potential political gain $[U(P_D) - U(P_R)]$ of all possible demonstrations from the point of view of our political archetypes, the pragmatist and the purist. The two axes in the diagram both represent the political spectrum; the horizontal axis denoting policies available to the regime, and the vertical axis describing potential dissident demands. Resting over the horizontal axis are the cardinal utility functions from Figure 8.1, which measure the political preferences of a pragmatist and purist who share the common ideal point, P_I.

The points in the plane below collectively represent every possible demonstration, each as an ordered pair of the form (P_R, P_D). Keep in mind that we are describing policies being demonstrated against, not the government's concessions to radical demands. The plane is partitioned into several regions, only one of which invites careful attention. All of the demonstrations lying below the 45° bisector lodge demands that fall to the right of the government's position on the horizontal axis. For leftist movements, these points can be disregarded (without any loss of generality). The area above the 45° line contains leftist demonstrations. This region is itself partitioned into two pieces by the perpendicular ray that intersects the bisector at the point (P_I, P_I). This ray describes demonstrations where the policy P_I happens to lie exactly halfway between the radicals' demand and the regime's policy. Because of the symmetry of their utility functions, both the pragmatist and the purist will regard these protests with indifference. On the left of this ray, we have protests in which the movement's demand lies farther from our potential recruits' ideal point, P_I, than the prevailing policy of the government does. (This area is labeled $U(P_D) < U(P_R)$.) Successful demonstrations in this subset of the plane leave people who aspire to P_I worse off, and therefore without any incentive to participate in them.

There remain, finally, the demonstrations on the right of the perpendicular ray whose demands are preferable to the government's policy from the perspective of the individuals at P_I. Here our friends become potential activists in a leftist movement, remembering, however, that the appeal of demonstrations in this region varies considerably. In some cases, the demand is significantly more attractive than the government's position, while in others it is only barely so. To convey a more precise, quantitative impression of how each individual will evaluate these protests, we have constructed two sets of indifference curves—the "fatter" set belonging to the pragmatist and the tighter set belonging to the purist. Each set includes three representative curves, which connect demonstrations whose potential political gain, $[U(P_D) - U(P_R)]$, equals $\frac{1}{4}$, $\frac{1}{2}$, and $\frac{3}{4}$ respectively. Thus, the middle curve in each set joins all the demonstrations whose demands are preferable to the government's policy by a difference of $\frac{1}{2}$ on the individual's utility scale. Taken together, the indifference curves describe how each individual ranks in order of preference those leftist demonstrations whose potential gain is positive. They also tell us exactly how the political activities of these two people will be curtailed as repression becomes more severe.

Attractive Sets and Their Properties

AN IMPORTANT feature of Figure 8.2 is that the demonstrations lying inside each indifference curve are more attractive than those on the curve itself, while demonstrations lying outside the curve are less attractive. According to our recruiting model, prospective recruits will accept the hardships of repression only when the potential benefit of the radicals' protest outweighs them. If the brand of repression meted out by the regime yields a value of $\frac{1}{2}$ on the individual's disutility scale, he will be willing to join *only* those demonstrations that lie inside the indifference curve labeled $\frac{1}{2}$ (where the potential political gain exceeds this value). If the disutility of repression increases to $\frac{3}{4}$, the individual's participation will be limited even further to those demonstrations lying inside the curve labeled $\frac{3}{4}$, and so on. In every case, the set of attractive demonstrations associated with a particular level of repression is equivalent to the interior of the corresponding indifference curve. Thus, by studying how the indifference curves collapse as we move to higher numerical levels of potential gain, we learn at the same time which political activity will be deterred by increasing levels of repression. Notice that when the disutility of repression equals zero, both the pragmatist and purist will join all of the demonstrations in the region labeled $U(P_D) > U(P_R)$. Thus, the intensity of individual preferences only becomes a relevant political consideration when participation is costly, and all of our earlier analysis can be subsumed under the more general recruiting model as a special case where the net costs of repression equal zero.

These preliminaries aside, let's now study the structure of our two indifference maps more carefully. Suppose first that the government holds its repression constant at a level whose disutility equals $\frac{1}{4}$. In this case, the pragmatist and purist will only be motivated to join protests that lie inside the outermost of the horseshoe-shaped indifference curves. Thus, only the demands that fall in the interval between the two legs of the horseshoes will mobilize their support against each particular policy. What happens, then, as the government moves its policy from a position far to the right toward these individuals' ideal point, P_I? Initially, both of them will support demands at some distance from their ideal policy. As the government converges toward their preferred position, however, the range of attractive demands becomes narrower. The more appealing official policy becomes, the fussier people get about the causes they support. The span of attractive demands collapses altogether at the apex of the horseshoe, in each case *before* the regime actually adopts the policy P_I. In other words, no demand will mobilize either the pragmatist or the purist when the government's policy is sufficiently close to ideal and the costs of repression are positive. Of course, dissent by the pragmatist is stifled sooner than dissent by the purist.

Next let's explore the consequences of escalating repression by studying how the attractive sets shrink as protesting becomes more perilous. In fact, the sets collapse in four distinct respects as shown in Figure 8.3. Each individual becomes less willing:

1. To oppose policies close to P_I

2. To support demands far from P_I

3. To support demonstrations that demand small changes

4. To support demonstrations when P_I lies close to the middle ground between the two sides

As repression becomes more intense, the only demonstrations that seem worthwhile press demands in a narrow interval around P_I against policies increasingly farther to the right.

Finally, it is interesting to compare the behavior of the pragmatist and the purist in a repressive environment. At each level of disutility, the attractive set of the purist spans a narrower range of demands than that of the pragmatist, but it extends closer to their common ideal point. The purist is therefore more tenacious in opposing policies that diverge only slightly from P_I but more reluctant to support demands that are less than ideal. The two political types also differ markedly

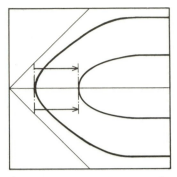

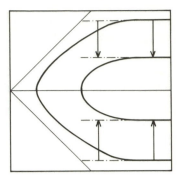

1) Less opposition to policies near the ideal point.

2) Less support for demands that diverge from the ideal.

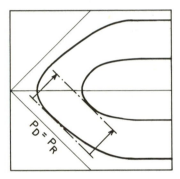

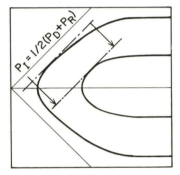

3) Less support for demonstrations that demand small changes.

4) Less support for demonstrations when the ideal point lies near the middle ground.

FIG. 8.3
The Effects of Escalating Repression

in their reactions to changes in the level of repression. This attribute is measured by how much the attractive sets shrink as repression becomes more intense. The political behavior of the purist is largely unaffected by costlier participation, while the pragmatist's political activities are fairly drastically curtailed.

The Span of Support

FIGURE 8.2 summarizes the micro-level impact of repression on the political activities of two particular individuals who share a common ideal point. The macrostrategic implications of repression depend, however, on how the total number of people joining demonstrations will be affected by punitive measures of the regime. Recall the steps by which we calculated the relative effectiveness of strategies in Chapter 3. In each case, the basic problem was to determine the number of people who would be mobilized by the strategy against every policy the government might adopt. This information defined a *mobilization curve*, which, when superimposed on the government's responsiveness map, told us exactly what concession the strategy would produce. When we allowed the movement's schedule of demands to vary, the mobilization curves changed, and so too did the policy conceded.

The ultimate objective in the analysis of recruiting, then, is to establish the mobilization curves of dissident strategies. Let's review more carefully the steps in their construction. First, the strategy itself assigns particular demands to all of the policies available to the regime. Whatever position the government adopts, the movement's strategy provides the demand to be lodged against it. The question then is how much support does each of these protests attract. To find out, we first determine the range of the ideological spectrum that will be mobilized (the span of support), and then add up the number of people whose ideal points lie inside the span (using the cumulative distribution that describes how the underlying population is arrayed politically). All of this was very easy when we assumed that participation was costless. In that case, the span of support included everyone to the left of the point halfway between demand and policy, and the cumulative distribution told us directly how many people maintained ideal policies inside the span.

It should be clear that deriving mobilization curves will become a much more difficult undertaking in a repressive society. The basic problem is that we no longer have a simple and definite rule for calculating spans of support, because it is no longer true that everyone on the left of the familiar halfway point will be mobilized in each demonstration. Unfortunately, it's not at all clear from the definition of our new recruiting model just what the spans of support will be when repression becomes a consideration for potential recruits. Such uncertainty is unfortunate, because it arises at a fundamental link in the chain of reasoning that connects inferences about individual behavior to inferences about strategic choice. If we don't know how to determine *exactly* where the boundaries of the spans of support lie, we won't be able to determine mobilization curves, and without mobilization curves, we can't say what each strategy will accomplish. A rigorous analysis of how repression affects the relative effectiveness of strategies therefore requires that we develop an explicit procedure for calculating spans of support. The key to the problem, as we shall see in a moment, is understanding the logical relationship between the structure of individual preferences and the boundaries of these spans.

Our problem can become overwhelmingly complicated if we try to accommodate every conceivable pattern of individual preference. To keep things manageable, then, let us consider a comparatively simple society whose population includes only two kinds of people—pragmatists and purists. We suppose that people of both types adopt ideal policies across the entire political spectrum, but that within each category the intensity of preference remains constant. In other words, people of the same type share identical utility functions except for location over the ideological spectrum. Furthermore, we shall assume that everyone weighs the various forms of repression identically with respect to the utility scale measuring political preferences.[5]

Adopting these constraints allows us to reanalyze Figure 8.2 from the aggregate perspective of the political strategist. The question is no longer what set of demonstrations will an individual support, but rather what set of individuals will support particular demonstrations. Figure 8.4 presents a geometrical reinterpretation of Figure 8.2 that answers this question. The basic idea behind the geometrical procedure is simple. Since everyone's utility function has one of two shapes, the span of support for a particular demonstration can be ascertained simply by shifting the policy axis under the two prototype utility functions. Doing so allows us to examine the attractiveness of the demonstration from every conceivable ideological perspective.

Perhaps the easiest way to understand the approach is by exploring a concrete example. Since our analysis proceeds by translating the axes in Figure 8.2, let's fix our political bearings more precisely by labeling policies with numbers (not to be confused with utilities) rather than letters. Call the objective of the dissident movement 100 and the regime's ideal point 0. Now suppose the radicals are pressing a sincere demand and the government is holding fast to its ideal policy. Figure

---

[5] A more complicated model might disaggregate the population even further according to its tolerance for repression. Then we might have cowards and adventurers, as well as pragmatists and purists, in our theory.

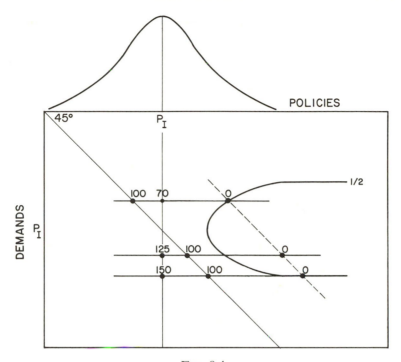

FIG. 8.4
Calculating Spans of Support

8.4 shows how to calculate the span of support for the particular demonstration (0, 100) when the level of repression has a value of $\frac{1}{2}$ on
the disutility scale. The diagram shows a $\frac{1}{2}$-level indifference curve that
defines the set of attractive demonstrations for an individual (here a
pragmatist) whose utility function is centered over the arbitrary ideal
point, P_I. Since the 45° bisector establishes the relationship between
the two coordinate axes ($P_D = P_R$ along this line), the scales of both
axes are fully defined as soon as the particular value of P_I is specified.

Three scales appear in the center of Figure 8.4, representing individuals of different ideological persuasions. (Admittedly, this is a rather
unorthodox way of labeling axes.) Consider the middle one first. This
scale defines the outlook of a person whose ideal policy, 125, lies
somewhat to the left of the movement's demand. Note that the scale
reads 125 directly beneath the peak of the utility function. The scale
is positioned in the plane below so that the policy demanded by the
radicals, 100, lies exactly on the 45° bisector. Relative to the vertical

(demands) axis, then, the scale is located at 100. In this position, it tells us directly whether or not this individual will join the demonstration in question. The key thing to notice is how the point on the scale representing the regime's policy (0) really occupies the point (0, 100) in the two-dimensional space. Since this point lies inside the attractive set, this person takes to the streets.

To find the full range of support for the demonstration (0, 100), we slide the scale along the bisector, anchoring the dissidents' demand to it as we go. There is nothing mysterious happening here. As the position of the policy scale changes in relation to the prototype utility function, we are simply adopting the perspective of individuals with different ideal points. Again, the important geometrical idea is that the demonstration enlists support as long as the government's policy (0) remains inside the attractive set. The remaining scales in Figure 8.4 fix the zero point exactly on the boundaries of the attractive set and thereby establish the ideological limits of support for this particular protest. The upper scale defines the rightward boundary of the span of support at the ideal policy $P_I = 70$. The lower scale locates the leftward limit at the policy $P_I = 150$. Thus, every pragmatist whose ideal point lies between 70 and 150 will join the demonstration (0, 100) when the disutility of repression equals $\frac{1}{2}$. Clearly, we can repeat this procedure to calculate the span of support for any demonstration, at any level of repression, among pragmatists and purists alike. In Figure 8.4, then, we have a geometrical representation of the logical relationship between individual preferences and spans of support.

A Digression on the Continuity of the Radicals' Support

AN IMPORTANT feature of our example is that the target of the radicals' protest (the policy labeled 0) remains continuously inside the attractive set as the policy scale slides along the bisector from the upper to the lower position. The political importance of this geometric fact is that everyone inside the span of support finds the protest attractive. In other words, the demonstration mobilizes support from a continuous interval along the ideological spectrum. This observation raises the general question of whether the span of support for every demonstration in a repressive political climate must be continuous.

A sufficient condition to assure continuity is that the attractive sets associated with each level of repression be convex. Geometrically, a set is convex if, and only if, all the points on a line segment connecting two points in the set also belong to the set. In Figure 8.2, all of the horseshoe-shaped indifference contours define convex attractive sets. Thus, when we apply the method of Figure 8.4, the broken line segment connecting the two boundary points on the indifference contour lies completely inside the attractive set. Clearly, the span of support for every protest, at every level of repression, will be defined by a similar line segment running parallel to the 45° bisector. The spans of support for every demonstration in this society will therefore be continuous.

It is not true, however, that every single-peaked (quasi-concave) utility function defines convex attractive sets. The continuity of the radicals' support therefore cannot be taken for granted. This problem is a bit vexing for two reasons. First, the construction of mobilization curves becomes vastly more complicated when the movement draws its support from several disconnected ideological neighborhoods rather than from a single continuous interval. Second, while it is easy enough to find particular single-peaked utility functions that generate non-convex attractive sets, it is difficult to describe in general when non-convexities will arise. In the analysis that follows, we shall simply assume that the political preferences of our hypothetical pragmatists and purists define attractive sets that are convex. While this assumption guarantees that spans of support for every demonstration will be continuous, it is not altogether clear what constraints must be imposed on individual preferences to insure that the assumption holds.

Spans of Support and Their Properties

THE GEOMETRIC reasoning of Figure 8.4 can be applied to any demonstration for any level of repression. It therefore provides the analytical machinery we need to calculate the span of support (not amount, of course) for any strategy the dissidents might pursue. Figure 8.5 has been constructed by applying this machinery to the pair of utility functions considered above. We have two sets of curves, one for purists, the other for pragmatists, which define *exactly* how the span of support for an arbitrary demand ($P_D = 100$) will vary with the government's policy and its repressiveness. In both diagrams, the vertical axis represents the government's position along the policy spectrum and the horizontal axis describes the ideal policies of the movement's potential recruits. Each curve defines the span of the political spectrum that the

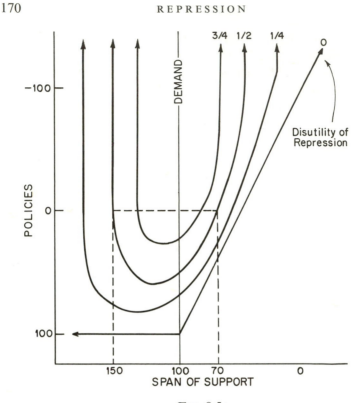

FIG. 8.5A
Ideological Recruiting under Repression
(Pragmatists)

movement can mobilize with its demand against every policy of the
regime. Recalling our earlier example, we see that when the government adopts the policy 0, and the disutility of repression equals $\frac{1}{2}$, the
demand 100 mobilizes all the pragmatists whose ideal policies lie between 150 and 70. Each curve represents a fixed level of repression, the
inner curves arising from more severe forms. We are interested, of
course, in the shapes of the curves, while the scales are used simply
for reference. Were the dissidents to adopt another demand, note that
the only change would be a translation of the axes. The diagram is
therefore a general representation of the process of ideological recruiting in a repressive society.

Figure 8.5 is rich in strategic implications, some quite immediate
and others more remote. In order to learn how these diagrams are
interpreted and to appreciate their relevance to important historical

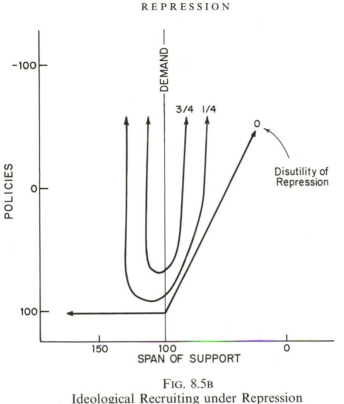

FIG. 8.5B
Ideological Recruiting under Repression
(Purists)

problems, let us consider the political strategy of revolution that Lenin
developed during the period between 1898 and 1905. Lenin's political
thought is often interpreted as an adaptation of Marxism to the harshly
repressive climate of tsarist Russia. As we shall discover, many of the
pivotal arguments in his master plan for a vanguard proletarian party
rest directly on reasoning about repression that is captured by our
graphs.

Repression and Lenin's Revolutionary Strategy

BECAUSE it departed so radically from the kind of society Marx portrayed as the natural setting for a socialist revolution, tsarist Russia
confronted revolutionary socialists with an acute strategic crisis. Capitalist development was barely under way at the turn of the century,
the proletariat, though rapidly growing, was still small and politically

immature, and the regime was anything but a liberal, democratic, bourgeois republic. The keystone of Lenin's revolutionary plan was a tightly-knit vanguard party of the proletariat. His organizational design for the party was partially motivated by the threat of "opportunist" intrusions, but its rationale, in fact, went much deeper. Lenin's strategic calculations were also a natural response by a radical and politically isolated movement to a violently repressive climate. As our model will help explain, his reasoning about repression produced a new vision of the proletarian revolution—a vision that decisively rejected the classical Marxian formulae and called into question the deepest articles of the Marxian faith, including the doctrine of historical inevitability.

Spans of Support under Escalating Repression

WE CAN BEGIN to appreciate how repression enters the strategic calculus by comparing the curves in Figure 8.5 that represent positive levels of repression to the single curve describing costless participation. When repression is absent, there is no leftward limit on a demand's appeal. Thus, the curve labeled 0 simply identifies the rightward boundary of the span of support at the position halfway between demand and policy. The strikingly different appearance of the other curves results mainly from the fact that spans of support are bounded on *both* sides of the movement's demand when demonstrating carries a price. People on the movement's left naturally prefer its demand to the government's position, but not necessarily by enough to undergo hardships on its behalf. Repression therefore imposes a constraint on the impulse to moderate unsuccessful demands by undermining the radicals' ability to attract new support on the right without sacrificing old support on the left.

Naturally, this constraint is not especially relevant for groups like the Bolsheviks who occupy the leftward fringes of the ideological spectrum. Far more important from their perspective is the rightward reach of their demand's appeal. But here, too, significant new constraints arise in a repressive environment. On one hand, the support curves collapse around the movement's demand as repression intensifies. The spans of support become narrower on both the right and the left as the political climate grows harsher. Another change with far-reaching strategic implications involves the ideological extension of the radicals' appeal as the regime drifts into extremism. In a costless world, the span supporting a fixed demand grows continuously wider as the government moves to the right. (The familiar halfway point trails relentlessly after the regime's position.) This is decidedly not the case, however, in a repressive atmosphere. As the policies of a repressive regime recede from the movement's demand, the support curves approach a maximal width.[6] Once the maximum is attained (or nearly so), any further radicalization of the regime's policy adds (virtually) nothing to the movement's appeal.

If we accept this reasoning, serious complications arise in a theory of revolution like Marx's in which the drive to the revolutionary threshold depends on historical forces that propel the old regime to politically untenable extremes. In the absence of repression, any demand can mobilize demonstrations that exceed the threshold of insurrection, providing the government's policy becomes sufficiently excessive. In a repressive climate, however, no guarantees exist. When regimes command a formidable repressive capacity, the historical necessity of political excesses on their part no longer implies the historical inevitability of their revolutionary demise. A movement with revolutionary ambitions simply cannot depend on rallying a broad political coalition around its revolutionary slogans—no matter how removed the regime may be from the political mainstream. In order to mount a successful uprising under its own political banner, the radical movement must draw the requisite forces from its own ideological neighborhood. Moreover, the heavier the yoke of repression, the narrower the neighborhood becomes. Mounting an ideologically "sincere" insurrection therefore becomes far more problematical than a theory that ignores repression might suggest.

Lenin's Caveat and Revolutionary Agitation

As THE TSARIST regime entered the twentieth century, Lenin was painfully aware that committed adherents of socialism were a rare breed among the Russian proletariat. Nor did he doubt that the tsar's repression curtailed support for the Social Democrats, even among its friends in the working class. Deploring the amateurism of his party's

---

[6] This conclusion follows from the idea that people become essentially indifferent among policies that lie far away from their ideal point (purists sooner than pragmatists). This idea is reflected in the shape of our prototype utility functions.

organizers, Lenin dolefully admitted in *What Is To Be Done?* that

> the workers begin to lose faith in the intellectuals and to avoid them; the
> intellectuals, they say, are much too careless and cause police raids.[7]

The question, then, was how to achieve a socialist revolution when the number of genuine socialists was negligible and the appeal of the socialist program was attenuated by brutal repression.

The dilemma was particularly acute in light of Lenin's well-known caveat about the second crucial dynamic in the Marxian revolutionary scenario—the radicalization of the masses as capitalism matures. Where Marx assumed that the swelling of the proletariat would spontaneously create a genuinely revolutionary army, Lenin argued that "the working class, exclusively by its own effort, is able to develop only a trade union consciousness."[8] Hardly the stuff of revolution, he hastened to add, trade unionism meant "ideological enslavement" to the bourgeoisie.

Taken in concert with the constraints implied by repression, Lenin's caveat deprived Marx's historical reasoning of its revolutionary vitality. No longer could the forces of history be depended upon to guarantee the revolutionary ascendancy of the proletariat, either by driving the regime to one extreme or the population to the other. However reluctant he may have been to put it in so many words, this was the logical implication of Lenin's political reasoning and the basis of his political strategy.

The Leninist Organization

THESE considerations defined the two central objectives of Lenin's political strategy against tsarism. The first was to radicalize the proletarian base by undertaking a comprehensive program of political agitation and propaganda among the workers. The second was to cast off the yoke of repression or at least to neutralize its evil effects. Both endeavors were responses to the challenge of mounting an insurrection in a repressive society. The first sought directly to increase the number of people inside the Social Democrats' span of active support. The second sought to extend that span across a broader range of the political spectrum (and thus to make the first task easier).

---

[7] V. I. Lenin, *Selected Works*, Vol. 1: *What is To Be Done?* (New York: International Publishers, 1967), p. 181.

[8] Ibid., p. 122.

The cornerstone of Lenin's strategy for realizing these goals was a tightly drawn and rigorously centralized political organization, built around an ideologically cohesive core of professional revolutionaries. If "the character of any organization is naturally and inevitably determined by the content of its activity," as Lenin suggests in *What Is To Be Done?*,[9] the character of his organization was determined by a thorough awareness of the political imperatives in a police state.

To appreciate more fully how Lenin adapted his revolutionary organization to the rigors of a repressive climate, we need to explore another facet of Figure 8.5. The intensity of individual preferences is politically irrelevant when dissent is tolerated by state and society (the zero-cost curve is identical for pragmatists and purists alike), but the distinction between the two political types becomes highly relevant when dissident activity carries a price. Political mobilization among pragmatists and purists follows markedly different patterns when joining a radical movement is dangerous, and it is upon these differences that Lenin's organizational blueprint rests.

One striking contrast between the two political types is the relative narrowness of the ideological neighborhood from which purists are mobilized, regardless of the level of repression. Because they are highly sensitive to deviations from their political ideals, the purists who rally behind a particular demand are more ideologically cohesive than the pragmatists. The spans of support for the latter group extend more broadly across the political spectrum, embracing a politically more diverse universe.

The purists tend also to be more intensely committed to the causes they support, in several distinct senses. When repression escalates, for example, the spans of support for the purists contract less violently than those of the pragmatists, providing a more stable foundation upon which to build a strategy of disruption. The purists are similarly less vulnerable to immobilization by partial concessions. While the pragmatists may retire from the battlefield as soon as the regime moderates its position even slightly, the purists are inclined to resist a broader range of policies extending closer to their movement's ultimate objective (i.e. they are more stubborn). And finally, the purists are far less willing to transfer their support from sincere demands to demands outside the immediate neighborhood of their ideal points.

[9] Ibid., p. 179.

These attributes made the purists natural candidates to carry out the arduous political tasks Lenin envisioned for his revolutionary party. "We must train people who will devote the whole of their lives, not only their spare evenings to the revolution," he wrote.[10] Only the leadership of a "compact core of the most reliable, experienced, and hardened workers"[11] could, in his estimation, resolve the political dilemma facing revolutionary socialism in tsarist Russia.

Building the Base

THE MOST urgent priority on Lenin's political agenda was imbuing the proletariat with a genuinely Marxist perception of society and politics. "We must take up actively the political education of the working class and the development of its political consciousness," he insisted.[12] "The workers [are] not, and [can] not be, conscious of the irreconcilable antagonism of their interests to the whole of the modern political and social system. Theirs is not yet a Social-Democratic consciousness."[13] By a system of reckoning very much of the kind in Figure 8.5, Lenin concluded that the task of educating the masses could never be left to a broad-based and open party without inviting disastrous consequences. The political education of the proletariat demanded, above all, absolute ideological coherence and unswerving devotion to principles—attributes that could only be found in the movement's purist core.

> Any subservience to the spontaneity of the mass movement, any degrading of Social-Democratic politics to the level of trade-unionist politics mean preparing the ground for converting the working-class movement into an instrument of bourgeois democracy.[14]

> If [a strong organization of tried revolutionaries] existed, one built on a firm theoretical foundation and possessing a Social-Democratic organ, we should have no reason to fear that the movement might be diverted from its path by the numerous "outside" elements that are attracted to it.[15]

> The broader the popular mass drawn spontaneously into the struggle, which forms the basis of the movement and participates in it, the more urgent the need for a ... [stable organization of leaders maintaining con-

---

[10] V. I. Lenin, *Selected Works*, Vol. 1: "The Urgent Tasks of Our Movement," p. 95.
[11] V. I. Lenin, *What Is To Be Done?*, p. 195.
[12] Ibid., p. 144.   [13] Ibid., p. 122.   [14] Ibid., p. 176.   [15] Ibid., p. 204.

tinuity], and the more solid this organization must be—for it is much easier for all sorts of demagogues to side-track the more backward sections of the masses.[16]

Thus, only the ideologically most reliable elements could be admitted to the revolutionary vanguard party, because the fate of the socialist revolution depended on the fundamental reorientation of the workers' consciousness. This was not work for "amateurs" and "windbags." It required "genuine Social Democrats."

Negating Repression

THE SECOND objective of Lenin's political program was to combat the debilitating effects of repression. Perhaps this imperative, even more than ideological coherence, accounted for the compact and centralized structure of his revolutionary organization. Again exploiting the special attributes of the purist core, Lenin devised an ingenious plan to isolate both the leading elements in his movement and the broader masses from the disruptive harassment of the tsar's political police.

To those who argued that the best defense against repression was the safety of numbers, Lenin retorted that "it is far more difficult to unearth a dozen wise men than a hundred fools."[17] Far from protecting the movement from disruption by the police, a broad-based organization only made their work easier. "If we begin with a broad workers' organization which is supposedly most 'accessible' to the masses (but which is actually most accessible to the gendarmes and makes revolutionaries most accessible to the police) ... we shall remain scattered and our forces ... constantly broken up."[18] The question, then, was how to reconcile "the contradiction between the need for a large membership and the need for strictly secret methods."[19]

The essence of Lenin's plan was to partition the movement into a two-tiered organizational structure. The most dangerous, and by necessity secret, facets of the movement's work ("the drawing up of leaflets, the working out of plans, the publication of an illegal newspaper") were to be left in the hands of the organization of professional revolutionaries. "Such an organization must perforce not be very extensive and must be as secret as possible.... It must consist first and foremost of people who make revolutionary activity their profession."[20]

[16] Ibid., p. 200.   [17] Ibid., p. 199.   [18] Ibid., p. 196.
[19] Ibid., p. 191.   [20] Ibid., pp. 189–190.

The "organization of the workers," on the other hand, "must be as broad as possible, and . . . as public as conditions allow. . . . We must have such circles, trade unions, and organizations everywhere in as large a number as possible and with the widest variety of functions; but it would be absurb and harmful to confound them with the organization of revolutionaries."[21]

The rationale for this organizational stratagem was twofold. First, it ensured the movement's political stability and ideological continuity by centralizing the vital functions of strategy making and ideological leadership in the hands of a committed core. The people in the core, "the organization of revolutionaries," were not only more willing to absorb the repression such activities invited, but more importantly, they were capable of avoiding it by accepting the hardships of a secret life underground and devoting the time necessary to acquire "professional training in the art of combating the political police."[22]

At the same time, the doors were opened to broader mobilization of the rank and file, who would no longer be forced to accept the hazards of participating in an illegal, "revolutionary" organization if they wanted to help the party. By assuming responsibility for the illegal and dangerous tasks, the core shouldered the yoke of repression for the masses. The movement's span of support would thereby be extended to embrace less committed sympathizers on its ideological fringes (as in Figure 8.5).

> Had we a real party, a real militant organization of revolutionaries, we would not make undue demands on every one of these "aides"; we would not hasten always and invariably to bring them right into the very heart of our "illegality," but on the contrary, we would husband them most carefully.[23]

Thus, by boiling down the vanguard party to the most intensely committed core, Lenin hoped to enhance mass participation in the party's peripheral organizations. "The active and widespread participation of the masses will not suffer, on the contrary, it will benefit by the fact that . . . experienced revolutionaries will centralize all the secret aspects of the work."[24]

Extending the Social Democrats' span of support would do more, of course, than enhance its immediate following. It also made the arduous job of radicalizing the masses easier by reducing the ideologi-

---

[21] Ibid., pp. 189–201.   [22] Ibid., p. 200.   [23] Ibid., p. 204.   [24] Ibid., p. 201.

cal distance moderate elements needed to travel before they reached
the boundary of the party's span of support. Thus, less time would be
required to assemble the critical mass for insurrection in the party's
ideological orbit.

Historical Inevitability and the War with the Compromisers

A SYSTEMATIC awareness of repression shaped Lenin's perception of his
movement's objectives and informed the organizational blueprint he
devised to accomplish them. His political reasoning suggested, on one
hand, an innovative solution to the fundamental dilemma facing every
politically isolated movement—how to proceed in the absence of mass
support. It also provided analytical leverage in the struggle against
political rivals who championed alternative responses to the dilemma.

Above all, Lenin broke decisively with the enervating doctrine of
historical inevitability, which left the development of a revolutionary
situation to the grand forces of history. In his aggressively interven-
tionist model of insurrection, laying the groundwork for revolution
became instead a conscious object of political strategy. His efforts to
overturn the conceptual foundations of Marx's theory invited determined opposition from Marx's more literal interpreters, who mobilized
the double-edged doctrine of historical inevitability to defend their
own vision of socialism's revolutionary mission. Their challenge resulted in a series of violent polemical disputes, which raged in Russian
socialist circles throughout the period between 1898 and 1905.

The target of Lenin's most rancorous blasts were the so-called
Economists.[25] This group sensed the political possibilities in the wave
of labor unrest that was then sweeping across Russia's industrial centers, and argued that Social Democrats should abandon their grand
political designs against the tsarist autocracy in favor of less ambitious
struggles aimed toward redressing the workers' economic grievances.
Their slogan, "Struggle for economic conditions,"[26] betrayed a conviction that the Russian workers were far more interested in alleviating
their economic distress than they were in radical political change. The

---

[25] The following account of the Economist position is gleaned mainly from the
documents Lenin presents in *What Is To Be Done?*. See also Donald Treadgold, *Lenin
and His Rivals* (New York: Frederick A. Praeger, 1955); Adam Ulam, *The Bolsheviks*
(New York: Collier Books, 1965); and Isaac Deutscher, *The Prophet Armed: Trotsky
1879–1921* (New York: Vintage Books, 1965).
[26] Cited in *What Is To Be Done?*, p. 127.

main thread in the Economists' political reasoning was therefore a conventional pragmatic appeal to enhance socialism's mass support by moderating its political program. "We must concentrate not on the 'cream' of the workers," they argued, "but on the average mass workers."[27]

The Economists assaulted Lenin's position with ammunition from Marx's arsenal of historical reasoning. The revolutionary struggle against the feudal tsarist regime was the historical mission of the liberal bourgeoisie, they insisted, and no business of the proletariat. From the perspective of Marx's theory of historical development, Lenin's revolutionary strategy appeared not only to be politically harmful but gratituously so. The Economists dismissed his plan to build a revolutionary, socialist base as a futile attempt to defy historical necessity by "substituting subjective plans for objective development."[28]

> Just as human beings will reproduce in the old-fashioned way despite all the discoveries of natural science, so the birth of a new social order will come mainly as the result of elemental outbursts, despite all the discoveries of social science and the increase in the number of conscious fighters.[29]

Ironically, then, the Economists found an alternative to Bernstein's reformist defense of a compromising strategy in the doctrine of historical inevitability. Without arguing that socialism could be reached by a road of gradual reform, they nonetheless rationalized their moderate strategy as a legitimate reflection of the historical situation. Revolutionary consciousness evolved, they said, by a historical process of continuing struggle. Socialism must therefore adapt its demands to the historical era, accepting the prevailing constraints on the workers' consciousness rather than seeking artificially (and futilely) to bend that consciousness to its ultimate demands. Adopting a classical pragmatic posture, the Economists proclaimed:

> That struggle is desirable which is possible, and the struggle which is possible is that which is going on at the given moment.[30]

With little regard for comradely feelings, Lenin denounced the Economists as the "trend of unbounded opportunism which passively adapts itself to spontaneity."[31] His detailed rebuttal of their position went far beyond a simple purist insistence that principles be main-

---

[27] Ibid.   [28] Ibid., p. 138.   [29] Ibid., p. 139.   [30] Ibid., p. 137.   [31] Ibid.

tained at any cost. By refuting systematically the doctrine of historical inevitability, by explaining rigorously the imperative need to raise the workers' consciousness, and by designing an organizational methodology for accomplishing this objective, Lenin articulated a coherent alternative to the compromisers' strategy for securing mass support—an alternative that did not depend on brokering to the "spontaneous" political aspirations of the masses. His arguments resolved, from a purist perspective, the multifaceted intellectual dilemma of how to proceed in an immature political setting without sacrificing ideological steadfastness. The answer, Lenin said, was building the base.

Historical Inevitability and the Bourgeois Democratic Revolution

THE SAME issues surfaced again in Lenin's debate with the Mensheviks about the frightfully complicated question of what strategy to pursue during the Revolution of 1905. Adhering closely to Marx's theory of historical development, the Mensheviks portrayed the uprising as a "bourgeois democratic" revolution and nothing more. Echoing the Economists' arguments, they insisted that the mantle of leadership in the struggle against tsarism fell by historical necessity to the liberal bourgeoisie. Any attempt to deny the liberals' political destiny and to place a proletarian stamp on the revolution therefore invited disaster. "Social Democracy must not set itself the aim of seizing or sharing power in the provisional government, but must remain the party of extreme revolutionary opposition," the Mensheviks resolved at their conference in 1905.[32] Brandishing the "red phantom" would only cause the liberal bourgeoisie "to recoil from the revolution and thus diminish its sweep,"[33] while participating in the provisional government promised to disillusion the masses when the party found itself "unable to satisfy the pressing needs of the working class."[34] The Menshevik strategy was essentially to stand aside and "unloose the revolution," rather than trying to guide it. Their slogan was at once an expression of faith that history was on their side and a tacit admission that its ebb and flow was beyond their control. With Rosa Luxemburg, and indeed with Marx himself, the Mensheviks shared the view that "an

---

[32] Cited in V. I. Lenin, *Selected Works*, Vol. 1: *Two Tactics of Social Democracy in the Democratic Revolution*, p. 481.
[33] Ibid., p. 525.   [34] Ibid.

82REPRESSION

uprising is not artificially 'made,' not 'decided' at random, not 'propagated,' but it is a historical phenomenon, which at a given moment, results from social conditioning with historical inevitability."[35]

As we might now expect, Lenin's radically more assertive approach to the bourgeois democratic revolution rested on close reasoning about repression and a consuming preoccupation with building a proletarian base for revolution. During the bourgeoisie's revolution, he argued, the proletariat must strive not primarily for economic concessions but to secure the absolute political liberty necessary for organizing the struggle that lay ahead. The proletariat's paramount concern should therefore be to destroy the tsarist apparatus of repression once and for all:

> A socialist revolution is out of the question unless the masses become class-conscious and organized, trained and educated in an open class struggle.... Achievement of this organization and the spread of this socialist enlightenment depend on the fullest possible achievement of democratic transformations.... Only in the event of a complete victory of the democratic revolution will the proletariat have its hands free in the struggle against the bourgeoisie.[36]

For this very reason, Lenin concluded, the bourgeoisie could not be trusted to carry out its own revolution decisively.

> The bourgeoisie looks backward in fear of democratic progress which threatens to strengthen the proletariat.... They stand in too great a need of Tsarism with its bureaucratic, police, and military forces for use against the proletariat, to want it to be destroyed.[37]

If left to their own devices, then, the outlook was not for a decisive victory over tsarism but "a wretched deal," "a travesity of a constitution," "a miscarriage," "an abortion."[38] The answer, in Lenin's view, was not to abandon the leadership of the revolution to the treachery of the bourgeoisie but to seize the initiative from them. Raising the banner of a "revolutionary-democratic dictatorship of the proletariat and peasantry," Lenin proposed, by mobilizing the peasants and the proletariat in a united front for democracy, to "settle accounts with the monarchy in a 'plebian way,' ruthlessly destroying the enemies of lib-

---

[35] Rosa Luxemburg, "The Mass Strike, the Political Party, and the Trade Unions," in *Rosa Luxemburg Speaks*, ed. Mary-Alice Waters (New York: Pathfinder Press, 1970), p. 153.
[36] V. I. Lenin, *Two Tactics of Social Democracy*, pp. 468, 495.
[37] Ibid., pp. 487, 491.   [38] Ibid., p. 493.

erty, and crushing their resistance by force."[39] Only if the proletariat "dared to win" could the democratic revolution be carried through decisively, and the repressive apparatus of the tsar be smashed forever. If this meant casting the liberals aside in their own revolution, so be it.

> Undoubtedly the revolution will teach us, and teach the masses of the people. But the question that now confronts a militant political party is: shall we be able to teach the revolution anything? Shall we be able . . . to put a proletarian imprint on the revolution, carry the revolution to a real and decisive victory, not in word but in deed, and to paralyze the instability, half-heartedness, and treachery of the democratic bourgeoisie?[40]

The same brand of reasoning he used to refute the doctrine of inevitable victory impelled Lenin in 1905 to abandon the underlying theory of historical stages. Unwilling to concede the political initiative (and state power) to the hateful liberals, and not at all persuaded of their inevitable demise, Lenin cast Marx's historical timetable to the winds, arguing, in effect, that the proletariat (or rather its vanguard party) should seize power regardless of the historical era. Although his plans failed to materialize in 1905, the analytical groundwork was laid for the bold plan to seize power under a socialist banner in 1917.

Lenin and Marx

MARX was primarily a theorist of history, Lenin a theorist of political strategy. Their radically dissimiliar visions of revolution ultimately reflect the profound discontinuities in these analytical perspectives.

Marx was beguiled by the idea that socialism must triumph inevitably. Ironically enough, the elaborate theory of historical development he invented to sustain this unverifiable article of faith snared his followers in a web of confusion and paradox when they sought out its strategic implications. On one hand, the theory was curiously indifferent to their choice of strategy. It absolved every strategic tendency of its political sins by rendering them all impotent before the grand march of history. The doctrine of historical inevitability became something of a mercenary soldier in Social Democracy's factional wars, supporting every trend in the self-consuming struggle to dislodge the opposition from its favored course.

[39] Ibid., p. 494.   [40] Ibid., p. 458.

At the same time, Marx's theory of stages damned its unlucky adherents in backward areas of the world to a hellish wait for historical developments that seemed at once fantastically remote and politically repugnant. To those who were drawn to his theory by an unrelieved hatred for capitalism and its bourgeois directorate, Marx offered the bitter medicine of making socialism's final victory conditional upon the political triumph of the bourgeoisie. Thus, the bridge between the historical and the strategic systems of reckoning was strewn with paradox, contradiction, and ambivalence, making the crossing treacherous indeed.

Lenin's efforts to define a strategy for revolutionary socialism in the unfriendly Russian climes brought him to a radically new vision of the road to socialism. Animating his vision was the unwavering conviction that strategy mattered, a conviction that sapped his faith in Marx's presumption of historical inevitability. Recoiling from the theory his rivals used to justify the politically unthinkable, Lenin attacked the doctrine of inevitable victory with close reasoning about repression and the dynamics of political mobilization. By casting a strategically enlightened political organization in the role Marx reserved for history, Lenin tried to circumvent the unpalatable strategic implications of "inevitabilism." The ultimate casualty of his reasoning was the theory of historical stages upon which the doctrine rested. From a conviction that strategy mattered, there emerged an essentially ahistorical vision of revolution—a vision that liberated the struggle for socialism from rigid historical fetters and paved the way for a remarkable diffusion of the socialist political banner in the economically underdeveloped world.

Repression and Programmatic Choice

THE FOREGOING sketch of Lenin's strategy of revolution demonstrates that our highly schematic formal model is more than rich enough to generate his central arguments about repression and mobilization. It is also enlightening to see how the behavioral precepts embodied in Figure 8.5 inform Lenin's position on so many fundamental questions, including historical inevitability, revolutionary organization, political leadership, and class collaboration. The diverse applications of these precepts are further evidence of the pivotal role played by reasoning about spans of support in all rigorous theories of strategy. Neverthe-less, it is important to remember that Lenin's analysis proceeds from a hardened purist perspective whose basic canon is that principles must be maintained at all costs. In his quest to place a steadfastly Social Democratic strategy on sound logical footing, Lenin therefore applies his reasoning about repression and mobilization to problems of organizational design and building the base. In doing so, he largely ignores the political questions that pragmatic strategists like the Ger-man revisionists or the Russian Economists would find most interest-ing; namely, how are less than ultimate demands ranked in order of effectiveness, and where is the optimal demand located along the poli-tical spectrum?

In Chapter 3, we were able to derive clear and definite answers to these questions from very weak assumptions about the structure of in-dividual preferences (single-peakedness) and the distribution of politi-cal opinion (continuity). When repression is negligible, the most radical of the successful demands, P_{max}, produces the largest concession, while other demands secure continuously smaller returns as their distance from P_{max} increases. In other words, the association between the con-tinuum of demands and the concessions they produce is always single-peaked in a world of costless participation.

It should be evident from the elaborate structure of Figure 8.5 that the relationship between demands and concessions will be neither as simple in form nor as easy to calculate when repression deters mobili-zation. All of the monotonic orderliness we discovered in Chapter 3 resulted directly from the fact that *everyone* is mobilized on the left of the point halfway between demand and policy when participating in protests is costless. The logic of simple ideological recruiting implied that the number mobilized increases monotonically as the movement's demand converges toward the government's policy, and this result was, in turn, the cornerstone of all the reasoning in Chapter 3 that demon-strated the efficacy of compromising unsuccessful demands (the moder-ation rule).

The situation changes considerably when we introduce repression (or costs in general, whatever their origin) into the recruiting model. Figure 8.5 shows us that the mobilization span becomes bounded on both sides of the movement's demand, left and right, and that the span becomes narrower on both sides as repression increases. It is then no longer true that moderating demands will necessarily produce monotonically increasing mobilization. Instead, as the radicals' demand moves to the right, both boundaries of the mobilization span (not just the right boundary) will be translated with it across the ideological spectrum. Thus, as new support is gained on the right, old support will be lost on the left. If the distribution of opinion is "lumpy" (continuous but nonuniform), the number mobilized will rise and fall as the mobilization span travels over the more densely and the more sparsely populated stretches of the political spectrum. Moreover, the span of support will collapse altogether before the movement's demand finally converges to the government's policy. The greatest mobilization will therefore be achieved by demands that are centered over the heaviest concentrations of popular opinion, not by minimal demands as before. As a result, we can no longer say in general which demand will mobilize the largest demonstration against each policy. The answer will depend on the particular structure of individual preferences (which determines the spans of support), and the particular form of the distribution of ideal points.

The upshot of these new complications is that no simple (single-peaked) association necessarily exists any longer between demands and concessions. Instead of nice, neat strategy-potential curves like the ones we get in Chapter 3 (Appendix B), we get curves that can assume virtually any form (as long as the only restriction is that ideal points be distributed continuously). Consequently, we cannot make general statements any longer about the effectiveness of moderating unsuccessful demands or the location of the optimal demand.

These difficulties arise because the assumptions of the model (single-peaked preferences and continuously distributed ideal points) are now too weak to produce general conclusions, given the more complex pattern of recruiting (compare Figure 8.5 to its analogue from the theory of peaceful protest, Figure 2.3). The political logic that determines the equilibrium outcomes of strategies hasn't changed, but a significantly more detailed description of the political situation is necessary to produce unambiguous empirical predictions. To achieve clear and definite results like those in Chapter 3, the specification of the model now must be constrained. Thus, the particular shape of the distribution of ideal points has to be specified *in detail* for both pragmatists and purists (continuity alone is no longer a strong enough restriction). Likewise for the utility functions of each political type (single-peakedness is no longer enough; the precise shape of the utility functions has to be described in detail). This is the *only* way to determine what shape the strategy-potential curve will have in particular situations. And, of course, defining the relative effectiveness of strategies is only the first step in predicting what strategy will be followed (recall the analyses of Chapters 4 and 6).

These relatively discouraging conclusions lead us to several final observations. First, it should be clear now that the apparently modest revision of the ideological recruiting scheme introduced in this chapter is really not so modest after all. Even if we maintain the simplest imaginable model of how repression affects individual behavior, a rigorous understanding of how repression affects strategic choice will require a broad and open-ended inquiry into a large number of specifically defined situations. Nevertheless, the reasoning and methods developed here provide all of the building blocks such an inquiry will require and, in particular, demonstrate how the basic conceptual problem of defining spans of support under repression can be resolved. Thus, we now have a solid foundation on which to build a careful understanding of how repression affects radical behavior. Until this work is completed, however, we must remain wary of the casual and unsubstantiated speculations about these questions that now abound in the literature.[41] In no analysis with which I am familiar are the detailed calculations required by this theory even approximated.

[41] For a review of existing theory and evidence, see Douglas A. Hibbs, Jr., *Mass Political Violence* (New York: Wiley Interscience, 1973), Chapter 6.

CHAPTER NINE

The Political Strategy of Violent Disruption

IN THE THEORY of peaceful protest, we have deliberately shunted aside the tactical elements of strategy making so that basic dynamics that shape the radicals' demands might receive the undivided attention they deserve. The political fate of most radical movements depends far more on the size of their following than on tactical finesse. It should not be surprising, then, that many of the grand questions of strategy in protests and insurrections show up readily in a theory that equates power with numbers.

Despite its broad analytical utility, the power-in-numbers approach remains completely silent about the political rationale for waging violent demonstrations. To understand when violent strategies become more effective than peaceful ones and what patterns of political reasoning lead to escalation, we must return to the more general models of recruiting, strategy, and responsiveness set forth in Chapter 2. These models include both demands and tactics (the latter described as points in the unit interval), and rest upon a broader conception of disruption.

Responsiveness and the Incentive to Escalate Tactics

IN CHAPTER 2, we argued that official reactions to demonstrations depend on how violent the protesters become, as well as on their numbers. According to this scheme of reckoning, it makes sense to represent official responsiveness by nested indifference surfaces in a three-dimensional space whose coordinate axes describe the number of people in the streets, the violence of their tactics, and the policy against which they are protesting. The general distaste for violent disruptions among those in authority implies that such indifference surfaces must slope downward into the violence dimension (as the surface in Figure 9.1 does). Whatever its policy may be, a regime cannot maintain an

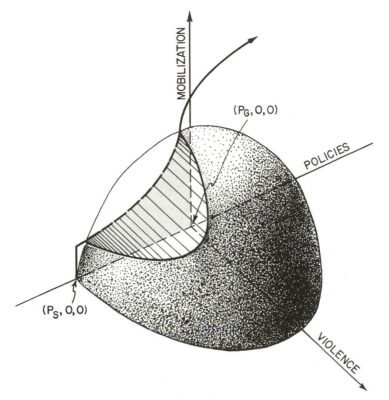

FIG. 9.1
Substitution of Violence for Support

initial level of satisfaction or utility if protests do not become smaller as they grow more violent. It follows that radical movements can use violence to win new concessions *without* mobilizing more people. In other words, the regime's aversion to violent disruptions allows the radicals to substitute violence for support.

This elementary, though fundamental, idea is illustrated by Figure 9.1. In this picture, the dissidents' objective is the policy P_S. The indifference surface passing through the point $(P_S, 0, 0)$ defines the minimum amount of disruption the movement must foment against other policies to make P_S the regime's most attractive alternative. Now suppose that a sincere strategy based on peaceful tactics does not generate enough disruption to be successful (as shown by the mobilization curve lying in the policy-mobilization plane where violence equals zero). We have already discussed how the movement might undertake a compromising strategy or a campaign of ideological persuasion to eliminate the political deficit. Figure 9.1 suggests another way to repair the shortfall. By escalating its tactics until the mobilization curve emerges from inside the indifference surface, the movement can achieve its goal without recruiting new people.

Thus the generalized model of responsiveness readily explains how the incentive to use violent tactics arises, and suggests some of the factors that influence how intense those tactics might become. Note, for example, how the amount of escalation required against each policy in Figure 9.1 depends on the size of the original deficit. Naturally, as the regime's aversion to violence increases (and the indifference surfaces slope more steeply into the violence dimension), less escalation is required to achieve the same results (and vice versa). Despite these important lessons, there remains much to be explained. After all, if radical movements could always compensate for inadequate support by escalating tactics, they would invariably achieve their goals.

Two Constraints on Escalation

THE SCENARIO described in Figure 9.1 raises the question of why all struggling movements do not become more violent. The answer, of course, is that violent tactics carry substantial political costs that constrain the impulse to escalate. Generally speaking, these costs fall into two categories. The first includes the *costs of generating* violence. When radical leaders want to escalate beyond the level of improvised unruliness in the streets (rock throwing, looting, barricading, and the like), they find that violence becomes increasingly difficult to manufacture. Weapons, ammunition, and explosives require lots of money or daring to obtain and special training to use. Because money is hard to come by and people with training in theft, munitions, military planning, and sabotage are scarce political resources, no movement has an unlimited potential for disruption. These constraints narrow the movement's options to the set of feasible strategies that lie within its physical capacity. Usually this capacity depends on the underlying ideological appeal of the cause, though foreign patrons are sometimes only too happy to finance domestic difficulties for their political rivals.

The second general class of constraints on political violence includes the *costs of participating* in violent demonstrations. Violence invites repression and offends moral sensibilities. It therefore complicates the process of recruiting and forces the radical strategists to assess the stability of their support. In order to understand the strategic ramifications of violent tactics, we must therefore reconsider the political dynamics of mobilization.

Ideological Recruiting in a Violent Uprising

As PROTESTS and rebellions become more violent, the decision to join them grows more complicated and difficult. The following model of ideological recruiting is a plausible generalization of the earlier recruiting models. It captures many of the political dynamics set in motion by strategies of violence and repression, and provides interesting new interpretations of the analyses presented earlier.

The new model rests on the assumption that three independent considerations influence decisions about joining a demonstration. These considerations will be represented by a cardinal utility function containing three additively separable components.

Substantive Political Preferences. The cornerstone of ideological recruiting is the individual's relative preference for the regime's policy and the radicals' demand. Let the term $\Delta U_I = U(P_D) - U(P_R)$ represent the difference in utility between the two sides' political positions (as discussed in earlier chapters). Assigning a value of one to each person's ideal policy and a value of zero to an extremely unattractive benchmark policy yields a measure of ideological appeal that varies between plus and minus one ($-1 \leq \Delta U_I \leq 1$).

Moral Evaluation of Tactics. Politicians are judged by their means as well as their ends. Most people find violence repellent and something of a taint on the political program of those who use it. History abounds with examples of regimes and movements that have alienated potential allies by relying on excessively violent tactics. When demonstrators become the victims of brutal repression, their movement often gains sympathy and even material support from people who have not suffered directly from the government's excesses. By the same token, radical groups that let themselves go on a rampage of destruction and killing often find their political base withering away.

Accepting the idea that "moral" (i.e. other-regarding) concerns influence popular sympathy for the government and its opponents, let us define the relative moral attractiveness of the two sides' tactics by the quantity.

$$\Delta M = L(R) - L(T)$$

where

R   is the level of repression meted out by the regime (measured along the unit interval so that $0 \le R \le 1$);

$L(R)$ is the moral distress or disutility created by the regime's repression (measured on the utility scale for political preferences so that $0 \le L(R) \le 1$);

T   is the tactic used by the radicals, $(0 \le T \le 1)$;

and

$L(T)$ is the level of moral distress aroused by the tactic T, $(0 \le L(T) \le 1)$.

Recall that our measuring rod for violent events (the unit interval) assigns a value of zero to peaceful demonstrations and the absence of repression, and a value of one to instances of horrendous violence as defined in the political culture. We suppose that moral preferences about violence and repression obey the following constraints:

1. $R = 0 \Leftrightarrow L(R) = 0$ and $T = 0 \Leftrightarrow L(T) = 0$
Moral distress evaporates when both sides use peaceful means.

2. $R > R' \Leftrightarrow L(R) > L(R')$
          $T > T' \Leftrightarrow L(T) > L(T')$
Moral repulsion increases continuously with the level of violence.

3. $T = R \Leftrightarrow L(T) = L(R)$
When the government's repression is commensurate with the movement's tactics, neither side gains an advantage in moral sympathy (i.e. $\Delta M = 0$).

4. $R > T \Leftrightarrow \Delta M > 0, T > R \Leftrightarrow \Delta M < 0$
Otherwise, moral sympathy swings to the side whose tactics are least violent. The ΔM term ranges in value from $+1$, when a regime uses horrendous repression against peaceful protesters, to -1, when a movement deploys horrendous violence against a nonrepressive regime.

The salient feature of these moral outrages is that they are experienced by everyone who observes the protests, whether they participate or not.

Personal Costs of Repression. Those people who join demonstrations must also face up to the personal consequences of suffering repression. These costs can be forbidding, indeed, though the political police rarely succeed in visiting them upon everyone who takes to the streets. Accordingly, let $[C(R) \cdot Pr(R|\text{Participation})]$ be the direct personal costs of experiencing violent sanctions at level R, weighted by the conditional probability of suffering repression given an active role in the protest.[1] If the personal costs of repression are measured on the utility scale for political preferences (so that $0 \leq C(R) \leq 1$, $R = 0 \Leftrightarrow C(R) = 0$, and $R > R' \Leftrightarrow C(R) > C(R')$), then the cost of suffering horrendous repression equals the difference in utility between the benchmark policies. In other words, politics involves life and death issues.

Given these criteria for deciding whether to join a radical cause, a new recruiting function can be defined as follows: Let

$$Pr(\text{Participation}|P_D, P_R, R, T, P_I)$$
$$= \begin{cases} 1 & \text{if } \Delta U_I + \Delta M - [C(R) \cdot Pr(R|\text{Participation})] > 0 \\ 0 & \text{otherwise} \end{cases}$$

If political preferences in our theoretical society are sufficiently similar in structure—in particular, if the population includes two political types (pragmatists and purists) and if people react similarly to repression and violence—the analytical machinery we developed for calculating spans of support in a repressive political climate can be used with the new model of recruiting. Each term in the recruiting model varies in value between plus and minus one. To determine the span of support for a particular demonstration, we first calculate the net level of disutility arising from the violence of the conflict. The terms

$$\Delta M - [C(R) \cdot Pr(R|\text{Part.})]$$

---

[1] Conspiratorial tactics such as terrorism and guerrilla war often increase the probability of suffering repression for people who are not active in the movement. In these instances a better model might be

$$C(R) \cdot [Pr(R|\text{Part.}) - Pr(R|\overline{\text{Part.}})]$$

where $Pr(R|\overline{\text{Part.}})$ is the probability of suffering repression for people who do not participate. When repression becomes indiscriminate, the two probability terms approach equality and the deterrent effect of repression is negated.

measure the level of (dis)utility associated with the violence of the movement's tactics and the regime's repression. The (discounted) personal costs of repression to participants may be compounded or canceled out by moral sympathies, depending upon whether the movement is more or less violent than the regime. When the probability of repression approaches one or the regime's repression is roughly commensurate with the movement's tactics, the sum of these terms varies (roughly) between minus one and zero. The particular level of (dis)utility, whatever it happens to be, defines attractive sets in the fashion of Figure 8.2, which in turn determine spans of support for all possible combinations of demands and policies (as in Figure 8.5). Thus, the logic of calculating the spans of support remains unchanged as the representation of the costs of participation becomes more complicated. Before we can make use of this machinery, however, two thorny problems need to be resolved.

The generalized model of ideological recruiting assumes that potential demonstrators can anticipate the level of repression they will face and estimate the probability that it will be visited upon them. This probability surely depends on the repressive capacity of the regime—something that is generally known in most places—but also on the number of people who ultimately take to the streets. Because there is safety in numbers, each potential recruit must estimate the likely size of the protest. But how can a protest be mobilized if nobody acts without knowing how others will act? If everyone must guess what everyone else is going to do, we need a recruiting model within our recruiting model and the ugly possibility of an infinite regress then looms up in our theory.

Those who would throw up their hands in despair at this point should take comfort in two facts. People find a way to cope with the problem in real life, so there must be a way to cope with it in theory. And, furthermore, everyone's behavior does not depend on everyone else's. Some people are so committed to radical causes that they willingly join demonstrations even though repression is a certainty (that is, regardless of the safety in numbers or lack of it).

The existence of such a political hard core suggests the following conservative approach for estimating the safety of numbers. Let everyone assume that repression will be unavoidable for all who participate in the movement's announced demonstration (i.e. that $Pr(R \mid \text{Part.}) = 1$). Each person can then estimate the size of the radicals' core following.

The core accepts the hardships of repression because the ideological appeal of the protest outweighs them. Note that the size of the core varies with the movement's strategy, the government's policy, and the level of repression. Recruiting can then be conceptualized as a two-stage process:

STEP 1: Determine the size of the movement's core following. Use this figure to estimate the safety in numbers.

STEP 2: Make a personal decision about joining the protest based upon the estimate in step 1 and the other criteria in the recruiting model.

A Two-Stage Recruiting Model

THESE steps can be readily incorporated into our formal model of recruiting. First, though, we need to specify how the probability of suffering repression depends on the size of the core. Any number of sensible interpretations for the probability term are conceivable. One useful possibility goes as follows:

$$Pr(R \mid \text{Participation}) = \begin{cases} \dfrac{K}{M^*} & \text{if } K < M^* \\ 1 & \text{if } K \geq M^* \end{cases}$$

where K is the regime's repressive capacity (i.e. the number of protesters the police are equipped to abuse);

and M^* is the size of the movement's core following (for the particular demonstration).

When the size of the movement's core exceeds the regime's repressive capacity, the costs of repression are discounted by the safety of numbers. Thus,

$$C(R) \cdot Pr(R \mid \text{Part.}) = C(R) \cdot K/M^* \to 0 \qquad \text{as } M^* \to \infty$$
$$\text{or } K \to 0$$

Nevertheless, the danger of repression weighs on the decisions of potential recruits as long as the regime's repressive apparatus remains intact. As Trotsky explains in *Terrorism and Communism*, repression intimidates even when it is less than a certainty. Describing the "state terror" of a victorious revolutionary class, Trotsky compares repression to the violence of war:

> War, like revolution, is founded upon intimidation. A victorious war destroys only an insignificant part of the conquered army, intimidating the remainder and breaking their will. The [state terror] works in the same way: it kills individuals but intimidates thousands.[2]

Thus, extraordinarily violent repression can deter would be oppositionists, even though its probability remains low for any individual demonstrator. And as the core shrinks toward the regime's repressive capacity, less violent repression accomplishes the same intimidation:

$$C(R) \cdot Pr(R|\text{Part.}) \to C(R) \qquad \text{as } M^* \to K$$

Our two-stage model of recruiting thus takes the following form. In the first step, everyone assumes that repression is a certainty and estimates the number of people, M^*, who will nevertheless take to the streets.

STEP 1: Set $Pr(R|\text{Part.}) = 1$, and find the number of people, M^*, for whom the quantity $\Delta U_I + \Delta M - C(R) > 0$ given the demands and tactics of the movement, the policy and repressiveness of the regime, and the distribution of preferences.

Then, in step 2 each person makes a personal decision about whether to join the demonstration.

STEP 2: Join the demonstration if

$$\Delta U_I + \Delta M - [C(R) \cdot Pr(R|\text{Part.})] > 0$$

given the strategies of the two sides and one's own ideal point P_I. Let M be the total number so mobilized.

This model appears to demand formidable analytical powers on the part of potential recruits—powers that might seem out of the ordinary to say the least. If we understand the core to be the group who are certain to engage in disruption, however, the first step of the recruiting process can be interpreted as a reconnaissance mission. The interested but wary elements on the movement's ideological periphery visit the site of the demonstration and circle around its fringes. The size of the

---

[2] Leon Trotsky, *Terrorism and Communism* (Ann Arbor: University of Michigan Press, 1961), p. 58.

core is revealed in the crowd's dense nucleus, which contains the people who are most determined to make their views known. By gauging the extent of the nucleus, the peripheral sympathizers can readily assess the safety of numbers and decide whether to join the demonstration or not. Our two-stage model therefore enjoys a fair degree of realism because the concentric structure of crowds reflects the ideological structure of the underlying population.

Anticipating Repression

OUR THEORETICAL scenario still leaves one important question unresolved. How do potential demonstrators anticipate the level of repression they will face in the streets? Some may argue that such estimates must inevitably be uncertain and unreliable, but this objection is largely irrelevant to the problem at hand (nor is it correct). Surely most people develop fairly concrete expectations about the dangers in store when they comtemplate joining a demonstration—the more so as their ideological commitment grows weaker. And surely these expectations, rather than the eventual repression itself, govern their calculations about participating in the radical cause. After all, the actual level of repression only becomes apparent when the demonstration is under way. The question, then, is what patterns of political reasoning underlie these expectations.

In our theory, we shall assume that familiarity with the regime's strategy of repression determines the sense of danger surrounding a protest. A strategy of repression is a rule or function that assigns various forms of physical harassment to dissident activities. Such strategies can be inferred over time by observing the regime's reactions to protests and uprisings. As long as the government's strategy remains consistent, experience provides the best evidence for anticipating the likely response to a new wave of unrest. Of course, all kinds of strategies are conceivable. In this introductory analysis, however, we shall focus on two that seem particularly interesting and important.

The Legalist Strategy of Repression

LET US GIVE the name *legalist* to regimes that mete out repression according to the tactics used by the protesters, as prescribed by a legal code that assigns punishments to crimes. Under a legalist strategy of repression, we suppose that

$$R_T = T \qquad \text{for all } T$$

In other words, the level of repression under a legalist regime is commensurate with the violence of the movement's tactics, whatever they may be. Of course, the sense of what is commensurate may vary from one culture to another, but the important point for our purposes is that all movements are treated equally before the law. In a legalist system, repression is administered according to what the dissidents do and not according to what they think. Thus, the level of repression carries the subscript T in a legalist system because repression is strictly a function of the movement's tactics.

The Tyrannical Regime

A TYRANNICAL regime punishes its opponents for their political ideas as well as for their transgressions in the streets. Thus, a tyrannical strategy assigns repression according to the dissidents' demands as well as their tactics. Extremist groups suffer especially harsh retribution, while groups with more "reasonable" demands receive friendlier treatment. A tyrannical strategy can be represented by the following rule:

$$R_{D,T} = T + \delta_D$$

where $\delta_D \to 0$ as the dissidents' demand converges to the regime's ideal point;

and $\delta_D \to 1$ as the demand becomes less attractive to the regime

subject to the constraint that $0 \le R_{D,T} \le 1$

Here δ_D represents the tyrannical component of repression. It measures the degree to which the actual repression, $R_{D,T}$, exceeds the legalist norm (whereby $R = T$). We assume that δ_D increases continuously as the movement's demand diverges from the regime's ideal point until the level of repression reaches its physical limit (i.e. until $R_{D,T} = 1$). Conversely, the tyrannical component of repression shrinks to zero as the movement's demand converges toward the regime's preferred policy. Of course, the level of repression increases whenever the dissidents escalate their tactics, whatever their demand. The repressiveness of a tyrannical regime therefore increases with both demands and tactics;

hence the subscripts for $R_{D,T}$. By this definition, a legalist regime is one that never becomes tyrannical ($\delta_D = 0$ whatever the movement's demands). Our equations conform roughly to the distinction made by political philosophers between "tyranny" and the "rule of law." According to Hannah Arendt, this distinction has been drawn since the end of antiquity when

> tyranny was understood to be the form of government in which the ruler rules out of his own will and in pursuit of his own interests, thus offending the private welfare and the lawful, civil rights of the governed.[3]

While our mathematical definition captures this idea fairly straight-forwardly, the political interpretation of the equations requires caution. For example, it is a canon of Marx's social theory that all legal systems are tyrannical. Marx assumes that the ruling class designs and uses the law to further its own interests. Clearly, "equality before the law" becomes an irrelevant measure of ideological impartiality when the law itself is contaminated by political bias and social favoritism. This surely is no place to undertake an extensive evaluation of Marx's legal reasoning or its empirical validity. The point to remember is that "applying repression strictly according to a legal code" should not be accepted uncritically as a literal interpretation of our mathematical idea of legalism. Some legal systems assign retribution for dissent that is not at all commensurate with the violence of the "crime." How often, for example, are the same penalties attached to political disorders as to similar levels of drunken disorderliness? Only rarely do legal systems remain truly indifferent about the political origins of disruptions in the streets. Those who regard Marx's analysis of this point with suspicion might find the homelier reasoning of Saul Alinsky more persuasive:

> The Haves develop their own morality to justify their means of repression . . . [and] usually establish laws and judges devoted to maintaining the status quo. Since any effective means of changing the status quo are usually illegal, . . . the Have-Nots from the beginning of time have been compelled to appeal to "a law higher than man-made law."[4]

Therefore, we too must sometimes appeal to a "higher law" in order to decide whether repression is commensurate with the dissidents' tactics.

[3] Hannah Arendt, *On Revolution* (New York: Viking Press, 1963), p. 126.
[4] Saul Alinsky, *Rules for Radicals* (New York: Vintage Books, 1972), p. 42.

Violent Strategies against Legalist Regimes

WE NOW HAVE enough machinery in place to analyze the tactical elements of strategy making against two important kinds of regime. Because violence can be used to compensate for inadequate support, it is easy to understand why escalation appeals to strategists who prefer not to compromise demands. For this reason, and for the sake of clarity, we shall assume in the discussion to follow that our hypothetical movement pursues a steadfast, sincere strategy. We can then focus on the dynamics set in motion by escalating violence, without attending to confounding effects caused by shifting demands. Let us also direct our attention to societies where political preferences are distributed continuously. This simplifies the exposition without affecting the basic logic of the analysis.[5]

When a movement confronts a legalist regime, the level of repression is commensurate with tactics ($R_T = T$ for all T). Therefore neither side gains an advantage in moral sympathy and the two-stage process of recruiting boils down to the following form:

STEP 1: $\Delta U_I - C(R_T) \rightarrow M_T^*$

STEP 2: $\Delta U_I - [C(R_T) \cdot Pr(R_T | \text{Participation})] \rightarrow M_T$

Before we consider the tactical implications of this model, let us suppose the movement adopts a peaceful strategy. Then $T = 0$, $R_T = 0$, $C(R_T) = 0$, and all that remains in the recruiting model is a simple binary comparison of the two sides' political positions (the ΔU_I term). The process reduces to the most basic form of ideological recruiting, which then becomes the cornerstone in the theory of peaceful protest. Note that M_0, the level of support mobilized under a peaceful strategy, is the entire set of people who sympathize with the movement's demand.

When the dissidents' tactics become violent, however, the recruiting process is complicated by calculations about the likelihood of repression and its disutility. The model assumes the more general form associated with a repressive climate, and we can rely on the reasoning represented by Figure 8.5 to understand the effects on mobilization as tactics escalate. When preferences are distributed continuously, this

---

[5] When the population is clustered in discrete groups, changes in the level of mobilization cannot be inferred from changes in the span of support. The story must then be complicated to admit this possibility.

graphic representation of ideological recruiting implies that the number of people supporting the radicals' demand must diminish steadily as their tactics become more violent. Here, then, is the crucial difficulty in any scheme to win quick and easy concessions by resorting to violence. Before we attend to anything else, it is important to understand in detail how this difficulty arises.

Consider first those movements whose sincere demands attract too little support to strain the regime's repressive capacity (so that $M_T^* \leq K$ for all T). The following expressions describe the recruiting process for these groups:

STEP 1: $\quad \Delta U_I - C(R_T) \rightarrow M_T^* \leq K$

STEP 2: $\quad \Delta U_I - C(R_T) \rightarrow M_T = M_T^*$

Because the core support for a sincere strategy is too small to provide safety in numbers, every participant in the movement's demonstrations suffers the full measure of repression prescribed by the law. As a result, only core supporters ever join the struggle (i.e. those people who willingly accept the legal consequences of their actions). With each successive round of escalation (for each $T' > T$), the legal penalties increase $(R_{T'} = T' > R_T = T)$, and their disutility increases as well $(C(R_{T'}) > C(R_T))$. As this happens, the spans of support collapse around the dissidents' demand and the level of mobilization diminishes (if preferences are distributed continuously, $M_{T'} < M_T$ for all $T' > T$). Thus, the number of people in the streets grows steadily smaller as the movement's protests assume a more violent character.

The same problem arises in larger movements that enjoy the safety of numbers (at least initially). Their recruiting can be described as follows:

STEP 1: $\quad \Delta U_I - C(R_T) \rightarrow M_T^* > K$

STEP 2: $\quad \Delta U_I - C(R_T) \cdot K/M_T^* \rightarrow M_T > M_T^*$

When the core support for a protest exceeds the regime's capacity to inflict sanctions, the costs of repression are discounted by the safety of numbers. The actual level of mobilization (M_T) then exceeds the size of the core (M_T^*) because the span of support extends further across the ideological spectrum than it would if repression were a certainty. Despite the initial safety of numbers, however, the movement still loses support if it becomes more violent. This happens in two ways. In the first step of the process, the anticipated level of repression increases with the violence of the turmoil in the streets. Hence the core shrinks ($M_{T'}^* < M_T^*$ whenever $T' > T$), and the safety of numbers becomes more tenuous. In the second step, then, both elements of the term $C(R_T) \cdot K/M_T^*$ approach unity as the level of violence escalates. Each new round of escalation narrows the movement's appeal even further, causing additional defections along its ideological periphery.

The Relative Effectiveness of Violent Tactics

GIVEN our reasoning about responsiveness and recruiting, the natural question to address at this point is whether any simple (monotonic or single-peaked) association exists between the level of violence used by the movement and the concession it receives. Are tactics ranked in effectiveness, for example, strictly according to their proximity on the continuum of violence to the optimal choice, in such a way that the dissidents will converge directly on the best tactic by a simple process of trial and error?

The answer to this question is that no simple relationship necessarily exists between tactics and concessions (at least at the level of generality on which our model is now developed). On the contrary, the optimal tactic can in general lie anywhere along the continuum of violence, and more importantly, there can be no assurance that other tactics will smoothly diminish in effectiveness as they diverge in either direction from the optimal choice. It follows that locating the optimal tactic will often be no easy matter for dissident leaders and that a highly detailed assessment of the political environment (probably unattainable in most cases) will be necessary to predict in advance the relative potential of each kind of violence. Let us be clear about why this is so.

Our model imposes two kinds of monotonic regularity on the strategic situation. First, taking the government's policy and the demand lodged against it as given, the movement's support will decline continuously as its tactics become more violent (assuming that ideal points are distributed continuously. If not, mobilization will decline in fits and starts). If we consider all the policies along the political spectrum simultaneously our recruiting function will define a *mobilization surface* that describes how many people will be mobilized against every possible policy in protests using each kind of tactical violence. (For an illustration, see Figure 9.6 ahead.) These surfaces will invariably slope downward into the violence dimension, but their particular shapes are completely undetermined by the assumptions we have made. They could be linear, convex, concave, or irregular; given only that violence erodes support, we can't say for sure. Only by specifying in detail the shape of individual utility functions and the distribution of ideal points can we determine precisely what shape the mobilization surfaces will have (using the reasoning of Chapter 8).

The second kind of monotonic regularity in the model arises in the description of the government's preferences. The indifference surfaces, which define the government's responsiveness to disruption, also slope downward into the violence dimension. Whatever its policy, the government cannot maintain an initial level of utility (remain on the same indifference surface) unless demonstrations against it become smaller as they grow more violent. In technical parlance, the slopes of these indifference surfaces describe the marginal rate of substitution, in the government's eyes, between mobilization and violence. These slopes, we assume, are invariably negative, but the particular shape of the indifference surfaces is again undetermined.

Now, given these two distinct kinds of regularity that we've imposed on the situation, what can we conclude about the relationship between tactics and concessions? To pursue an optimal strategy, the dissidents must locate the most effective tactic against every policy the government might adopt (recall that we have assumed for simplicity that the movement's demand will be sincere). Let us consider, then, how the optimal tactic will be determined against each particular policy. Since the same logic will apply to all of the policies available to the regime, even this simple problem will reveal the indeterminacy that resides in our general model.

To describe the optimal violent strategy, we will have to consider as a whole the relationship between the radicals' mobilization surface and the government's indifference surfaces. When we are interested only in the optimal tactic against a particular policy, however, we can restrict our attention to a two-dimensional cross section of these surfaces (where we hold the government's policy constant). In each case, we will have a picture something like the one in Figure 9.2. Here the solid curves are cross sections of the nested indifference surfaces of the regime, while the broken curve is a cross section of the movement's mobilization surface. The broken curve describes the amount of support that can be mobilized against the particular policy in question by

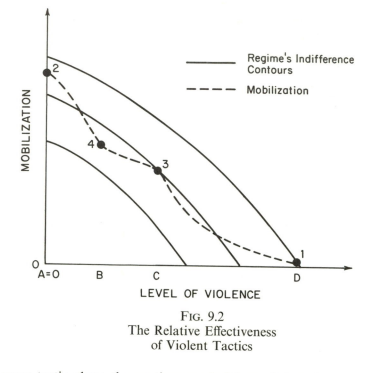

FIG. 9.2
The Relative Effectiveness
of Violent Tactics

every tactic along the continuum of violence (when the movement's demand is sincere).

From the movement's point of view, that tactic is best which achieves the highest indifference surface (or curve in this partial analysis where the government's policy is taken as given). The higher the reach on the responsiveness map, the more unpleasant the demonstration becomes and the larger the concession the regime will be motivated to make in return for tranquility. Of course, we must remember that a powerful demonstration against a single policy will not be sufficient to secure the concession desired by the movement's leaders. Instead, they must foment enough disruption against *all* of the policies along the political spectrum to make their demand the most attractive alternative to the government. It is therefore a bit premature to talk about concessions in a partial analysis of tactical choice. Nevertheless, the *potential* for achieving concessions varies directly with the amount of disruption created against each policy. For the time being, then, it should be understood that our discussion of "concessions" refers only to this potential.

Now consider the four tactics *A* through *D*, which become progressively more violent. The amount of mobilization they achieve declines steadily (violence erodes support) as indicated at the appropriate points along the broken mobilization curve. However, the four tactics do not produce monotonically decreasing disruption (as defined by the regime's own preferences). Instead, tactic *D* produces the most unpleasant demonstration from the regime's point of view (and thus is ranked first in effectiveness), tactic *A* (the peaceful demonstration) is second, *C* is third, and *B* is fourth. In this case, the dissidents will receive rather confusing signals as they escalate from a peaceful tactic. Initially, they will observe their demonstrations becoming generally less effective, though not without occasional reversals of the general trend. Only after they pass tactic *C* and the low ebb shortly beyond it will the radicals finally achieve more disruptive demonstrations than their peaceful protest, and this after sacrificing most of their mass support. Thus, we have none of monotonic regularity that characterized the relationship between demands and concessions in the theory of peaceful protest. There, successive demands secured continuously larger concessions as they approached the optimal choice from either direction. Here, successive tactics obey no simple ordinal ranking in effectiveness.

This is not to say, of course, that simple relationships between tactics and (potential) concessions might not arise in some situations. It should be clear that by varying the particular shape of either the movement's mobilization curve or the government's indifference map, we can observe virtually *any* relationship between tactics and concessions while still adhering to our assumptions about recruiting and responsiveness. The diagrams in Figure 9.3 illustrate situations where violent tactics decrease monotonically in effectiveness, increase monotonically in effectiveness, and define a single-peaked pattern (first increasing, then decreasing in effectiveness). But this is just the problem. Without a *detailed* description of the structure of individual political preferences, the distribution of ideal points, the government's responsiveness to all forms of disruption, and its strategy of repression, it is impossible to predict the relationship between tactics and concessions or to identify the optimal level of violence. Lacking such detailed information, the slopes of the relevant curves simply won't be known.

Our reasoning implies that efforts to predict how violent movements will become from a general aggregate description of their political environment will usually be doomed to failure. In every case, the

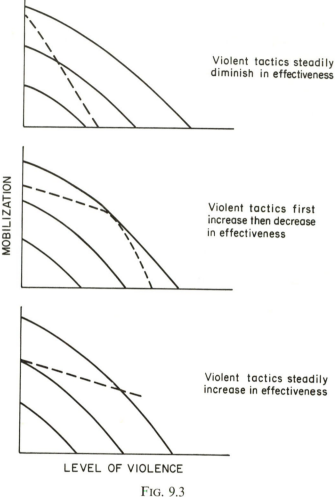

FIG. 9.3
Patterns of Disruption in Violent Conflicts

outcome of tactical escalation depends specifically on how rapidly the movement sacrifices support relative to the marginal rate of substitution, in the government's view, between violence and mobilization. Measuring these quantities requires an extraordinarily detailed understanding of the political situation; far more detailed, in fact, than would normally be available in practice. Thus, efforts to predict the intensity of violent behavior from the assumption that dissidents adopt the most effective tactic will often founder on the intractable empirical problem of defining what tactic actually is optimal in the political arena under study.

In Chapter 11, we shall return to the problem of predicting how violent radical groups might become. The outlook for deriving testable predictions from our theoretical reasoning improves considerably when we adopt a broader view of the dissident strategist's objectives. As we have already observed in Chapters 4 and 6, it is quite mistaken to assume that radical leaders evaluate strategies strictly according to the concessions they produce. And as we shall see later, when other considerations influence strategic decisions, the kinds and amount of information required to predict the likelihood of violence change significantly. Generally speaking, one needs substantially less information about the movement's external political environment, and much more information about its internal structure and composition. The reason is quite simple. When psychological predilections (like "purism") constrain strategic choice, dissident leaders will often adhere to essentially similar strategies in a broad range of circumstances. The problem then is to identify what kind of leadership the movement has, rather than to define the exact contours of its political situation. Before we address these new problems, however, much work remains to be finished here.

Strategy against a Tyrannical Regime

LET US NOW consider the logic of strategy against a tyrannical regime (one whose repression surpasses the legalist norm by larger and larger amounts as the movement's demand becomes more extreme). In this case, the movement derives moral sympathy from the government's excesses and the process of recruiting becomes somewhat more complicated than it was before.

Recall that our recruiting function has the following elements:

$$\Delta U_I + \Delta M - [C(R) \cdot Pr(R \mid \text{Part.})]$$

where ΔU_I defines the political gain to potential recruits from achieving the movement's demand, and the other terms jointly determine the net cost (direct and other-regarding) associated with the movement's violence and the regime's repression. The individual will join the demonstration only when the potential political gain exceeds the net cost of participation (that is, when the terms in the recruiting function sum to a positive quantity).

Recall that the term ΔM defines the difference between the moral outrage created by the regime's repression and the movement's violence ($\Delta M = L(R) - L(T)$). When the regime adheres to a legalist strategy, its repression remains commensurate with the movement's tactics (regardless of the radicals' demands) and the quantity ΔM equals 0. Tyrannical governments are given to incommensurate repression, however, and the term ΔM becomes positive, creating a new incentive to join the radical cause. Whether such a moral backlash will be sufficient to constrain the regime's repressiveness is the basic question to which we turn next.

We have conceptualized the mobilization of a protest demonstration as a two-stage process. The first stage determines the extent of the movement's core following (against the particular policy being targeted for disruption). The core following, it will be recalled, includes those people who are sufficiently committed to achieving the movement's demand (i.e. those for whom ΔU_I is sufficiently large) that they willingly accept the certainty of repression. Thus, the core following is the minimum who will participate when there is no safety in numbers. To determine the size of the core, we first assume that repression will be visited on all participants (i.e. we set $Pr(R|\text{Part.}) = 1$), and then calculate the movement's span of support (using our new recruiting function and the methods of Chapter 8).

We have then:

STEP 1: $\Delta U_I + [L(R) - L(T)] - C(R)$
            $= \Delta U_I + [L(R) - C(R)] - L(T)$

The vital question here is whether the disutility of experiencing repression directly (the $C(R)$ term) exceeds the moral outrage created by observing it applied to others (the $L(R)$ term). Certainly, the most favorable circumstance for which the movement could hope is that the two terms be equal ($C(R) = L(R)$). This condition would only obtain in highly altruistic societies where each person essentially said to all others: "It hurts me just as much to see you repressed as it does to experience the same repression myself."

In this case, the first stage of the recruiting process reduces to:

STEP 1: $\Delta U_I - L(T) \rightarrow M^*$

and the size of the movement's core following is *completely unaffected* by the amount of repression used by the regime (the deterrent effect is entirely canceled out by moral backlash). Nevertheless, the radicals continue to face a trade-off between violence and support, just as they would against a legalist regime. The movement sacrifices core support whenever it escalates tactics because it cannot escape a moral backlash ($L(T)$) against its own violence.

The dissidents' core following, M^*, provides a conservative benchmark from which to calculate safety in numbers in the second stage of recruiting. If M^* does not tax the regime's repressive capacity (i.e. if $M^* \leq K$), then the movement's peripheral support withdraws from the streets and recruiting is identical to step 1 (only the core participates). Otherwise, the deterrent effect of repression will be further attenuated by the safety of numbers, and the actual number mobilized will exceed the size of the core:

$$\text{STEP 2:} \quad \Delta U_I - L(T) + \left[L(R) - C(R) \cdot \frac{K}{M^*} \right] \to M > M^*$$

Now the personal disutility of repression ($C(R)$) is discounted by safety in numbers ($K/M^* < 1$). We see that in an altruistic society (where $L(R) = C(R)$), the quantity in brackets will necessarily be positive, and the net cost of participation will be less in step 2 than it was in step 1. The movement's span of support will therefore grow wider, and additional people will be mobilized who would not have joined had repression been a certainty.

More importantly, the positive quantity in the brackets will increase in magnitude as the government's repression grows more intense. Exploiting the assumption of altruism, we can substitute $L(R)$ for $C(R)$ inside the brackets to obtain $L(R) \cdot (1 - K/M^*) > 0$, a quantity that is strictly increasing with the level of repression R.[6] When the movement achieves safety in numbers (however slight), repression becomes entirely counterproductive. The more tyrannically the government behaves (the heavier its repression), the bigger the movement gets. In fact, the most prudent policy from the government's point of view is to use no repression at all, however violent the movement's tactics.

In a highly altruistic society, then, repression is never a paying proposition. When the movement is too small to enjoy safety in numbers, repression is simply gratuitous (its net impact on mobilization is

---

[6] Recalling that M^* remains constant for all levels of R.

zero). Otherwise, repression is strictly counterproductive, enhancing the movement's appeal whatever its tactic or demand.

Before we relax the assumption of altruism, it remains to inquire whether the dissidents will necessarily be forced to sacrifice support when they escalate tactics. We have already observed that escalation erodes support when there is no safety in numbers (step 1), but what happens when the movement's core following exceeds the repressive capacity of the government? In that case, we may rewrite the recruiting equation for step 2 as follows:

$$\text{STEP 2:} \quad \Delta U_I + \Delta M - C(R_{D,T}) \cdot \frac{K}{M_T^*}$$

$$= \Delta U_I + [L(T + \delta_D) - L(T)] - C(T + \delta_D) \cdot \frac{K}{M_T^*}$$

The latter terms in the equation, describing the deterrent effect of repression, necessarily increase in magnitude as the movement's tactic, T, becomes more violent. Not only does the repression of a tyrannical regime increase directly with tactics, but the movement's core following diminishes in step 1, reducing safety in numbers. Thus, the net cost of participation will certainly rise in more violent demonstrations, unless it happens that moral sympathy for the movement, ΔM, increases when it escalates tactics. But none of our assumptions implies that this will happen. In particular, we have assumed that the tyrannical component of repression (δ_D) depends only on the movement's demand, not its tactics. Thus, the excessiveness of the regime's repression will not increase as the radicals become more violent, and there is no reason to believe that moral sympathy for them will increase either.

The radical movement will therefore face a trade-off between violence and support even when it enjoys safety in numbers. This is a rather strong conclusion when we consider how weak the deterrent effect of repression is in an altruistic society. Not only have we assumed that the deterrent effect of repression is no greater than the moral backlash it creates, but the scope of the deterrent effect is often much less when we allow for discounting by safety in numbers. Meanwhile, the moral outrage created by excessive repression has not been assumed to vary with the number of people victimized by the political police. In this model, the government encounters the same backlash whether it overreacts against ten demonstrators or thousands. Thus, the cards seem to be heavily stacked in the movement's favor here, and yet it cannot escape the basic dilemma that violence erodes support.

This does not mean, of course, that the dissidents are best advised to pursue a Gandhian strategy of nonviolence against a tyrannical regime. As we have already explained, the fact that violence erodes support does *not* necessarily imply that more violent tactics are politically less disruptive. Whether they are or not depends on the particular relationship between loss of support and the regime's responsiveness. Thus, even in a highly altruistic setting, there is no guarantee that a strategy of nonviolence will be the most productive for the movement. A nonrepressive strategy is always best for the government, however.

Now let's consider the more realistic case in which the disutility of experiencing repression personally is greater than the moral outrage that arises from observing it applied to others (i.e. where the deterrent effect is stronger than the moral backlash effect). We need not assume that people are entirely self-interested, but it does seem reasonable to suppose that individuals attach more value to their own well-being than to the well-being of others, especially as the government becomes more ruthless and brutal. Let us assume, then, that the difference between the personal disutility of repression, $C(R)$, and the sense of moral outrage against it, $L(R)$, is positive and increases with the level of repression, R. While the two effects, deterrent and backlash, might be similar in magnitude at low levels of repression, the concern for one's personal welfare becomes relatively more important as radical activity grows more dangerous.

If we let $\Delta_R = C(R) - L(R)$, then Δ_R is a positive, increasing function of R as illustrated in Figure 9.4. Once again we are interested in whether a tyrannical regime will be motivated to constrain its repression or not.

In the first stage of the recruiting process (and in general when the movement lacks safety in numbers), no such inhibition exists. We have:

STEP 1: $\Delta U_I + [L(R) - C(R)] - L(T) = \Delta U_I - \Delta_R - L(T) \rightarrow M^*$

and it is immediately apparent that the net costs of participation will increase directly with the level of repression (because Δ_R also increases with R). Thus, the government invariably undermines the movement's *core* support by intensifying its reprisals against demonstrators. If the radicals' core support remains sufficiently large to create safety in

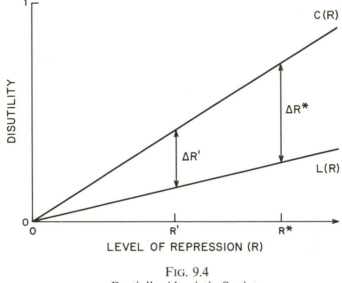

FIG. 9.4
Partially Altruistic Society

numbers, however, a tyrannical strategy may ultimately backfire when the second stage of the recruiting process is played out.

Let's examine first the extreme case in which the movement's core following so dramatically surpasses the regime's capacity to repress that the quantity K/M^* (describing the probability of suffering repression in the streets) approaches zero. Then the deterrent effect of repression is nullified, and the total mobilization in the demonstration will be given by:

STEP 2: $\Delta U_I + (L(R) - L(T)) - C(R) \cdot K/M^*$
$= \Delta U_I + (L(R) - L(T))$ when $K/M^* = 0$

Now the escalation of repression only increases moral outrage against the regime (assuming the movement's tactic remains fixed), without deterring anyone. Finding itself hopelessly overmatched, the government does best by not repressing at all (and hoping for the best).

But what happens in the more usual circumstance in which safety in numbers is less than absolute? In these situations, there is no general rule to describe whether escalating repression will undermine or enhance the movement's support. Instead, the outcome depends on the particular contours of the political situation.

To understand why our general model is inconclusive in these cases and how the specific consequences of escalating repression are determined, we can rewrite the recruiting model for the second stage as follows:

$$\text{STEP 2:} \qquad \Delta U_I - L(T) + \left[L(R) - C(R) \cdot \frac{K}{M^*} \right]$$

When the movement holds its demand and tactic constant, the first two terms remain fixed and the net impact of repression depends completely on the expression in brackets. In a partially altruistic society (where $C(R) > L(R)$), we have already seen that the sign of this expression is ambiguous. When safety in numbers is minimal, the term K/M^* approaches one and the net impact of repression is negative. When safety in numbers is pronounced, K/M^* approaches zero and the expression becomes positive. Whether repression intimidates and deters, or backfires against the regime, therefore depends critically on how much the deterrent effect is discounted by safety in numbers. In general, we can't say for sure which side will benefit from particular levels of repression.

The model is similarly ambiguous about the political impact of changes from lesser to greater amounts of repression. Our reasoning identifies two specific consequences that invariably follow when repression gets heavier: first, the positive difference between the deterrent effect, $C(R)$, and the backlash effect, $L(R)$, grows larger, and second, the size of the movement's core diminishes in step 1, reducing safety in numbers. Nevertheless, it is not necessarily true that deterrence *discounted by safety in numbers* will increase at a faster rate than moral outrage does. Thus, it is not clear whether the net impact of repression will change positively or negatively.

To understand this important point more fully, and to appreciate the richness of the possibilities here, let's explore the specific example illustrated in Figure 9.5. The upper panel in the diagram shows, for all demonstrators in the streets, how the probability of becoming a victim of repression varies with the level of repression, R. We have already seen that the probability must increase with R, because the movement's core will shrink with escalating repression. As it does, the ratio K/M^* (which defines safety in numbers) will approach one. We have called the particular level of repression where safety in numbers finally disappears R'. At higher levels of repression than R', the movement's core

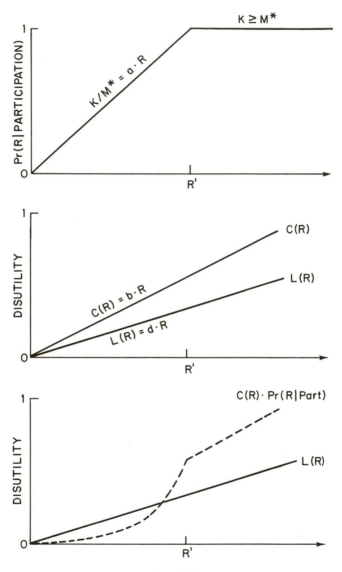

FIG. 9.5
Repression in Partially Altruistic Society

is smaller than the government's repressive capacity, and no demonstrator escapes punishment for his actions.

Of course, there are any number of functions that satisfy these general requirements. The particular relationship between repressiveness and safety in numbers portrayed here is notable mainly for its simplicity. Below the threshold R', the probability of becoming a victim is a simple linear function of the amount of repression.

$$Pr(R \mid \text{Part.}) = \begin{cases} K/M^* = a \cdot R & \text{if } R < R' \text{ with} \\ & a > 0 \text{ and } K/M^* < 1 \\ 1 & \text{if } R \geq R' \end{cases}$$

In this case, safety in numbers is virtually absolute when repression is close to zero (an essentially similar story follows if we include a positive intercept in the linear function). The probability of suffering harm in the streets then increases linearly with the level of repression until it becomes a certainty at R' and beyond.

The curves in the middle panel describe the deterrent and backlash effects of repression. As we have discussed previously, the difference between the two effects increases with the intensity of the government's violence. To keep things simple, however, we have assumed further that the deterrent and backlash effects are linear functions of the level of repression, so that:

$$C(R) = b \cdot R \qquad \text{with } b > 0 \text{ and } 0 \leq C(R) \leq 1$$
$$L(R) = d \cdot R \qquad \text{with } b > d > 0 \text{ and } 0 \leq L(R) \leq 1$$

Now the question of real interest to us is whether the net impact of represssion,

$$L(R) - C(R) \cdot Pr(R \mid \text{Part.})$$

changes positively or negatively when the regime becomes more heavy handed with demonstrators. When the backlash effect, $L(R)$, increases faster than the discounted effect of deterrence, the net costs of participation are reduced and the movement grows larger. On the other hand, when deterrence outpaces backlash, participation declines.

The lower panel of Figure 9.5 contains two functions, one describing the backlash effect and the other the *discounted* effect of deterrence. When the backlash curve lies higher than the deterrence curve, the net impact of repression is positive and the movement benefits from the government's excesses. When the deterrence curve is higher, then repression cuts into the movement's support (increasingly so as the distance between the two curves becomes greater).

The reader should notice that the backlash function comes directly from the middle panel, while the discounted deterrence curve is simply the product of the probability function in the upper panel and the $C(R)$ curve in the middle panel. When the probability of suffering repression equals one, the deterrent effect carries full weight and the discounted curve below is identical to the original $C(R)$ curve (for $R > R'$, $C(R) \cdot Pr(R|\text{Part.}) = C(R)$). When there is safety in numbers, however, the deterrent effect is weighted downward by a probability number smaller than one, and the discounted curve is lower than the original $C(R)$ curve. When repression is less intense than R', we have

$$C(R) \cdot Pr(R|\text{Part.}) = C(R) \cdot K/M^* = (bR)(aR) = abR^2$$

and the discounted effect of deterrence traces out a parabola. Thus, the deterrence curve in the lower panel includes two pieces, one parabolic and the other linear.

Let's explore what happens as the government escalates repression against the movement. Initially, the political backlash caused by the regime's repression exceeds the deterrent effect, and the movement actually mobilizes more people than it would have if there had been no repression at all. As the regime resorts to more extreme measures, however, the two curves eventually intersect (at which point the net impact of repression becomes zero again). Thereafter, the discounted effect of deterrence exceeds moral backlash, and the regime finds that each extra measure of repression reduces the movement's support even further.

We have, then, a situation that conforms with the widely held view in the literature that middling repression is less effective than either no repression at all or harshly draconian reprisals against demonstrators.[7] Nevertheless, it is clear that this pattern is only one of many that might arise in a society whose members are partially altruistic. For example, if the curve describing safety in numbers is displaced upward, the discounted effect of deterrence will approach $C(R)$ itself, and repression of every kind will reduce the movement's support. On the other hand, if we introduce nonlinearities into the model, all sorts of

---

[7] See Douglas A. Hibbs, Jr., *Mass Political Violence* (New York: Wiley Interscience, 1973), Chapter 6, for a review of existing reasoning and evidence on this point.

complicated patterns might arise (the curves in the lower panel might intersect in many places in such a way that escalating repression would produce oscillating results, first favoring one side and then the other). Thus, the assumptions of our model are not sufficiently strong to produce clear and definite general rules about the effectiveness of repression when the movement enjoys some safety in numbers.

Let us conclude our survey of violent politics in a tyrannical setting by returning briefly to the problem of tactical choice in the dissident movement. Given our earlier discovery that violence erodes support even in a fully altruistic society, it should come as no surprise that the same dilemma exists when people are only partially altruistic. On the contrary, all of our earlier arguments apply here, and radical leaders will continue to sacrifice support whenever they escalate tactics.

A Brief Review

WE HAVE STUDIED two quite different types of regime, one obeying legal norms and the other behaving tyrannically. When governments follow a legalist strategy, their repression is determined entirely by the movement's tactic and the problem of whether to use harsher or milder forms doesn't arise. When legal constraints are absent, however, the question is whether the tyrannical government will be motivated to limit its excesses or not. In a completely altruistic society (where $C(R) = L(R)$), the inhibitions against excessive repression will be very strong. There repression is at best gratuitous (when the movement is too small to strain the government's repressive capacity) and often counterproductive (whenever the radicals enjoy safety in numbers, however slight). When altruism is only partial, however, people attach higher weight to their own welfare than to that of others, and the deterrent effect of repression is greater than the moral backlash effect. The temptation to escalate repression will then be unconstrained, unless the movement has safety in numbers. In that case, the consequences of tyrannical behavior are ambiguous. Sometimes increasing repression will reduce the radicals' support; other times it will backfire against the regime.

Our conclusions about the movement's tactical choices are, by contrast, much simpler. Whether the government is tyrannical or legalistic, whether society is altruistic or self-interested, and whether there is safety in numbers or not, we have discovered that resorting to more

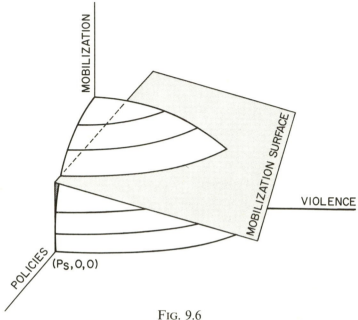

FIG. 9.6
A Situation That Rewards Escalation

violent tactics invariably diminishes the dissidents' support. It follows that none of the difficulties we encountered in defining the relative effectiveness of tactics in a legalist setting will disappear when backlash effects become important. In every case, establishing how much disruption each tactic creates will require a detailed knowledge of how rapidly violence erodes support in relation to the government's responsiveness to violence (i.e. in relation to the slopes of its indifference surfaces). We see, then, that the assumptions we have made about recruiting and responsiveness are simply too weak to define a specific association between tactical choice and policy outcomes, even when we disaggregate the net impact of repression and violence quite explicitly.

The Dilemma of Political Violence Defined and Illustrated

IT REMAINS now to characterize the general process that determines a regime's choice of concession in the face of violent opposition. We have already examined the logic of political disruption against a single

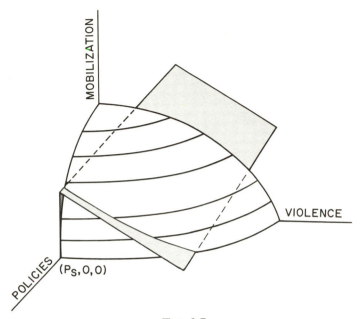

FIG. 9.7
A Situation That Punishes Escalation

policy, but this reasoning is not sufficient to establish the ultimate outcome of the movement's struggle for change. Instead, it is necessary to consider the relative attractiveness of all the policies from which the government may choose, given the level of disruption against each one.

Although the movement will not have to employ the same amount of violence against each policy to achieve its objective, the basic dilemma confronting the dissident leaders remains always the same. When the radicals lack enough support to achieve their objective peacefully, they are enticed to escalate tactics by the regime's aversion to violence. This impulse is constrained, however, by the erosion of support occasioned by repression and moral backlash. The crucial question, therefore, is whether the government's additional responsiveness to violent protests will provide sufficient compensation for the movement's smaller size.

To understand this fundamental dilemma more clearly, let's examine Figures 9.6 and 9.7. While the main ideas underlying these illustrations are already familiar, perhaps a brief review of basics will be helpful before we get into details. The space defined by the three coordinate axes contains the entire universe of possible demonstrations against the government, each described according to size, degree of violence, and the policy being opposed. Given the government's relative preference for alternative policies and its aversion to disruption in the streets, we can construct an indifference map that describes how the government ranks all possible demonstrations in order of distastefulness. Naturally, the ideal situation from the government's point of view is to adopt its most preferred policy with no disruption (peaceful or violent) mobilized against it. As it adopts less attractive policies or faces more disruption in the streets (either growing mobilization or violence), the situation becomes less appealing. We shall have, then, successive indifference surfaces nested infinitely close to each other (resembling the layered skins of an onion). Each surface defines a set of demonstrations (varying in size, violence, and target) among which the regime is indifferent. Lower surfaces describe less distasteful demonstrations, while higher surfaces contain more unpleasant possibilities. In adjusting its policy, then, the government always wants to wind up on the lowest indifference surface it can possibly achieve.

Figures 9.6 and 9.7 illustrate the political situations of two radical groups whose common objective is the policy P_S. We have chosen to portray the particular indifference surface that passes through the point $(P_S, 0, 0)$ because this surface defines the minimum amount of disruption the movement must inflict upon other policies in order to compel the government to adopt P_S. The question for the government is whether it will be most satisfied at P_S with absolute tranquility in the streets (violence and mobilization at zero), or at a policy closer to its ideal point with some positive amount of disruption. Only if the demonstrations against other policies are severe enough to place the government on higher surfaces than the one shown here will it be motivated to concede P_S. Notice that at each policy along the political spectrum, the amount of mobilization required to achieve the desired result diminishes as the radicals' demonstration becomes more violent. It is in this sense that governments are said to become more responsive as the movement's tactics grow more intense.

Now, of course, the radical movement does not enjoy the luxury of being able to create any amount of disruption it desires. The severity of its protests is constrained by the availability of mass support. Once demands are selected (here we assume each movement presses the sincere demand P_S), the number of people mobilized against each policy depends on the tactic employed in the streets. We have for each movement, then, a *mobilization surface* describing the number of people who can be rallied against every policy in demonstrations using every degree of violence. These surfaces determine the movement's potential to create disruption. In essence, the movement's leaders will trace out a mobilization curve, lying along the surface, as they select the particular tactic to be used in each protest. In other words, their *strategy of violence* assigns a unique tactic to every policy along the political spectrum. The disruptiveness of the strategy can be summarized by a mobilization curve, which describes precisely the kind of demonstration that will transpire in every situation.

The burden on the regime, then, is to locate that policy which is most palatable given the disruption created by the movement's strategy of violence. This equilibrium policy will be defined by the *lowest* tangency of the mobilization curve with the responsiveness map. The paramount question is whether the radicals can find a schedule of tactics that will force the government to accede to their demand (i.e. establish equilibrium at P_S). If not, will resorting to violence at least achieve a larger concession than the one available under a peaceful strategy?

In Figures 9.6 and 9.7, the answers to these questions differ dramatically. First, notice in both situations that P_S cannot be secured peacefully. The mobilization *curve* for a peaceful strategy lies on the front edge of each mobilization surface (in the policy-mobilization plane where violence equals zero). We see that some of these peaceful protests lie inside the indifference surface passing through the point $(P_S, 0, 0)$. It follows immediately that P_S cannot become the equilibrium concession under a peaceful strategy, because other policies will necessarily place the government on lower indifference surfaces).

Both movements therefore confront the dilemma of escalation. The radical leaders must ask themselves whether violent tactics will create enough additional pressure on the regime to outweigh the support lost by using them. From a formal point of view, the question is whether there exists a strategy of violence whose mobilization curve lies higher on the indifference map than the curve defined by strictly peaceful tactics.

Even though violence erodes support for both movements, the rate of loss is much higher for the second (Figure 9.7) than for the first (Figure 9.6). As a result, the political effectiveness of escalation is dramatically different in the two situations. By adjusting its tactics

accordingly, the leaders of the first movement can define a mobilization curve that lies strictly higher than the indifference surface through
$(P_S, 0, 0)$. The more violent demonstrations are sufficiently damaging
from the government's perspective that it finally capitulates in full to
the demand P_S. In contrast, the second movement's support erodes
so rapidly when it becomes more violent that the perceived disruptiveness of its demonstrations diminishes. The movement actually sacrifices
concessions when it abandons a peaceful strategy because its mobilization surface slices downward into the regime's responsiveness map (i.e.
into progressively lower indifference surfaces) as tactics become more
violent.

In Figures 9.6 and 9.7 the two regimes are identically responsive to
demonstrations, peaceful protests attain essentially similar results, and
yet violent strategies have dramatically different outcomes. The remaining question is how to account for the discrepancy. Clearly, the key to
the puzzle lies in the distribution and composition of each movement's
political support. When a movement adopts a more violent strategy,
its span of support collapses around its demand. The crucial strategic
question is whether the people within the initial span are concentrated
near the center or on the margins. If the radicals' following is largely
drawn from ideologically peripheral elements, defections can be preci-
pitous if the span of support contracts even slightly. Such a configuration of forces places a tight constraint on tactics. Conversely, the
movement can escalate its tactics with minimal defections if it draws
a large fraction of its support from the immediate vicinity of its
demand. A related consideration is the relative proportion of purist
and pragmatic types in the original span of support. Purists are recruited from a narrower ideological spectrum than pragmatists, and
their personal involvement in the movement is less sensitive to the
regime's repression and concessions. Having a large purist following
therefore makes it easier to escalate tactics without suffering debilitating defections.

Summing Up

Two DISTINCT constellations of forces determine whether violent strategies will be more or less effective than peaceful ones. The responsiveness of the regime determines how readily the movement can substitute
violence for support, while the distribution of preferences around the

dissidents' demand determines how much support will be lost as the costs of participating escalate with tactics. When a large bloc of un-mobilized support lies on the movement's ideological periphery, the political imperative is to extend the span of support until the bloc is recruited. Such situations clearly favor moderate tactics. When the bulk of the movement's potential support lies near its demand, however, the constraints on escalation are relaxed considerably. Choosing tactics effectively therefore requires a balanced appraisal of (1) the regime's relative sensitivity to the various forms of disruption and (2) the sensitivity of the movement's following to the costs of repression and the safety of numbers.

A Closing Footnote

BEFORE we turn to some examples that illustrate this reasoning in action, it is important to understand why the political logic of escalation does not change fundamentally if a movement's goals are revolutionary rather than reformist. The preoccupation of revolutionaries is to cross the insurrectionary threshold rather than to manipulate the responsiveness map lying below it. When disruption depends solely on numbers, the threshold may be represented by a curve in the policy-mobilization plane (as in Chapter 5) defining the level of mobilization the government can tolerate before it topples. If disruption depends on violence as well as numbers, however, then the threshold must be represented by a surface in the three-dimensional space shown in Figure 9.1. The surface describes the minimal combinations of mobilization and violence that will drive the regime from power. Now surely the level of mobilization that a government can withstand diminishes as its opponents become more violent. Certainly it takes more peaceful protesters to unseat a regime than would be required if the dissidents were well-armed and highly trained in the art of war. The threshold must therefore slope downward into the violence dimension just as the indifference surfaces do. The dilemma of escalation is therefore formally identical in structure for the two kinds of movement. For the revolutionaries, the question is whether the threshold of insurrection or the mobilization surface slopes more steeply into the violence dimension (i.e. whether escalation brings the movement closer to the threshold or not). For reformers, the concern shifts from the threshold to the indifference surfaces that govern concessions.

*Choosing between Violence and Support: Notes
on the Boston Tea Party*

THE POLITICAL dilemmas surrounding violent strategies are especially
well illustrated by the history of the Boston Committee of Correspondence.[8] The committee coalesced in 1772 to mobilize the people of
Massachusetts in a struggle for colonial autonomy against the British.
The increasingly contentious policies of the British regime—including
the Stamp Act of 1765, the Townshend duties, the effort to control the
colonial judiciary, and the decisive Tea Act of 1773—reinforced the
opinion that colonial interests could only be defended by mobilizing
active resistance against the Parliament's encroachments. No sooner
had they decided to follow the road of resistance, however, than the
leaders of the Boston committee confronted a delicate strategic decision. While they desperately needed the support of outlying towns to
challenge the formidable authority of the crown, the widespread ambivalence toward "tumults and discords" among the relatively less
radical country folk severely constrained the committee's choice of
tactics. The question was whether to accommodate moderate opinion
by choosing "softer" tactics or to follow the aggressive course favored
by the more radical Bostonians.

Preserving Unity

THE COMMITTEE quickly decided that preserving unity among the colonists was essential to a successful strategy. In accord with the reasoning of our theory, the committee's leaders appealed to two threads of
reasoning to support a moderate tactical course. On one hand, they
argued that Parliament would remain unresponsive to unrest if the
colonists did not press their demands as a united front. Without unity,
they said, legitimate grievances would be dismissed as "imaginary" and
"seditious" while "Boston would be singled out as the discontented
seat of faction."[9] Beyond the power of numbers, there are safety in
numbers as well—a critical concern given the stark imbalance in the

---

[8] Our account draws upon the evidence presented by Richard D. Brown in *Revolutionary Politics in Massachusetts* (New York: W. W. Norton, 1976). Unlike most historians, Brown approaches revolutionary politics with an eye to strategy rather than
causes.
[9] Ibid., p. 82.

military forces of the two sides. A united opposition made it difficult for the British to crush the resistance by focusing their repressive capacity on the capital city. If the moderate elements could be rallied to the cause, the British would be forced to spread their troops thin. And as the ratio of troops to protesters became more unfavorable to the regime, the radicals' span of support could be extended even further. Thus, the committee believed that preserving the safety of numbers was critical to mobilizing a broad coalition against the crown. As Sam Adams pointed out to the committee, every town was reluctant to make itself stand out unless it could be sure of general support.[10] Recognizing that the less militant people in the province "would not act hastily," the committee understood that "they must see thro' the matter to its utmost termination ... and compute the chances with the nicety of a DeMoivre before they will engage in anything dangerous."[11] Still, the committee remained confident that "when they are satisfied they will proceed gently, but with constancy, and finally attain their end."[12] Thus, it strove always to find the most aggressive tactics that preserved unity among the opposition.

Choosing Tactics

PRESERVING unity turned out to be an extraordinarily difficult task that demanded untiring efforts to rein in the radicals while pressing the moderates to wage a more vigorous struggle. The committee maintained close contacts with the towns and continually experimented with more assertive tactics in an effort to exploit the shifting policies of the regime (mostly for the worse) and the evolution of public opinion (mostly to the "left"). Over and over again, it discovered that escalating tactics was a risky and highly delicate political course, which endangered the movement's cohesion by alienating the support of sympathetic moderates. Because assertive tactics appeared to be politically necessary, the committee went to exceptional lengths to cultivate and preserve that support, an endeavor that vividly illustrates the central political dilemma arising in our analysis of political violence.

[10] Ibid., p. 83.
[11] Ibid. Abraham DeMoivre (1667–1754) was a Huguenot mathematician and a pioneer in developing the mathematical theory of probability. His book *The Doctrine of Chances* was published in London in 1716.
[12] Brown, p. 83.

The committee's first major campaign against the regime began in 1772. Its purpose was to prevent the Parliament from transferring the salaries of the Massachusetts Superior Court justices from the payroll of the colonial assembly to the payroll of the crown. Recalling the unfavorable popular reaction to violent attacks on the home of the lieutenant governor during the Stamp Act crisis, and recoiling from the disorderly mob violence that resulted in the Boston Massacre in 1770, the leaders of the opposition were determined this time to follow "a maturated plan . . . within a regular mode of procedure."[13] The committee's first priority was to "stop the mouths of every bellower against mobing, pulling down houses & c."[14] By proceeding instead in "a slow and steady manner," they hoped to enhance the appeal of their demands to the moderates in the towns. At the same time, they undertook a campaign of political persuasion designed to move the townspeople closer to their own position. This was the only sure way to make possible further escalation without suffering defections. By striving always to appear "so reasonable that the governor's high tone would put him in the wrong," the committee hoped to make more aggressive tactics "reconcileable even to cautious minds, & thus we may expect the unanimity we wish for."[15]

The judiciary crisis was still unresolved when the British Parliament passed the notorious Tea Act in May 1773. Resolving that the tea of the East India Company "shall not be landed," the leaders of the resistance launched a new campaign of disruption, which culminated in the famous Boston Tea Party. As the evidence presented by Professor Richard Brown clearly shows, the Tea Party did not in any sense transpire haphazardly in a fit of defiant indignation. On the contrary, it was part of a calculated strategy of escalation, designed to preserve colonial unity while exerting greater pressure on the British authorities.

The crisis reached a peak in November 1773 when tea-bearing ships arrived in Boston for the first time after the act was passed. The leaders of the resistance convened a "Meeting of the People," which adopted an aggressive resolution banning the importation of tea. The problem then was to mobilize general support for the boycott. Toward this end, the committee circulated a package of documents that manipulated all of the elements in the recruiting process defined by our theory. Nat-

[13] Ibid., p. 52.   [14] Ibid.   [15] Ibid., p. 56.

urally, the finest rhetoric was devoted to the evilness of the regime's policy and the virtue of the movement's demand. The tax had been passed solely "to support the extravagance and vices of wretches whose vileness ought to banish them from the society of men," the circular advised. If the tax was not repealed, it would result in corruption and slavery "more to be dreaded than plague or pestilence." The call then was to "impress upon the minds of your friends, neighbors, and fellow townsmen, the necessity of exerting themselves in the most zealous and determined manner, to save the present and future generations from temporal and (we think we may with seriousness say) eternal destruction."[16]

The committee also tried to reduce the townspeople's qualms about repression and violence by stressing the "regularity" and reasonableness of the resistance, and the complete absence of "riots and tumults" in Boston. It also recruited representatives from Roxbury, Dorchester, Brookline, and Cambridge to coauthor the circular and included a copy of the Philadelphia Resolves in the package. These measures were calculated to enhance the moderates' estimates of the size of the movement's core.

The committee, finally, pursued every opportunity for the peaceful redress of its grievances. By following "every procedure, however futile" to have the tea returned, the radical leaders hoped to convince potential recruits that the colony's only alternatives were accepting defeat or conducting an active resistance. The circular to the towns depicted the political options in the starkest terms; either the people could "sit down quiet under this . . . as good natured slaves, or rise and resist . . . as becomes wise freemen."[17] Only after these steps were completed was "every last ounce of the tea . . . immersed in the Bay, without the least injury to private property" as Sam Adams judiciously, if not quite accurately, explained in a letter to fellow oppositionists.[18]

Evidently, the committee's efforts to preserve support while escalating tactics were rather successful on this occasion. A letter from the Philadelphia Friends of Liberty praised the Bostonians for their steadfastness and courage, assuring them that the destruction of the tea had been "justified by a strong necessity . . . [caused by] Inveterate Enemies . . . who seek their own advantage in compelling you to any

[16] Ibid., p. 160.   [17] Ibid., p. 161.   [18] Ibid., p. 165.

measures of violence,"[19] Even better evidence for the success of the strategy was the inability of the royal government to arrest the perpetrators of the Tea Party, owing to the "practically unanimous public approval of the resistance to the tea in Boston."[20]

The history of the Boston committee provides numerous examples that show how tactical decisions resulted from a calculated balancing of violence and popular support, given the responsiveness of the regime and its strategies of repression on one hand, and the distribution of political opinion and the safety of numbers on the other. Sometimes the committee was able to employ fairly severe tactics without alienating its sympathizers (as in the case of the Boston Tea Party). In other instances, it was forced to moderate its course in order to prevent defections. Its efforts to enforce a general boycott on all British goods as well as a secondary boycott against those who purchased them, for example, created widespread anxiety in the towns about "breeding discord among the inhabitants . . . a Discord of Sentiment [that] may be destructive to the good effect proposed."[21] In any event, the leaders' choice of tactics was very much constrained by moderate opinion throughout the struggle. When recruiting is ideological, the presence of a sizable bloc of moderate opinion on the movement's periphery constraints tactical extremism just as it checks programmatic extremism.

[19] Ibid., p. 180.   [20] Ibid., p. 167.   [21] Ibid., p. 202.

CHAPTER TEN

The Logic of Terrorism

TERRORISM has much in common with other forms of political violence, but its logic nevertheless demands special attention. The fundamental difference, of course, is that terror emanates from the underground, while rioting, looting, trashing, and pillaging rage in the streets for all to see (including the police). The element of conspiracy is essential in explaining how terrorism originates, its political rationale, and the quandaries it creates, both for its perpetrators and its targets.

Like all violent tactics, terrorism can be interpreted as an effort to create more disruption without mobilizing more people. That terrorism often springs from groups on society's political fringes—groups who have not been able to mobilize mass support—suggests that political isolation is an important motive for its use. Consider, for example, the gloomy political assessment in the first number of *Narodnaya Volya* ("People's Will"), the underground journal of the famous Russian terrorist group that coalesced in 1878 after the enormous populist drive to "go to the people" failed quite utterly to rouse the Russian peasantry against the tsar's regime.[1]

> Vast, covered in impenetrable darkness, ahead of us there lies the marsh of Russian life: and far off like some will-o-the wisp there float the illusions which seduce the inexperienced to come to the warm, light corner. But these illusions only lead to some cold dark pit. Political illusions ruin peoples and are ruining our parties.[2]

Looking back on the ruthless suppression of the naive student organizers, the terrorists of Narodnaya Volya were determined not to fall prey to the same "illusions" about the revolutionary aspirations of the masses. All the same, it would be a drastic oversimplification to dismiss

---

[1] The evidence about the Russian terrorists reported in this chapter has been culled from Franco Venturi, *Roots of Revolution*, trans. Francis Haskell (London: Weidenfeld and Nicolson, 1960).

[2] Ibid., p. 666.

terrorism as just another way to substitute violence for support by exploiting the aversion to disruption among those in authority. In most cases, this motive is only one element in a far more complicated and interesting chain of reasoning.

Repression and Terror

THE IDEA that violent tactics result from repression as often as they provoke it is by now a commonplace in the literature of political violence. A noteworthy feature of the extended model of ideological recruiting is the way it brings life to this tired generalization. The model lends substance to the commonplace view by untangling the numerous threads that bind up strategies of terror and strategies of repression in a complicated reciprocal relationship.

A Defense against Repression. For movements that do not enjoy the safety of numbers, conspiratorial tactics offer another defense against the ravages of repression. By waging their struggle behind a veil of secrecy, the dissidents can drastically reduce the probability of suffering harm at the hands of the authorities. When peaceful tactics provide no reprieve from the clubs and prisons of a tyrannical regime, conspiracy may become the only way to save a small movement from decimation. This motive was surely an important impetus driving the Russian terrorists of the nineteenth century. At his trial for the assassination of Tsar Alexander II, one of the young leaders of the Narodnaya Volya, Andrey Ivanovich Zhelyabov, explained to the court how terrorism was a consequence, rather than a cause, of the regime's tyrannical strategy of repression.

> We have tried several different ways to act on behalf of the people. At the beginning of the seventies we chose to live like workers and peacefully propagate our Socialist ideas. The movement was absolutely harmless. But how did it end? It was broken only because of the immense obstacles in the form of prison and banishment with which it had to contend. A movement which was unstained by blood and which repudiated violence was crushed. . . . From metaphysics and dreams we moved to positivism . . . instead of a peaceful fight we applied ourselves to a fight with deeds."[3]

Zhelyabov had fallen victim six years earlier to the wave of repression that engulfed the populist movement in Odessa. In a letter to a

[3] Ibid., p. 719.

friend describing that catastrophe, he sketched the same reasoning even more pointedly:

> It was the winter of 1875, the prisons were crammed with people. Hundreds of lives had been shattered ... everything collapsed. The old, enticed by the advantages to be derived from keeping on the right side of the law, were slow to abandon their sheltered nests. Excellent men perished. ... But the movement did not die. The only thing to change was our tactics.[4]

Thus, it can be quite misleading to construe terrorism as a desperate means to compensate with violence for a dearth of support, when terrorism may be the radicals' only way to protect their support from violence.

Boiling Down Dynamics. Heavy repression can drastically affect the composition of a radical movement and, in the process, fundamentally transform the prevailing balance of power among its various factional trends. Our reasoning about repression suggests that sympathetic moderates and pragmatists—the principal spokesmen for compromising strategies—are the first to succumb to intimidation from the forces of repression. When this happens, the purist elements, who are most willing to employ dangerous tactics and for whom violence offers an attractive alternative to compromising demands, suddenly find themselves unchecked by countervailing pressure within their own movement. Thus, by a process of boiling down under the heat of repression, a movement may arrive at a strategy of terror even though the external balance of forces remains stable.

The official reign of terror that followed an unsuccessful attempt on the life of the tsar in 1879 seems to have had this effect on the Russian populist movement. Recalling the hangings and persecutions that befell his comrades, Alexander Mikhailov, a leading figure in the terrorist section of Zemlya i Volya and its successor Narodnaya Volya, later explained how:

> The government's repression had weakened the party as far as numbers were concerned but had helped to make it five times stronger from the point of view of quality. It had created a remarkable unity of spirit and aims. Everywhere the majority had only one desire; a bloody fight with the government.[5]

[4] Ibid., p. 646.   [5] Ibid., p. 639.

In this fashion, a strategy of repression designed to induce passive submission resulted instead in a campaign of terror that finally struck down the tsar himself on March 1, 1881.

A Spur to Mobilization. When peaceful agitation fails to mobilize a sizable following in a repressive atmosphere, the dissident leaders can appeal to either of two explanations for their political difficulties. They might, of course, attribute the passivity of the masses to ideological hostility, disillusioning as such an assessment must be. Or they can embrace the more palatable explanation that the masses, though politically friendly, are immobilized by the repression visited upon dissenters. Once this interpretation is accepted, an entirely new rationale for terrorism comes into play. By somehow undermining the regime's strategy of repression, the terrorists can unloose the pent-up political energies of the masses and destroy the artificial tranquility created by fear and intimidation. Terror can then be rationalized as the first step in a two-stage process of mobilization, without any appeal to arguments about securing concessions directly.

This reasoning is a recurring theme in the political writings of the Russian populists who used it to design a campaign of terror after their movement in the countryside collapsed. Vera Figner, another of the idealistic young socialists who joined Zemlya i Volya, develops this argument in her political memoirs:

> We saw that our cause in the countryside was lost. . . . It was not because we had an abstract programme which appealed to the people for purposes which did not concern it or for inaccessible ideals; it was not because we put excessive hopes in the state of preparation of the masses. No, no, we had to give up, knowing that our programme was vital, that our demands met with a real response in the life of the people. What was lacking was political freedom.[6]

Political freedom, that is, to carry on a program of agitation and propaganda without becoming the target of an official reign of terror. It followed, therefore, that a general uprising could only be carried off by disabling the repressive apparatus of the state. As an early manifesto of Narodnaya Volya put it:

> No activity aimed at the good of the people is possible given the despotism and violence which here reign supreme. There is no freedom of speech

[6] Ibid., p. 577.

or freedom of the press which would allow us to act by means of persuasion. . . . The Party draws from its ranks a fighting union which attacks the government, shakes and disorganizes and disconcerts it. In this way, the Party makes it easier for all those who are dissatisfied—for the people and the workers and all those who desire their good—to arise and carry out a general revolution.[7]

Our model of recruiting suggests several avenues by which a strategy of repression might be compromised, and it is striking that each of them caught the attention of the Russian strategists of terror. One possibility, of course, is to attack the agents of repression directly in an effort to reduce the regime's repressive capacity. Such was the intent of Zemlya i Volya's campaign to "disorganize the forces of the state"; a campaign later continued by Narodnaya Volya. This plan included efforts to subvert the officer corps, to infiltrate the tsar's bureaucratic apparatus "so as to paralyze its activities against . . . the revolutionary forces,"[8] and, above all, to carry out "the systematic annihilation of the most dangerous and important elements in the government."[9] So began, in 1878, a program of assassination directed against the tsar's military governors (including the sensational attack on General Trepov by Vera Zasulich) that led ultimately to the murder of the monarch himself.

A natural corollary of this approach involves tactics that demean the forces of repression rather than destroy them. This is a much easier job, of course, that can be equally effective. Terrorist groups frequently indulge in cat-and-mouse games just to show up the political police as bumbling and incompetent. The symbolic effect of executing a daring attack right under the authorities' noses can be far more devastating than the physical damage it causes. Naturally, the underlying rationale is to undermine the paralyzing aura of physical prowess with which the state can immobilize an atomized population. As an editor of the periodical *Zemlya i Volya* insisted (only slightly facetiously):

> The important thing is that some clandestine review should come out. The police look for it and are unable to find it—that's what strikes the public. It's of no importance what's written inside.[10]

Finally, it is important to understand how conspiratorial tactics can incapacitate a strategy of repression by compounding its debilitating side effects. Using repression as a weapon of intimidation becomes significantly more dangerous and expensive when the perpetrators of

[7] Ibid., pp. 649, 703.   [8] Ibid., p. 615.   [9] Ibid.   [10] Ibid., p. 620.

violence are difficult to identify. Unlike demonstrators in the streets who can be readily singled out for abuse, terrorists defy retribution with their anonymity.

Sometimes, the regime's inability to define responsibility for subversive acts strains its treasury to the breaking point. When the government finds it impossible to focus its repressive forces on a well-defined circle of activists, a difficult choice arises between diverting valuable resources from more worthy political endeavors in order to finance a bigger counterrevolutionary effort or stretching the existing repressive capacity thin. As the publicists for Narodnaya Volya pointed out, the tsarist regime was "unable to fight against groups of revolutionaries (described in its own words as insignificant) without setting a policeman on every single inhabitant."[11] Farfetched as this claim may seem, the demands of combating an extensive clandestine movement were taxing indeed. The records of the tsar's political police, the notorious Third Section, showed that a million rubles a year were paid for political information just to porters in St. Petersburg alone. Almost 7,000 people were subjected to direct supervision by the police for political reasons.[12] The clandestine tactics of the Russian revolutionaries created a fantastic drain on the tsar's budget by extending the movement's scope, in effect, from the set of active participants to the vastly larger set of potential sympathizers.

While the unproductive expenditures required to combat a conspiratorial movement can become a heavy burden, in most cases they probably pale in comparison to the political costs arising from harassing innocent people. In the absence of reliable intelligence about the identities of its adversaries, a repressive regime often falls into the trap of meting out punishment tyrannically. Because it is much easier to identify a movement's sympathizers than its active participants, the unfortunate tendency is to apply repression indiscriminantly among the people who share a radical ideological predisposition. This not only creates moral outrage, but destroys the incentive not to join the battle among the movement's weakly committed adherents.

Evidently, this dynamic worked to the rebels' advantage in 1879 when the tsar reacted to an attempt on his life by conferring unlimited police powers upon military governors in six regional capitals. Em-

[11] Ibid., p. 667.   [12] Ibid., p. 690.

powered to arrest, try, banish, or execute anyone they pleased, the reactionary generals proceeded with a vengeance. Progressive elements in Russian society soon found themselves under siege, regardless of their political activities. Describing the events in Odessa, the future terrorist Mikhail Frolenko explained how the "dark cloud oppressing the town" ultimately created wider sympathy and support for the radicals' cause.

> Everyone felt it; everyone was loaded with an oppressive nightmare. Everywhere one could hear the cry—no longer stifled, but violent and insistent—that "one could no longer go on living, it was essential to find some escape." People who until then had hardly even heard of the revolutionary movement were now on the move looking out for radicals, pointing out the way of escape, offering themselves for work, suggesting that the best, indeed the only, way to put an end to this suffocation was to kill the Tsar. [13]

Thus, terrorism can sometimes stimulate mobilization by provoking untoward repression against innocent people. The difficulty, however, is that campaigns of repression tend to be short-lived and quickly forgotten. They provide a far less stable source of support than persistent ideological grievances. The danger from the radical's point of view is misinterpreting sympathetic moral reactions against a regime's repressiveness as ideological commitment to the movement's demands. When this happens, disastrous errors in strategy often result.

Political Liabilities of Terrorism

WHILE our model shows that coherent reasons can be marshaled to defend a strategy of terror, it also provides ample entries for the deficit side of the ledger. Resorting to terror creates profound dilemmas for a radical party—dilemmas that generally result from forgoing the political advantages of broad support.

Unlike public demonstrations, where safety almost always resides in numbers, conspiracies become more dangerous as they grow bigger. No one has explained this phenomenon better than Machiavelli, who takes up the problem of conspiracy in *The Discourses*. [14] Machiavelli

---

[13] Ibid., p. 638.
[14] Niccolò Machiavelli, *The Prince and the Discourses*, trans. Luigi Ricci (New York: Modern Library, 1950). See especially Book 3, Chapter 6, "Of Conspiracies."

identifies two threats to the conspirators' enterprise, both of which increase with its scope. The first, "want of prudence," is essentially a sto-
chastic process in which the probability of accidents, carelessness, and
bad luck increase with the number of conspirators. This lesson is driven
home time and time again in the stormy history of the Russian populists, whose conspiracies were disrupted by an extraordinary variety
of unlucky occurrences. Consider, for example, the revolutionary cell
that was denounced from the grave (in a manner of speaking anyway).
One circle in the Workers' Union of South Russia had been lucky
enough to identify an agent provocateur in their midst before he betrayed them to the authorities. Their luck ran out when the police
plant, a certain Gorinowich, miraculously survived a bludgeoning with
a revolver and a dousing with sulphuric acid only to betray them anyway after being left for dead.[15] A leading figure in Narodnaya Volya,
Alexander Mikhailov, met his demise when he ordered photographs
of two comrades who recently had been hanged. The owner of the
photography shop happened to be a police agent, and Mikhailov was
arrested when he returned for his revolutionary souvenirs.[16] And so
it went.

The second threat Machiavelli considers is treachery. "You cannot
safely impart your project to any but such of your most trusted friends
as are willing to risk their lives for your sake," Machiavelli points
out.[17] Naturally, such people are difficult to find because "their devotion to you must be greater than their sense of danger and fear of
punishment."[18] Thus, political conspiracies remain secure only as long
as they embrace people with the deepest ideological commitment to
the cause. Unfortunately, ideological commitment is extraordinarily
difficult to measure without the litmus test of experience—experience
that can be disastrous if the litmus test proves negative.

> Men are very apt to deceive themselves about the degree of attachment
> and devotion which others have for them, and there are no means for as-
> certaining this except by actual experience.... If you attempt to measure
> a man's good faith by the discontent he manifests toward the prince, you
> will be easily deceived, for by the very fact of communicating to him your
> designs, you give him the means of putting an end to his discontent."[19]

[15] Venturi, *Roots of Revolution*, p. 581.   [16] Ibid., p. 708.
[17] Machiavelli, *The Discourses*, p. 416.   [18] Ibid.   [19] Ibid., p. 417.

Such was the unhappy fate of Dmitry Lizogub, who joined the Socialist movement despite (perhaps because of) the fantastic wealth of his family. Lizogub reached his Waterloo when he decided to donate his inherited property to Zemlya i Volya. No sooner had he entrusted his holdings to a friend, with instructions to sell everything and transfer the proceeds to the revolutionaries, than the friend went to the police and proposed the inevitable bargain. He would be happy to tell all he knew, the "friend" said, if he could keep the property for himself.[20] Lizogub's martyrdom is only one example of betrayal through fear or greed that plagued the Russian revolutionaries throughout their struggle. Dmitry Klements, a founder of Zemlya i Volya, was betrayed by a servant. The Pan-Russian Social-Revolutionary Organization was denounced by a worker. Nikolay Rysakov revealed the names and addresses of his fellow assassins as soon as the police arrested him for killing Tsar Alexander II. The difficulty always was finding people who were so deeply committed to the revolutionary cause that they could withstand the rigors of torture or the temptations of treachery. As Mahatma Gandhi once said, "There are nine hundred ninety-nine patrons of virtue for every virtuous man."[21]

This is not to say that the need for compactness and ideological devotion escaped the attention of the Russian terrorists. Zemlya i Volya, for example, took elaborate precautions in admitting people to its "fundamental group." Each candidate had to sustain "a rigid appraisal of his personality," secure a "guarantee" from five members of the group, and be elected by two-thirds of the organization.[22] Narodnaya Volya's procedures for constituting its executive committee were, if anything, even more strict. According to the articles of the organization's program:

A candidate for membership of the Executive Committee must be:
(a) In complete agreement with the programme, principles and statutes of the society.
(b) Autonomous in his convictions.
(c) Tenacious, experienced, and practical in action.
(d) Utterly dedicated to the cause of liberating the people.
(e) Before his admission he will have to spend some time as a second class agent.[23]

[20] Venturi, *Roots of Revolution*, p. 636.
[21] Louis Fischer, *Gandhi* (New York: Mentor Books, 1954), p. 39.
[22] Venturi, *Roots of Revolution*, p. 613.   [23] Ibid., p. 652.

Candidates also had to be recommended by five members and elected by "an open ballot in which each negative vote is equal to two positive ones."[24]

These precautions were usually only temporarily successful in defending the conspiracies from detection. They created permanent political difficulties of other sorts, however, difficulties inherent in the conspiratorial approach. Most fundamentally, a conspiratorial movement risks self-enclosure and loss of contact with its potential base in the larger population. This possibility was a perennial source of ambivalence among the Russian conspirators; it caused considerable factional tension between those who were committed to terrorism and others who retained the populist impulse to go to the people and build the party's base. The terrorists for the most part acknowledged the danger of political isolation but still defended the conspiratorial road as the only safe way to avoid detection and imprisonment. Building the base in their view was simply too dangerous until the state's repressive apparatus was destroyed. Remarking on the extraordinary narrowness of the "fundamental group" in Zemlya i Volya, A. A. Kryatkovsky defended it nevertheless as a necessary evil.

> The fundamental group is not the ideal kind of organization. Its conception and triumph represent, so to speak, a necessary evil. It is conditioned on the one hand by the inexperience of a considerable number of Russian revolutionaries, and on the other hand by the difficulties of the situation in which we have to carry on our activities.[25]

Others were less convinced, insisting that socialism had to restore its ties with the people if it hoped to survive. Eventually the centrifugal pressures became too great, and Zemlya i Volya split in two pieces. The terrorists formed the group called Narodnaya Volya, while the base-builders created another party called Cherney Peredel ("Black Partition"). A "Letter to my ex-Comrades," which appeared in Cherney Peredel's first newsletter from the underground, lucidly describes how Zemlya i Volya broke apart and calls to our attention a kind of fracture to which terrorist groups are especially prone.

> One of the two sides put all the emphasis on the war with the government, which it considered to be the problem of the day; while the other . . . absolutely denied the need for an immediate war of this kind and was convinced that all forces should be concentrated in the people.[26]

[24] Ibid.   [25] Ibid., p. 612   [26] Ibid., p. 659.

Interestingly enough, the leading figures in Cherney Peredel later founded the first avowedly Marxist party in Russia (known as the Emancipation of Labor group) and became an important influence on their younger colleague Lenin. Georgy Plekhanov especially is still remembered in the Soviet Union as the father of Russian Marxism in spite of his stormy falling out with Lenin and his subsequent disavowal of the Bolshevik's politics.

While the overriding need for secrecy imposes direct constraints on the ideological breadth and therefore on the size of conspiratorial movements, the political dynamics set in motion by these constraints greatly enhance the risk of political isolation. The conspirators may easily find themselves caught up in a vicious cycle—reducing their circle to the hardest of the hard-core purists in order to prevent detection, finding then that extreme tactics are the only way to compensate politically for diminutive size, and compounding the initial isolation by resorting to morally reprehensible tactics that alienate moderate support and justify, in the public mind, even harsher repression from the regime. For those who travel this perilous road despite its grave hazards, two questions become paramount. Can the conspiracy survive, and can it accomplish anything with a handful of people?

The apocalyptic tone in the writings of the Russian terrorists betrays a political consciousness that was preoccupied by the palpable and inescapable specter of catastrophe. "This situation cannot go on for long," declared the journal *Narodnaya Volya*. "Either the government explodes or the Committee and all the Party will be suffocated."[27] And, indeed, so it was. Because the security of a conspiracy depends so completely on secrecy, the more reliable safety of numbers is lost irretrievably. When a movement stakes its survival on invisibility, there arises a very real possibility of total annihilation. The simple words of a survivor capture all the horror and despair that an underground movement can suffer when its nucleus is destroyed by the political police (as Zemlya i Volya's was in October 1878):

> Those who were still at large had neither money nor passports, and had no chance of finding their comrades.[28]

The vulnerability and fragility of isolated conspiracies was a central charge in Lenin's indictment of Russia's terrorist heritage. Denouncing

[27] Ibid., p. 672   [28] Ibid., p. 618.

the idea "that it is possible to bring about a political revolution . . . by means of excitative terror . . . without training the proletariat in steadfast and stubborn struggle," Lenin deplored the "primativeness" of the student radicals whose premature and disorganized blows against the empire resulted in "immediate and complete fiasco."[29] "The masses of the workers literally lost all their leaders, the movement assumed an amazingly sporadic character, and it became impossible to establish continuity and coherence."[30]

The problem of survival becomes, then, the overriding concern in the political life of a conspiracy. For those who confront it successfully, the question of how to transform the dedication and political energy of an isolated cell into a vehicle of political change is no less fundamental or problematic. In practical terms, the problem is how a small circle of people can generate enough disruption to make a difference, either by pressuring the regime directly or by spurring mobilization. In the nineteenth century, the European anarchists were convinced that Alfred Nobel's invention of dynamite was the answer to this problem. Hailing the explosive as the "New Messiah," the anarchist periodicals extolled it with poetic refrains:

> At last a toast to science
> To dynamite that is the force
> The force in our own hands
> The world gets better day by day.[31]

These dreams now seem hopelessly naive and misguided, which is only one indication of how resilient state power has become and how immense are the difficulties, both technical and political, that arise in attempts to replace mass support with explosive force. On one hand, the problem of recruiting people to commit large-scale acts of violence is far more difficult than it might seem. As the Russian terrorist Dora Brilliant once said, "it is easier to die than it is to kill."[32] Nor is the technical capacity to generate violence easy to acquire. These difficulties in turn raise the question, How much is enough? For movements with revolutionary aspirations, this issue has provoked an enduring controversy about the nature of state power and the state's vulner-

---

[29] V. I. Lenin, *Selected Works*, Vol. 1: *What Is To Be Done?* (New York: International Publishers, 1967), pp. 179–80.

[30] Ibid., p. 181.

[31] Walter Laquer, *Terrorism* (Boston: Little, Brown, 1977), p. 59.   [32] Ibid., p. 124.

ability to violent disruption. Even in the early days of socialism, the problem excited heated exchanges between Marx and Engels and their anarchist rival, Bakunin. Although Marx finally prevailed in his quest for supremacy in the First International, the terrorist impulse was never laid finally to rest and the question of its political potential never fully resolved.

The terrorists gravitated to a personalist conception of the state, insisting that government amounted to nothing more than a collection of individuals, all of whom were mortal and therefore susceptible to intimidation or elimination through physical violence. The anarchist C. S. Griffen developed this view as boldly as anyone, arguing anthropomorphically that no government could exist without a head, and therefore

> by assassinating the head just as fast as a government head appeared, the government can be destroyed, and, generally speaking all governments can be kept out of existence.[33]

The same view prevailed among the Russian terrorists who identified the tsarist state with the person of the tsar himself. Their conviction ran so deep, in fact, that the plan to kill the tsar kindled angry debates about what the conspirators should do after they seized power. Some talked of handing power over immediately to the people, while others warned that a politically isolated coup would only replace "the policemen of the Imperial Department with the policemen of the Zemsky Sobor."[34]

When neither governmental collapse nor popular uprisings ensued upon the assassination of Alexander II, the detractors of terrorism insisted even more adamantly upon strategies of mass mobilization. Following the lead of Marx and Engels, the base-builders of Cherney Peredel (and later the Social Democrats) grounded their opposition to terrorism in a more abstract model of the state. According to the theory of class warfare that lay at the heart of Marx's analytical system, the state is a political manifestation of class rule. From this perspective, the personnel of government become interchangeable parts in the machinery invented by one class to dominate another. Accordingly,

---

[33] Ibid., p. 55.
[34] Venturi, *Roots of Revolution*, p. 663. The Zemsky Sobor was a constituent assembly, or council, long favored by Russian liberals and populists as the cornerstone of a new democratic state.

the threshold of insurrection appeared far higher than the terrorists supposed. "The classes whom the state serves will always find new men—the mechanism remains intact and continues to function," wrote Trotsky in 1911. "Far deeper is the confusion that terrorist attempts introduce in the ranks of the working masses. . . . If a pinch of powder and a slug of lead are enough to destroy the enemy, what need is there of a class organization?"[35]

Summing Up

ACCORDING to Article 9 in the party rules of Zemlya i Volya, "the end justifies the means, excluding those cases in which the use of certain means may harm the organization itself."[36] The article's clumsy language is eloquent testimony to the profound dilemmas occasioned by the use of terrorism. No other strategy invites harsher repression, greater moral censure, deeper alienation from the masses, or more potential for disaster. Still, our reasoning and evidence show that terrorism can be defended by cogent political reasoning, despite its maximal character. We must be careful, however, not to confuse the balance sheet of factors that make terrorism more or less effective with an explanation for why it happens. Like other strategies, terrorism cannot be explained in vacuo. Its attractiveness depends in part on the effectiveness of alternative forms of dissent, as well as on the other criteria used by radical leaders to choose among competing strategies. Spelling out the process of selection among alternative forms of disruption is our purpose in the pages ahead.

[35] Laquer, *Terrorism*, p. 67–68.
[36] Venturi, *Roots of Revolution*, p. 614.

CHAPTER ELEVEN

Violence and Factionalism

REASONING that simply describes the circumstances in which violent tactics are more or less effective should not be accepted as an explanation for why radical movements use them. A complete analysis must also consider the process of competition by which the radicals select violent measures from a broader menu of alternatives. Such decisions necessarily reflect the political aspirations and predispositions of the dissident strategists, aspirations that surely include tangible political concessions but rarely to the exclusion of other objectives. Thus, we shall often be misled about the likelihood of violence and the reasons for its appearance if we ignore the political psychology of the radical decision makers. The problem is analogous to the one encountered in Chapter 4 where the appeal of the various peaceful strategies depended only partially on their immediate effectiveness. The same holds for violent strategies, and once again it is the study of factional tensions that brings the additional psychological constraints into sharpest focus. Let us return, then, to the literature of revolutionary socialism and try to untangle the dynamics of factional struggle between the advocates of political violence and their opponents. By exploring how the question of violence excites factionalism in radical groups, we shall acquire a deeper understanding of the motivations that underlie both violent and peaceful campaigns of disruption.

When Peaceful Strategies Fail

OUR THEORY identifies three roads a dissident movement can travel if a sincere and peaceful strategy fails to achieve its objective. The radicals can devise a compromising strategy, seeking to rally moderate support by adopting less ambitious demands. Or they might try to transform the distribution of preferences with a campaign of agitation and propaganda; pursuing the prestrategy of building the base sometimes rejuvenates a sincere strategy when earlier it had failed. And, finally, the dissidents might escalate their tactics in an effort to stimulate mobilization or to replace it. Taken together, the three roads define the principal axes of factional cleavage in radical politics. Each one attracts as partisans the individuals whose political sensibilities are most compatible with the opportunities and obstacles it presents.

The road of compromise entices people who are hungry for immediate concessions, but it exacts a toll on the movement's principles. It appeals to pragmatic individuals like Bernstein who are impatient to move ahead, who are more concerned with "what can and ought to happen in the present, not what will happen in the distant future," and for whom "a kopek added to a ruble is worth more than any socialism." Compromise repels the purists, however, who not only cherish their principles but regard partial concessions with disdain.

This now familiar pattern of cleavage is the first of the great fault lines in radical political life. Those who refuse to travel the road of compromise are left with two alternatives—building the base or resorting to violence. Both strategies avoid the disagreeable prospect of compromising principles, but neither comes without a price. The road of violence entices the hotheads and the "bellowers" with the possibility of radical and immediate dislocations of the status quo, but it invites catastrophe by defying the fundamental axiom that power resides in numbers. Building the base, on the other hand, is a logical corollary of the fundamental axiom, but it requires patience for the arduous and tedious work needed to develop an organization and to arouse the masses. There arises, then, another kind of factional cleavage, partitioning the strategy-making core into its patient and impatient elements. As Mao writes in one of his early political essays:

> Some comrades suffer from the malady of revolutionary impetuosity;
> they will not take pains to do minute and detailed work among the masses,
> but, riddled with illusions, want only to do big things.[1]

The tendency among his impetuous followers, Mao quickly discovered, was to lapse into the "purely military viewpoint"; a political disease whose symptoms include "overconfidence in military strength and absence of confidence in the strength of the masses."[2] Disputes between base builders and the advocates of violence spring up along the

---

[1] Mao Tse-tung, "On Correcting Mistaken Ideas in the Party," *Selected Military Writings of Mao Tse-tung* (Peking: Foreign Languages Press, 1972), p. 55.
[2] Ibid.

second major fault line in radical politics. Together with the struggles between purists and compromisers, these disputes decide the political trajectory of most great radical movements.

A General Model of Factional Strife

WE CAN ACQUIRE a fuller understanding of the factional alignments in radical movements by elaborating the model of strategic decision making set forth in Chapter 4. The key revision comes by extending the dissident leaders' political calculus to include a third criterion for evaluating strategies—the time they take to bear fruit. Adding a temporal dimension to the model allows us to discriminate the essential political attributes of the three major strategic trends.

Figure 11.1 shows how the potential of all the strategies in a movement's arsenal can be represented by curves[3] in a three-dimensional space whose axes measure:

1. The (most radical) demand lodged by the dissidents' strategy

2. The concession attained by the strategy

3. The time required to implement the strategy

Each curve radiates from a point in the space labeled $(P_S, P_S{}^*, 0)$ that identifies the outcome of a sincere and peaceful strategy. Here a peaceful strategy demanding P_S results immediately in the concession $P_S{}^*$. The compromise curve, describing the effectiveness of peaceful strategies with less extreme demands than P_S, is familiar from Chapter 4. It lives in the plane formed by the demand and concession axes because compromise can be implemented without delay. Indeed, the principal rationale for moderating demands is to exploit the existing situation more effectively than a sincere strategy does. Violent strategies are similarly adapted to existing circumstances, though their demands are typically sincere. Therefore, the political violence curve also lies in the plane where time equals zero but along the ray that passes through the movement's sincere demand, P_S. Its end point defines the concession achieved by the most effective violent strategy, given the balance of forces in the movement's political environment. Presumably not all violent tactics yield optimal results, so experimentation might be needed to find the best one. Nonetheless, the outstanding feature

---

[3] We have portrayed linear curves in Figure 11.1 merely for convenience, not because linearity is implied by earlier reasoning.

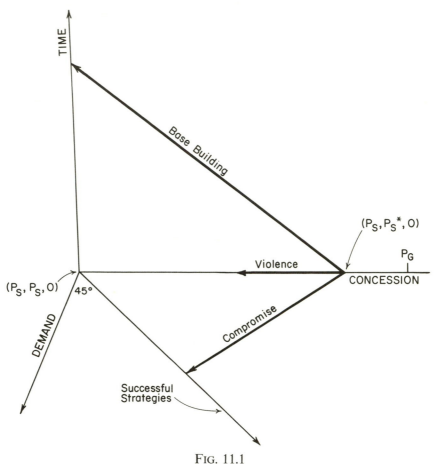

FIG. 11.1
The Avenues of Strategic Opportunity

of violent strategies is their immediacy. The third curve shows the results of building the base for various lengths of time and then returning to a sincere and peaceful strategy.

Naturally, the relative position of these curves will vary with the political situation. Whether one fares better than others depends on the responsiveness of the regime, its repressive capacity, the distribution of ideal points, and the intensity of political preferences in different ideological neighborhoods. Given an initial configuration of forces, however, the three curves will not usually evolve independently as the political situation changes. If the movement becomes more isolated

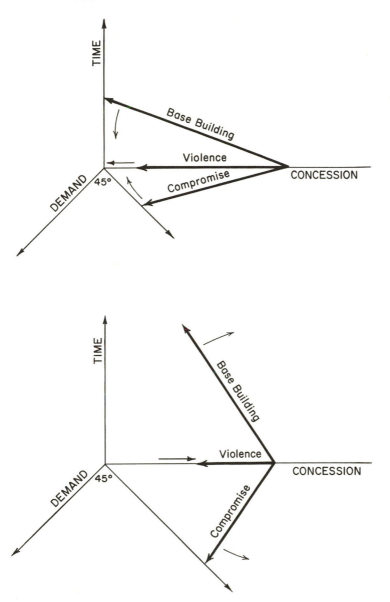

FIG. 11.2
Strategy in a Changing Environment

politically or the regime becomes less responsive, all three roads will be more difficult to travel. Likewise, changes that enhance the effectiveness of one strategy usually enhance others as well. Thus, we should expect the strategy-potential curves to covary in the fashion of Figure 11.2.

Friends and Foes of Violence: The Purists

THE LIKELIHOOD that factional stresses will develop in a particular situation depends, of course, on the composition of the movement's strategy-making core. The predilections of the various radical personalities can be represented in the three-dimensional space by indifference surfaces that describe an individual strategist's relative enthusiasm for

1. tangible concessions

2. ideologically sincere demands

3. quick results

Figures 11.3 and 11.4 contrast such indifference maps for purists of the impatient and patient varieties. As usual, each surface contains political outcomes among which the strategy maker is indifferent. Naturally, the ideal outcome is to pursue a sincere strategy to an immediately successful conclusion. The indifference surfaces contain more desirable outcomes, then, as they converge toward the point $(P_S, P_S, 0)$. Strategies that require more time, or more ideological compromise, or result in fewer concessions are less attractive. All of the surfaces obey these assumptions, individually and collectively. Their slopes measure the individual's willingness to substitute shortcomings in one respect for advantages in another. Differences in the slopes distinguish one kind of political personality from another.

The purist's aversion to compromising principles is captured in both pictures by the steep slopes of the indifference surfaces as we move on a tack that keeps time constant. From earlier reasoning, we know that purists abhor ideological instability and advocate compromise only when substantial new concessions can be achieved. Holding to the same indifference surface when time is fixed therefore requires a marked shift up the concession axis to compensate for each new departure from a sincere demand.

These attributes are common to the indifference maps of all purists. The rate at which the surfaces climb into the temporal dimension therefore distinguishes the patient from the impatient types. In these pictures, a shallower slope indicates relatively greater impatience. The impetuous strategist requires major new concessions to justify strategies that take only slightly more time. As an indifference map approaches a vertical pitch, on the other hand, it portrays a willingness to undertake vastly more time-consuming endeavors that return only small new concessions. It represents what Mao calls "the patience to carry on arduous struggles together with the masses."[4] When we superimpose the three strategy-potential curves upon these indifference maps, the potential for factional strife comes immediately to life. The pictures show clearly how leaders with different political temperaments can violently disagree about which strategy is best even though they share a common assessment of what each one will accomplish.

The impatient purist longs for quick results without compromising principles. Thus, in Figure 11.3, the impetuous strategist prefers only moderately effective violent tactics to the long-term drudgery of building the base—even though the organizational road is the only one that reaches the ultimate destination. In one sense, then, the psychological constraints of purism and impatience create a radical single-mindedness, not at all given to ambivalence or second thoughts. The strategic tunnel vision of the impatient purist can be readily appreciated by studying the indifference surface that contains the outcome of the peaceful, sincere strategy $(P_S, P_S{}^*, 0)$. This point establishes a floor on the movement's fortunes, while the surface passing through it defines the minimal requirements other strategies must satisfy to become active candidates in the search for a new course. Only strategies with enough potential to penetrate this barrier can ever seem preferable to maintaining the strategic status quo. In this political climate, the impetuous purist dismisses base-building and compromise out of hand, regardless of his opinions about violence. The strategic alternatives narrow to a choice between escalating tactics—a tack that is preferred whenever it seems likely to produce any additional concessions at all—and abandoning new initiatives altogether (if violence proves to be less effective than sincere peaceful protest).

[4] Mao Tse-tung, "On Correcting Mistaken Ideas in the Party," p. 62.

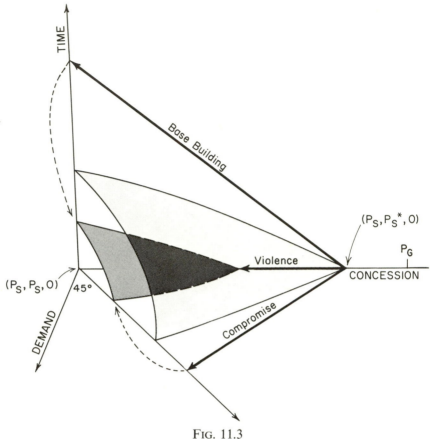

FIG. 11.3
The Impatient Purist

We have, then, in Figure 11.3 a formal representation of what Mao calls "the purely military viewpoint." For such people, judgments about the effectiveness of violence are the keystone in making decisions about strategy. As Mao says, "They become conceited when a battle is won and dispirited when a battle is lost."[5] To understand what he means, consider what happens as the assessment of violent strategies varies in Figure 11.3. When violent tactics appear to be even marginally more effective than the original strategy $(P_S, P_S^*, 0)$, as they do here, stringent new demands are imposed on the base-building and compromising alternatives. Given the indifference surface reached by the violence

[5] Ibid., p. 55.

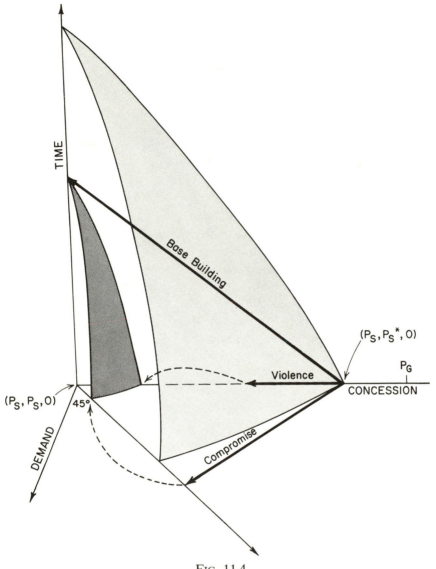

FIG. 11.4
The Patient Purist

curve, those alternatives remain unattractive until their potential increases dramatically, to the extent indicated by the broken arrows. Thus, in an atmosphere of uncertainty, the impatient purist needs only the slightest pretext to justify escalating tactics. He demands overwhelming assurances of extraordinary effectiveness, however, to embrace strategies of compromise or political agitation. In other words, an exceptionally wide range of estimates about the impact of base-building and compromise still leaves a modestly effective campaign of violence as the preferred strategy. When the political situation is unfriendly to violent tactics, on the other hand, the impatient purist is likely to withdraw from the struggle, abandoning the search for new initiatives altogether. The picture captures what Lenin calls the mentality of "the petty bourgeois driven to frenzy by the horrors of capitalism."[6] Such people "easily go to revolutionary extremes," he writes, but are "incapable of perseverance, organization, discipline and steadfastness. The instability of such revolutionism, its barrenness, and its tendency to turn rapidly into submission, apathy, phantasms—all of this is common knowledge."[7]

Despite these disparaging remarks, there can be little doubt about the pivotal role played by impetuous personalities in the history of Russian terrorism. The debates about strategy within Narodnaya Volya, Zemlya i Volya, the Workers' Union of South Russia, the Northern Revolutionary Populist group, the Pan-Russian Social-Revolutionary Organization, and a host of other terrorist cells all resonate with calls to violence, disdain for building the base, polemics against alliances with moderates, and an overriding sense of urgency. Take the Kiev Workers' Union of South Russia, for example. This group set out in 1880 to incite the workers to burn their factories and kill their employers.[8] Their manifestoes show clearly that the terrorists reached the road of violence by a systematic process of elimination cycling over the major strategic alternatives identified by the model. On one hand, they argued that alliances with the bourgeoisie were "hopeless" because the bourgeoisie was at once too weak and too dangerous. "In Russia the bourgeoisie is very disorganized. . . . And so

---

[6] V. I. Lenin, *Selected Works*, Vol. 3: "Left-Wing Communism—An Infantile Disorder," p. 346.

[7] Ibid., pp. 346–47.

[8] See Franco Venturi, *Roots of Revolution*, trans. Francis Haskell (London: Weidenfeld and Nicolson, 1960), pp. 518–23.

we must recognize that if the bourgeoisie were to become better organized and more united this would be extremely harmful to the workers themselves."[9] This argument reflects the enduring ambivalence about bourgeois liberalism among the Russian populists. Some argued that the liberals were too vacillating and cowardly to make worthwhile allies, while others feared that a political combination with the workers might hasten their ascendancy to power. The decisive consideration, however, seemed usually to be more simple. As the manifesto of the Workers' Union put it, "The bourgeoisie is the worker's natural enemy."[10]

If compromising strategies seemed unattractive, so too did further attempts to cultivate a revolutionary consciousness among the masses. Propaganda pure and simple was unlikely to accomplish anything until "the day Christ returns to Earth," the union declared.[11] Their attitude toward political agitation recalled the writings of Michael Bakunin, the revolutionary godfather of an entire generation of terrorists, who had complained as early as 1848 that Marx was "ruining the workers by making theorists of them."[12] The answer was not to "teach the people, but to lead them to revolt" Bakunin insisted. "Let the people emancipate themselves first and they will instruct themselves of their own accord."[13]

And so, violent insurrection became the union's favored strategy. A program of terrorism in the factories seemed best to its leaders, and as one said, "we worked rapidly, feverishly, well knowing that our days were numbered."[14] Inspired by a faith that "the revolution was imminent," the union's efforts to incite the workers continued until October 1880, when the police descended upon their organization and destroyed it.

Bakunin's compulsive impatience pervaded the Russian terrorist culture throughout its history. The ever-present feeling that the decisive moment had arrived, that is was now or never, and that history would not wait produced an extraordinarily narrow vision of political strategy—a vision that many young populists took to the grave. "We must act before it is too late," declared the journal *Narodnaya Volya*,

---

[9] Ibid., p. 521.   [10] Ibid.   [11] Ibid.
[12] James Joll, *The Anarchists* (Cambridge: Harvard University Press, 1964), p. 75.
[13] Ibid.   [14] Venturi, *Roots of Revolution*, p. 519.

"while there is a real possibility that power can in fact pass to the people—Now or never; that is our dilemma."[15]

The Patient Purist

FIGURE 11.4 shows how the purist's strategic vision is extended as the psychological constraint of impatience becomes less pronounced. While his impatient comrades search for opportunities in the set of strategies that take the political situation as a given, the patient strategist has wider horizons that encompass ambitious efforts to transform the political landscape. As time becomes less dear, campaigns of political education and ideological transformation appear increasingly preferable to more immediate strategies that deliver only partial concessions. Patience creates a high standard of strategic performance as the test for excellence shifts from what can be accomplished in the present to how long it will take to succeed in the future. Thus, patience skews the purist's inclinations away from violence toward building the base.

It should be noted in both diagrams that the constraints imposed by intense preferences eliminate compromising strategies from the purist's active consideration. From each point of view, the sincere strategy using peaceful tactics strictly dominates the moderate strategies, which sacrifice principles for support. Only when the optimal compromising strategy is markedly more effective than the sincere alternatives does it become an active contestant in the strategic competition. Karl Kautsky's polemic in 1898 against a revisionist parliamentary strategy provides a good summary of the purist's attitudes toward compromise (cf. the arguments of Lenin and Luxemburg in Chapter 4):

> For the present, propaganda and organization stand in the forefront. These are our most important "practical" tasks. . . . A programme of parliamentary action based solely on what is "realizable" without taking account of whether or not it compromises our future or endangers the unity or clarity of the party would be a highly impractical programme. For a party that pursues grandiose goals and presently finds itself in the minority, striving for the "unrealizable" can be more practical in the long run than seeking agreement over what is "realizable" under the rule of an imposing reaction.[16]

[15] Ibid., p. 671.
[16] Quoted in Massimo Salvadori, *Karl Kautsky and the Socialist Revolution, 1880–1938*, trans. Jon Rothschild (London: NLB, 1979), p. 44.

The purist's efforts to remedy the shortcomings of the strategic status quo therefore boil down to a choice among the uncompromising alternatives. The impatient types, finding the prospect of "minute and detailed work among the masses" too onerous to contemplate, must either resort to violence or abandon the struggle. The natural tendency, especially in the presence of uncertainty and flux, is to tout the violent course while demeaning the prospects of cultivating a mass following (i.e. to adopt what Mao calls the purely military viewpoint).

The patient elements, on the other hand, are less given to wishful thinking about the efficacy of violence because it does not represent their only active political option. Moreover, they require much larger concessions from a violent strategy before they adopt it. In Figure 11.3, the impatient purist pursues a violent course whenever it appears likely to return new concessions beyond P_S^*, however small they might be. The patient strategist in Figure 11.4 contemplates violence only when it appears significantly more effective than the original peaceful strategy (to the extent shown by the broken arrow). Violent tactics are not dismissed in principle, but the patient strategist demands much stronger evidence than his impatient comrades that violence will bring good results. Thus, Lenin roundly denounced the Socialist Revolutionaries for adopting a terrorist strategy in 1901 but immediately embraced a strategy of armed insurrection when the Russian workers took to the streets in 1905.

Terrorism, Lenin wrote in *What Is To Be Done?*, would achieve neither of the effects that its adherents proposed. Governments could not be intimidated or destroyed by isolated terrorist cells, he asserted in the traditional Marxist fashion, because governments were instruments of class rule whose personnel were interchangeable and replaceable. But, "the admission that the government cannot now be 'terrified,' and hence disrupted by terror, is tantamount to a complete condemnation of terror as a system of struggle."[17] After all, nothing was more bankrupt than the idea that terrorism could "excite the working class movement," providing an impetus to broader mobilization:

It is difficult to imagine an argument that more thoroughly disproves itself. Are there not enough outrages committed in Russian life without special "excitants" having to be invented? Is it not obvious that those

[17] V. I. Lenin, *What Is To Be Done?*, p. 161.

who are not, and cannot be, roused to excitement even by Russian tyranny will stand by twiddling their thumbs and watch a handful of terrorists engaged in single combat with the government?[18]

Thus, Lenin reached in 1901 the usual political conclusions favored by patient purists when the political situation seems unfriendly to immediate strategies of disruption:

> Calls for terror and calls [for compromise] are merely two different forms of evading the most pressing duty now resting upon Russian revolutionaries, namely, the organization of comprehensive political agitation.... Both the terrorists and the Economists underestimate the revolutionary activity of the masses, ... and whereas the one group goes out in search of artificial "excitants," the other talks about "concrete demands." But both fail to devote sufficient attention to the development of their own activity in political agitation and in the organization of political exposures. And no other work can serve as a substitute for this task either at the present time or at any other.[19]

This was not to say, of course, that violence should be disregarded in principle. Years later, Lenin recalled how the Socialist Revolutionary party

> considered itself particularly "revolutionary" or "left" because of its recognition of individual terrorism and assassination—something we Marxists emphatically rejected. It was, of course, only on grounds of expediency that we rejected individual terrorism, whereas people who were capable of condemning [it] "on principle" ... were ridiculed and laughed to scorn.[20]

Patient purists readily embrace a strategy of violence when a "revolutionary high tide" restores their confidence in its effectiveness. Even a resolutely committed base-builder like Lenin immediately endorsed a strategy of armed insurrection when the wave of strikes in 1905 convinced him that the workers were ready to revolt:

> Tailist revolutionaries fail to understand that when a revolutionary period has set in, when the old superstructure has cracked from top to bottom ... it is apathy, lifelessness, or else betrayal of the revolution and treachery ... to try to avoid action by pleading the need for "psychological conditions" and "propaganda."[21]

Nonetheless, the patient strategists, far more than their impatient comrades, remain cautious about resorting to violence. Their slogans and programs emphasize that things take time; that political success

---

[18] Ibid.   [19] Ibid., p. 162.
[20] V. I. Lenin, "Left-Wing Communism," pp. 347–48.
[21] V. I. Lenin, *Two Tactics of Social Democracy*, p. 504.

requires endurance, dedication, organization, and steadfastness; and that violent episodes of "adventurism" or "putschism" invite disastrous repression and alienation from the masses. As Plekhanov argued in opposition to the terrorists who formed Narodnaya Volya:

> If the people's forces are not organized and their consciousness ... not stimulated, even the most heroic fight by the revolutionaries will prove advantageous only to the upper classes.... We attribute the greatest importance to organizing the people's forces. In this way, we are choosing a road which is long but which is sure.... It demands not momentary and gigantic impulses, but a concentrated and inflexible energy.... Nature does not jump.... The liberation of the people must be the work of the people itself.[22]

This was Marx's stance against the anarchists, Lenin's stance against the terrorists, and Mao's stance against his followers who "refused to recognize that military affairs are only one means of accomplishing political tasks."[23]

The Pragmatic Attitude toward Violence

THE FOREGOING analysis of the purists suggests that casual impressions about the perpetrators of political violence frequently miss the mark rather badly. The propensity to use violent tactics arises not from fanatical ideological commitment per se, as the commentators usually assume, but from political impatience. Moreover, it is only because the tendency to be impatient occurs independently of the intensity of political preferences that debates about tactics often provoke deep splits in the purist core of radical movements.

Failing to appreciate this distinction can easily lead to misunderstandings, as shown by Lenin's exchanges with the liberal polemicist Peter Struve during the Revolution of 1905. In typical liberal fashion, Struve misrepresented Lenin's ideological passion as a craving for violence. "The fundamental political temper of the Bolsheviks," he wrote, "is abstract revolutionism, rebelliousness, and eagerness to stir up insurrection among the popular masses by any and every means.... The Leninists are thoroughly imbued with the narrow-mindedness of revolutionism; they renounce all practical work ... and any kind of practically useful compromise."[24] Having recently engaged in long polemics

---

[22] Quoted in Venturi, *Roots of Revolution*, pp. 666–67.
[23] Mao Tse-tung, "On Correcting Mistaken Ideas in the Party," p. 54.
[24] Quoted in V. I. Lenin, *Two Tactics*, p. 545.

against the terrorists, Lenin could only reply in frustration: "We should like to ask Mr. Struve whether he can point to any passage in, for instance, *What Is To Be Done?*—the work, from his standpoint, of an extreme revolutionary—which advocates rioting."[25] On the contrary, Lenin retorts, at the time *What Is To Be Done?* appeared "slogans advocating mass agitation *instead of* direct armed action, preparation of the sociopsychological conditions for insurrection *instead of* pyrotechnics were revolutionary Social-Democracy's only correct slogans."[26]

The idea that the predisposition to use political violence arises from impatience rather than from ideological intensity per se is further reinforced when we consider the pragmatist's strategic inclinations. Once again, first impressions can be deceiving. In fact, there are frequently strong political resonances between a violent and a compromising mentality—resonances that often rally pragmatists around a violent strategy long before the base-building purists come over. This apparent paradox is resolved when we recognize that pragmatists can be impetuous and impatient just as purists sometimes are. Such a predisposition narrows the pragmatist's strategic vision in a way that makes alliances with terrorists far more likely than one might suppose.

What Is There in Common between Economism and Terrorism?

LENIN's appreciation of these resonances motivated his persistent and apparently farfetched efforts to portray the compromising Economists as the political bedfellows of the Russian terrorists. In fact, the analysis and evidence that Lenin presents to support his position are entirely consistent with the predictions of the model. In Lenin's opinion, the political reasoning of both trends was fatally flawed by an impatient insistence that Social Democracy adapt its strategy to an immature political situation. "The Economists and the present-day terrorists have one common root," he wrote, "namely, subservience to spontaneity . . . i.e. that which exists at the present moment."[27] In Figures 11.3 and 11.5, we see how impatience creates more than a superficial resemblance between those pragmatists and purists who are possessed by it. Sometimes it becomes the political cement that bonds factional alliances around a strategy of assassination and terror.

---

[25] Ibid., p. 502.   [26] Ibid., p. 505.
[27] V. I. Lenin, *What Is To Be Done?*, p. 159.

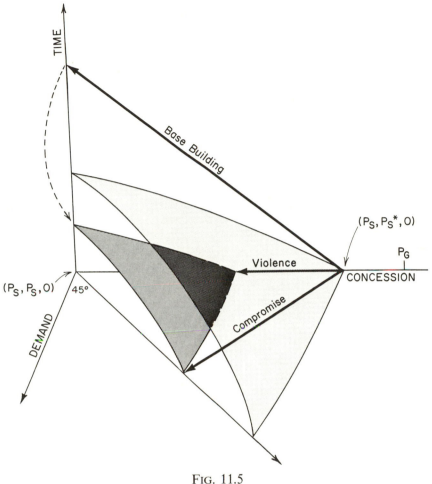

FIG. 11.5
The Impatient Pragmatist

Like all impatient strategists, the pragmatic types find an active
strategy, even if only modestly effective, far more appealing than passive
and time-consuming efforts to transform the ideological preferences of
an immature political base. Recall, for example, the Economists' arguments that Lenin's strategy of political agitation was nothing but a
futile attempt to substitute political organization for historical development. "The task of the revolutionary Social Democrat," they insisted,
"is only to accelerate objective development by his conscious work,

not to obviate it or substitute his own subjective plans for this development. . . . *Iskra*, owing to its doctrinaire view of tactics, belittles the significance of the objective or spontaneous element of development . . . and exaggerates the role of the conscious element."[28] The Economists' preference was to let the workers' political consciousness evolve through struggle, especially since "the only desirable struggle is that which is possible, and the struggle which is possible is that which is going on at the given moment."[29]

When a sincere and peaceful strategy falters, this kind of impatience narrows the pragmatist's options to a choice between moderating demands and escalating tactics. Although he remains open, far more than the purists of either type, to a compromising strategy, the impetuous pragmatist has a pronounced receptivity to violent measures (as shown in Figure 11.5). Unlike those purists who discount the value of time more heavily, this kind of strategist readily endorses violent methods of struggle whenever they appear more effective than a peaceful, evolutionary approach. While the impetuous pragmatist staunchly denounces violence if moderate demands return bigger concessions, he becomes a ready ally of the terrorists and the brawlers when the situation favors their techniques (even if neither course is very effective).

> A party which claims to have a future must base itself above all on an absolutely real relationship with life. The most rosy of ideals is not only useless but positively harmful, if by its nature it cannot be realized in life, and consequently deflects forces and labor from a reform which may be less grandiose but which is feasible. . . . A party of action must give itself concrete, realizable objectives which are of immediate use to the people. It must choose the most effective means at the right moment.[30]

These words were penned not by some determined compromiser of socialist principles but by the terrorists of Narodnaya Volya in the first issue of their undergound newspaper (note that the call is not for moderate demands but for immediate gains). That they could have been written by the Russian Economists or the German revisionists testifies to the close affinity between two political trends that seem, at first, to have little in common. In fact, both tendencies arose from a burning impatience for change—an impatience that aligned these wings of the Socialist movement against the forward-looking political

---

[28] Quoted in *ibid.*, pp. 129, 138.   [29] Ibid., p. 137.
[30] Quoted in Venturi, *Roots of Revolution*, p. 666.

organizers who insisted on a strategy of total victory. Long after the Narodnaya Volya had been destroyed, the Economists were still lecturing the advocates of political agitation about "being unable to cope with political tasks in the real and practical sense of the word, i.e., in the sense of the expedient and successful practical struggle for political demands."[31]

And so Lenin's spiteful notion of the "Economist-terrorist" is not at all farfetched. As he took great pains to document, the political viewpoint of the two trends often converged. "What is there in common between Economism and terrorism?" Lenin asked.

> There is not an accidental, but a necessary, inherent connection between the two. . . . The Economists and terrorists merely bow to different poles of spontaneity. . . . Surely it is no accident that many Russian liberals— avowed liberals and liberals that wear the mask of Marxism—wholeheartedly sympathize with terror and try to foster the terrorist moods that have surged up.[32]

A Brief Retrospective

THE EXTENDED model of strategic decision making and factional disputes has a striking capacity to untangle the bewildering debates and coalitions that develop when radical groups find their political objectives difficult to attain (i.e. most of the time). Although it relies on just three political attributes—location of ideal point, intensity of preferences, and political impatience—the model makes it possible:

1. To generate a useful typology of the various strategic mentalities

2. To calculate how people with different political temperaments will evaluate the strategic opportunities that the political situation presents

3. To decipher complicated patterns of factional alignment and the occasions for their formation and dissolution.

Moreover, the model accomplishes its purposes without any recourse to ad hoc or tautological notions like "a violent nature" or "a conspiratorial personality" that simply describe, after the fact, the behavior they

---

[31] Quoted in *What Is To Be Done?*, p. 184.   [32] Ibid., pp. 159–60.

are meant to explain. Consider Trotsky's characterization of Lenin and Martov in the days before they became implacable enemies heading rival factions. "One can say of Lenin and Martov that *even before the split* . . . Lenin was 'hard' and Martov was 'soft.' And they both knew it." Moreover, "Martov lived much more in the present, in its events, . . . in the political problems of the day; Lenin, on the other hand, although he was firmly entrenched in the present, was always trying to pierce the veil of the future."[33] But according to our theory, these are precisely the attributes that later propelled the Bolsheviks and Mensheviks along radically different strategic trajectories. That Trotsky was able to appreciate the essential differences between the two outlooks, even before they coalesced into distinct factions, testifies not only to his political insightfulness, which was extraordinary, but to the predictive utility of the constructs in the theory. They can be measured without observing the behavior they are meant to explain.

The extended model of strategic choice and factionalism represents the last major component in an analytical system that now contains the building blocks for understanding the strategic opportunities available to radical groups, the political forces that govern the effectiveness of these alternatives, and the relative appeal of the strategic options to the various political personalities. Despite the stark austerity of its structure, the theory provides a sobering antidote to the glib generalizations about protest and rebellion that now abound in the literature. As soon as one accepts the basic logic of the framework, no doubts can remain about the exceptional difficulties facing anyone who would explain the behavior of radical groups in particular historical situations and the impact they have on public policy and political institutions.

Two lessons especially seem not to be widely appreciated in the current literature. First, piecemeal accounts of radical activity that focus exclusively on one kind of strategy or another are inherently too narrow in focus. Neither mass political violence, nor terrorism, nor peaceful protest, nor nonviolent resistance can be explained in vacuo. To explain why one strategy is adopted is to explain why other strategies are not. But, the tunnel-visioned studies that comprise much of the literature lack enough analytical generality even to define the full range of strategies available to radical groups, much less to explain what makes one strategy more effective than others or how people

---

[33] Leon Trotsky, *My Life* (New York: Pathfinder Press, 1970), p. 151. Italics mine.

choose among them. Good theories must be general enough to consider all of the alternatives simultaneously.

Moreover, a coherent explanation of a radical movement's political activity requires a detailed appraisal of both its internal and external environment. The external environment defines the outcomes associated with different strategies, while the internal environment defines the movement's preferences among the outcomes. Accounts of protest and rebellion that focus entirely upon a movement's leadership or mass following fail to explain the opportunities and constraints residing in the political situation. Such accounts are logically just as incomplete as others that attribute a movement's behavior to its historical setting, without attending to its internal composition and structure of authority.

It follows that understanding a movement's strategic course in a dynamic political environment is truly an arduous undertaking. First, one must evaluate the potential effectiveness of *all* the strategies at the movement's disposal, not just the one it finally adopts. To generate strategy-potential curves of the kind shown in Figure 11.1 requires detailed evidence about the configuration of social forces, including the distribution of political opinion and its intensity, the political constraints that govern the regime's responsiveness, the nature of the regime's repressive capacity, and its inclination to use one strategy of repression rather than another.

Explaining which of these strategies the movement actually prefers requires additional evidence about its internal composition and organizational structure. To argue that one strategy brings more concessions than others is not to explain why it is adopted. Radical leaders pursue other objectives besides concessions when they select strategies—and all radical politicians do not weigh these objectives identically. One must therefore assess the relative frequency of the different strategic personalities inside the movement's strategy-making core, and describe the patterns of decision-making authority by which their preferences are aggregated (or which lead the movement to split).

A dynamic story requires finally that the ebb and flow of all these variables be continuously monitored as they experience both exogenous shocks (wars, famines, economic development, population growth, migration, etc.) and endogenous pressures from the conduct of the struggle itself (transformations of public opinion, changes in the movement's composition occasioned by repression or flux in demands and tactics, shifts in the regime's responsiveness after co-optation or purges, and so forth). The striking thing about the historical literature on protests and rebellions is how little we know about the basic political elements described by the theory. That we have only fragmentary information about most radical movements, however momentous their accomplishments, counsels the greatest skepticism toward casual arguments that purport to demonstrate historical necessity or inevitability. Perhaps the historical evidence we need to build coherent explanations is now lost forever. If we are lucky, it is still waiting for those who ask the right questions.

Library of Congress Cataloging in Publication Data

DeNardo, James, 1949–
Power in numbers.

Includes bibliographical references and index.
1. Government, Resistance to.   2. Revolutions. I. Title.
JC328.3.D44 1985   321.09   84-42880
ISBN 0-691-07682-0